Personalities and Problems

Interpretive Essays in World Civilizations

Volume Two

Personalities and Problems

Interpretive Essays in World Civilizations

Third Edition

VOLUME TWO

Ken Wolf
Murray State University
Illustrations by John Stephen Hatton

Boston   Burr Ridge, IL   Dubuque, IA   Madison, WI   New York
San Francisco   St. Louis   Bangkok   Bogotá   Caracas   Kuala Lumpur
Lisbon   London   Madrid   Mexico City   Milan   Montreal   New Delhi
Santiago   Seoul   Singapore   Sydney   Taipei   Toronto

Higher Education

PERSONALITIES AND PROBLEMS: INTERPRETIVE ESSAYS IN WORLD
CIVILIZATIONS, VOLUME II

Published by McGraw-Hill, a business unit of The McGraw-Hill Companies, Inc.,
1221 Avenue of the Americas, New York, NY, 10020. Copyright © 2005, 1999,
1994, by The McGraw-Hill Companies, Inc. All rights reserved. No part of this
publication may be reproduced or distributed in any form or by any means, or
stored in a database or retrieval system, without the prior written consent of The
McGraw-Hill Companies, Inc., including, but not limited to, in any network or
other electronic storage or transmission, or broadcast for distance learning.

Some ancillaries, including electronic and print components, may not be
available to customers outside the United States.

This book is printed on acid-free paper.

2 3 4 5 6 7 8 9 0 DOC/DOC 0 9 8 7 6 5 4

ISBN 0–07–256566–7

Publisher: *Lyn Uhl*
Editorial assistant: *Sean Connelly*
Senior marketing manager: *Katherine Bates*
Project manager: *Destiny Rynne Hadley*
Production supervisor: *Janean A. Utley*
Designer: *Cassandra J. Chu*
Associate supplement producer: *Meghan Durko*
Manager, Photo research: *Brian J. Pecko*
Art manager: *Robin K. Mouat*
Art director: *Jeanne M. Schreiber*
Cover design: *Cassandra J. Chu*
Interior design: *Michael Remener*
Typeface: *10/12 Palatino*
Compositor: *Shepherd-Imagineering Media Services Inc.*
Printer: *R. R. Donnelley and Sons Inc.*

Library of Congress Cataloging-in-Publication Data
Wolf, Ken, 1943–
    Personalities and problems : interpretive essays in world civilizations /
Ken Wolf; illustrations by John Stephen Hatton.—3rd ed.
        p. cm.
    Includes bibliographical references.
    ISBN 0-07-256564-0 (v. 1 : softcover : alk, paper)—IBSN 0-07-256566-7
(v. 2 : softcover : alk. paper)
    1. Civilization—History. 2. Biography. I. Title.
    CB69.W63 2005
    909—dc22   2004040189

www.mhhe.com

*To my family, my colleagues at Murray State
and
the students, faculty, and staff of the
Commonwealth Honors Academy,
2001–2004*

and to my grandchildren,

*for helping me give meaning to the phrase
"life-long learning."*

Contents

Preface

Dear Reader:

The people you will meet in these pages illustrate the richness and variety of human history over the past five centuries. The personalities range from a Portuguese adventurer, Prince Henry, to a twentieth-century Russian physicist and political activist, Andrei Sakharov. One explored the oceanic frontiers; the other worked on the frontiers of modern physics. If history is the study of the human beings who make it, *Personalities and Problems* is an introduction to world civilizations that focuses upon some of the most interesting men and women that the written records of these civilizations allow us to meet. This book assumes no previous knowledge of history; it does assume that the lives of exciting people have a certain magic that captures our attention across the boundaries of space and time.

But most of you know that history is more (sometimes less) than the study of interesting people. If all the interesting historical figures were included in our history texts, the books would be too large to carry, much less read. The people we choose to include in our histories must also be considered memorable or important—by someone. Whether great in the traditional textbook sense of the term or not, each of these personalities was included in this work because I found them interesting and thought their lives could help you better understand some of the issues that historians and other scholars have struggled with in their teaching, research, and writing. Before you can assess their importance for yourselves, it will be helpful for you to begin to classify or organize them.

Twelve of the people you will meet in these pages were rulers or political leaders—people such as Otto von Bismarck, Ito Hirobumi, Tecumseh, Elizabeth I, Akbar, M. K. Gandhi, and Ho Chi Minh. Another six were primarily intellectuals (writers, thinkers, religious leaders); this list includes Francis Bacon, Galileo Galilei, Nicholas Condorcet, George Sand, and Harriet Beecher Stowe. You will also meet several explorers, two World War I soldiers, and two modern scientists.

Putting people in such broad categories is, of course, only one way to describe them—and not necessarily the best way. For one thing, in history as in life, people have a way of breaking through our neat categories. Gandhi was a political leader who tried to exert a profound influence on the religious life of his people. Andrei Sakharov will be remembered at least as much for his political views as for his creation of the Soviet H-bomb. And most of those we call intellectuals were memorable precisely because they were concerned with religious, political, and social/cultural issues (Harriet Beecher Stowe's work falls into all three categories). In a larger sense, this book is interdisciplinary; its author is committed to the idea that, whatever lines we might draw between subjects in schools, we cannot understand human beings adequately if we separate their political behavior from their religious beliefs, their social position, or their economic concerns.

A second way of classifying people is to ask about the nature and extent of the impact they made on their society. Some, like Otto von Bismarck and Golda Meir, were important because they reflected in their actions the dominant values of their society. Others, such as Nelson Mandela and Andrei Sakharov, were significant because they challenged those dominant values. Occasionally, we find people who both reflected the beliefs of their time and place and tried to change the way people think about the world. Chinese mariner Zheng He did not change the direction of Chinese history in the fifteenth century, but his voyages of exploration offer a fascinating look at what might have been. His counterpart, Prince Henry of Portugal, both reflected European attitudes toward overseas exploration, and, by his work, helped Europeans become even more outward-looking. People such as George Sand and Harriet Beecher Stowe challenged people in their respective societies to live up to the standards they professed.

These are only two ways of classifying the personalities in world history. As you read these essays, I invite you to devise some of your own. Your determination of what makes an individual a success or a failure, admirable or deplorable, will be based upon your personal values. I ask only that you also consider the times in which these individuals lived and the problems they faced. If you consider both their problems and the values they brought to bear in trying to solve them, you will begin the process of thinking historically. You will become historically minded.

To help you with this task, all of these personalities are presented to you in relation to a particular issue or issues that they had to face or that their careers raise for us—as thoughtful citizens of an increasingly interdependent world. These issues—noted by the questions that begin each essay—include such things as the role of religion as a social force, the problems faced by females in male-dominated societies, and the relative importance of money and personality when one is appealing to voters. Each personality is also paired with a contemporary who faced a similar problem or issue, either in the same civilization or country or in another one. These pairings are often cross-cultural and should help you understand that human problems really do transcend the boundaries of race, creed, and nation. When we begin to see that individuals as different as German Otto von Bismarck and Japanese Ito Hirobumi had to face similar problems in constructing a modern government, we can appreciate the fact that our history is world history and not only a history of individual nations or even civilizations.

Historical greatness, then, is not just a matter of how talented we are (or how lucky) but also a matter of when and where we live. History helps make us as surely as we help make history. If this book challenges you to think about just how and why this happens, it will have served its purpose.

Because this book does not assume any prior knowledge of history, or even prior college-level work, I use brackets [] to define terms which might be unfamiliar to a beginning student. You also should know that each chapter is designed to stand independently; chapters need not be read in order. You can start at any point and read in either direction, after checking with your teacher, of course!

This third edition of *Personalities and Problems* has been enlarged and altered in direct response to teachers who used the second edition and suggested the addition of Martin Luther King Jr. and Nelson Mandela. Beyond this, all chapters have been corrected and edited where appropriate. As in the first two editions, I invite readers to suggest people who might be included or omitted. Your comments have been taken seriously, and will be again, should this work appear in a fourth edition.

In addition to all those colleagues and students whom I thanked in the first edition, I would like to again thank all the faculty members in the Department of History. For this edition, I am grateful to Melinda Grimsley-Smith, whose hard work as my graduate assistant made the job of revision easier. I would also like to thank the reviewers of the second edition whose comments helped shape this third edition: Robert Blackey, California State University, San Bernardino; Myles L. Clowers, San Diego City College; Nancy Erickson, Erskine College; Norman O. Forness, Gettysburg College; Paul E. Gill, Shippensburg University; David Grier, Erskine College; Dane Kennedy, University of Nebraska, Lincoln; Fred Nielsen, University of Nebraska, Omaha; Melvin E. Page, East Tennessee University; Jon Stauff, Saint Ambrose University; and Steven F. White, Mount Saint Mary's College. My thanks as well to the fine librarians at both Murray State and the Hesburgh Library at the University of Notre Dame, where I have been privileged to work several summers. Lyn Uhl and her wonderful staff at McGraw-Hill have been very supportive and helpful in suggesting revisions, in surveying users of the first and second editions, and in helping with last-minute improvements. Any errors which remain after all this help can only be due to my own carelessness or stubbornness— and all those mentioned above should be absolved of any errors and credited with trying to save me from myself. We all join, however, in hoping that this work offers you pleasant reading, new insights into the past, and intellectual excitement.

Sincerely,

Ken Wolf

Department of History
Murray State University
Murray, KY 42071

Personalities and Problems
Interpretive Essays in World Civilizations

CHAPTER 1

Prince Henry and Zheng He: Sailing South

How do the structures and values of a society affect the way people view contact with other cultures? Why did Europeans benefit more from the voyages of Prince Henry that the Chinese did from those of Zheng He?

It somehow doesn't seem fair. Prince Henry of Portugal (1394–1460), who was land-bound, is known to history as Henry the Navigator, while Chinese admiral Zheng He (ca. 1371–1433), who commanded fleets with hundreds of ships, is remembered as a eunuch [castrated male]. Of course, Henry's personal ability to navigate—if he had any—is not what made his life significant. Zheng He's condition as a eunuch did not affect his ability to lead men or manage fleets. Each man is remembered as he is because of the conditions and values of his society. These conditions and values helped to determine how the Chinese and Portuguese reacted to the voyages of their remarkable explorers.

Between 1405 and 1424, the Ming dynasty ruler Yongle created a fleet and ordered it to make seven expeditions into the "Great Western Sea," or Indian Ocean. The man selected to command these voyages, the most ambitious in Chinese history, was born Ma He, a member of a Muslim family of Mongol descent in the province of Yunan. When the first Ming emperor incorporated this Mongol province into his empire in 1381, Ma He was captured, castrated, and taken to the imperial capital of Nanjing, probably to serve as a harem guard. At age twenty, Ma He entered the service of the royal prince, Zhu Di, and very soon distinguished himself as a junior officer in a civil war that brought Zhu Di to power as the new Yongle emperor. The new ruler promoted Ma He to the position of superintendent of the office of eunuchs and honored him with the Chinese surname Zheng. The new head eunuch was described as tall and handsome, with "glaring eyes, teeth as white as well-shaped shells, and a voice as loud as a huge bell." He was a man who "walks like a tiger and talks in a commanding voice."[1]

It was this commanding figure whom the emperor chose to lead his new fleet. In this role, Zheng He was to undertake seven voyages, each of which lasted nearly two years. On his first voyage, in 1405–1407, he commanded twenty-eight thousand men on 317 ships, many of them large "treasure ships" 400 feet long and 160 feet wide. By contrast, Columbus "discovered" America 85 years later with 120 men and a fleet of three ships, one of which was 75 feet long.

Zheng He's first expedition traveled to India, with stops at Java and Ceylon. The fourth expedition, in 1413–1415, reached Aden and Hormuz on the Persian Gulf, and on the seventh expedition, in 1431–1433, the Chinese sent a small group to visit Mecca; they also touched the east coast of Africa as far south as Malindi near the modern state of Kenya. At each stop, Zheng He presented lavish gifts to the local rulers from "their" emperor and recorded information about interesting customs and creatures he encountered. An "Overall Survey of the Ocean's Shores Annotated" was written by Zheng He's fellow Muslim, Ma Huan; it was based on a diary that Ma Huan kept during several voyages.[2] Ma Huan's book shows the great interest the Chinese took in the dress, food, language, marriage and death rituals, and flora and fauna of the countries they visited. According to most modern historians of China, however, anthropological research was not the primary purpose of these costly trips.

There were a number of reasons the court of the Son of Heaven initiated these voyages, discounting for the moment the exuberance of a young ruler and a natural curiosity about his neighbors to the south and west. To consolidate his power won in a civil war, the emperor decided to send what the Chinese called tribute missions to all neighboring countries to set up diplomatic and economic exchanges. Owing to their advanced civilization, the Chinese, like other people before and since, believed that all other cultures were inferior and that, once foreigners became familiar with Chinese culture, they would realize it was the source of all wisdom and political power. While some representatives of foreign states felt the Chinese claim was unwarranted, many kowtowed [bowed] before the emperor because they either regarded it as appropriate or because it enabled them to establish trade relations with the Chinese. Zheng He's voyages, then, were part of the Yongle emperor's effort to demonstrate his own power. Perhaps more important was his desire to bring money into the imperial treasury by expanding foreign trade. The voyages were also designed in part to curb Japanese piracy along the eastern coast of China, to check on possible Mongol activity in western Asia, to search for needed medicinal herbs and spices, and to overawe a few "barbarians."

Zheng He accomplished these aims in visits to at least thirty-seven countries, many more than once. At the end of his fourth voyage, in 1415, he brought back the envoys of thirty states to do homage to the Chinese emperor.[3] He also brought back a giraffe and a zebra to astonish the court; this latter creature, whose Swahili name sounded similar to the Chinese word for unicorn, was celebrated at court as a good omen for the dynasty and as an "emblem of Perfect Virtue, Perfect Government and Perfect Harmony in the Empire and in the Universe."[4] Zheng He's work had clearly boosted Ming prestige, as well as increased Chinese trade with south and west Asia.

Therefore, from a Western perspective, it is surprising that Chinese overseas voyages were abruptly halted at the end of the seventh voyage, in 1433, and were never resumed. Zheng He himself had died on this last voyage and was buried at sea. The exact date of his death, like that of his birth, is uncertain. After this, the Chinese went back to fighting nomads on the northern land frontier, something they had done for centuries. Japanese pirates soon reappeared along the southern coast. Zheng He's name lived on as the name of a Buddhist temple in Thailand and as the name of a well in Malacca.[5] In China, however, Zheng He and his travels to the "Western Ocean" were soon forgotten. A generation after his last voyage, an official in the Ministry of Defense even burned the log books of the expedition, whether deliberately or by accident, whether at the command of the emperor or on his own, no one seems to know. By 1500, it had become a capital offense to even build a boat of more than two masts, and in 1525 an edict ordered the destruction of all remaining ocean-going vessels. "In less than a hundred years the greatest navy the world had ever known had ordered itself into extinction."[6]

We do know that a far different fate awaited the work of Prince Henry of Portugal, a man who became a legend in European history.

Born in 1394 as the third son of King John I and Queen Philippa of Portugal, Henry became famous as the man whose sailors explored the west coast of Africa during the first half of the fifteenth century. Every grade school student knows that, without the pioneering explorations of Prince Henry the Navigator, Bartholomeu Dias would not have been able to round the Cape of Good Hope in 1487–1488, Vasco da Gama would not have sailed to India and back in 1497–1499, and Columbus would not have sought a sea route to the Indies in 1492.

Although he never personally navigated any ships south, Henry did make it his life's work to send out ship after ship from his rocky outpost of Sagres on the Atlantic coast of Portugal. Henry either outfitted the ships himself or granted a license to private captains who would repay him with a fifth of everything valuable they brought back. In the early years, when his ships were hugging the African desert lands, Henry usually spent far more than he earned. Although his ships were much smaller than the government-built and -outfitted vessels of Zheng He, Henry's record was impressive for his time and place. Men working under his direction settled in the Madeiras and discovered and settled the Azores and some of the Cape Verde Islands. In 1434, Gil Eanes finally sailed beyond Cape Bojador on the west coast of Africa after other Portuguese sailors had refused or been unable to do so on fourteen earlier trips. Many men feared sailing too far south. Current rumors included the belief that anyone passing Cape Bojador would turn black, that the sea boiled in the tropics, and that the sun's rays descended in the form of liquid fire as you approached the equator. Once the Portuguese passed Cape Bojador, a barrier more psychological than physical had been breached.

The Portuguese caravels [light, fast, maneuverable ships that could be sailed inshore] continued their journeys south in the late 1430s and 1440s. Alfonzo Goncalves Baldaia went 300 miles beyond Bojador in 1435, and in 1441 Nuno Tristao went down as far as Cape Blanco, halfway between Sagres and the equator. It was in this decade that Cape Verde was rounded, although it was not until the year of Prince Henry's death in 1460 that Pedro de Sintra reached Sierra Leone. In the early years, Henry constantly had to urge his sailors "to go back and go further." It was easier and more profitable to pirate Muslim vessels in the north than it was to take the more fearful route southwest along the barren desert coast.

However, after several blacks were brought back to Portugal as slaves in 1441, the number and willingness of Henry's sailors grew. The slave trade and African exploration became intertwined, and Henry built the first European trading post used for slaves on Arguin Island in 1448.

While Prince Henry did not set out to secure slaves, the new trade in human beings did not trouble him greatly. Slaves had souls that could be saved, and that appealed to Henry as much as did the selling and "civilizing" of them. Unlike his Chinese counterpart, whose voyages had no religious aims at all, Henry had a strong desire to spread his faith and fight the infidel Moors [Muslims in northwest Africa]. Zheng He, by contrast, made no attempt to offend the religiosity of those he encountered. Personally, he offered sacrifices to a Chinese sea goddess before each voyage, but, on a tablet he placed in Ceylon in 1409 with inscriptions in Chinese, Persian, and Tamil, he offered thanks to Buddha, Allah, and the Hindu god Vishnu—all of whom were worshipped on that island. Writing such an "ecumenical" inscription would have been literally unthinkable to Henry of Portugal. Indeed, his early interest in West African exploration was stimulated by the Portuguese conquest of the Muslim city of Ceuta on the North African coast in 1415; in 1437, Henry and his brother Fernando unsuccessfully attacked the city of Tangier, near Ceuta in Muslim Morocco.

The word *crusader* has medieval associations that contrast with our image of Henry as one of the first modern explorers, but the objectives of Henry the Navigator make him a crusader in the typical Iberian fashion. A major objective of his African expeditions was to "get behind," or outflank, the Moors by sea. Like other medieval Christians, he had heard about the legendary Prester John, a Christian king in Africa somewhere south of the Sahara. If the Portuguese could reach Guinea, as they called black western Africa, they might be able to find an ally who could attack the infidel Muslims from the south. His desire to secure military allies contrasts with that of Zheng He, who sought only a formal acknowledgment of Chinese sovereignty, trade in rare goods, and political and nautical information.

Although his explorations failed to secure Henry's military and diplomatic objectives against the Moors, they provided new geographical knowledge that improved future map-making and encouraged further Portuguese exploration. They also allowed him to promote trade, control many Atlantic islands, and increase Portugal's political power at Spain's expense. In sum, Henry the Navigator's program mixed religion with economics in a way designed to appeal to the various components of Portuguese society, all of whom, unlike their Chinese counterpart, were strongly driven by the expectation of profits. His brother, King Duarte I, supported Henry's work by granting him several royal monopolies. These gave him a fifth of everything of value brought back from south of Cape Bojador and made him the "landlord" of the Madeiras, the Azores, and Cape Verde. Henry also held the monopoly on all fishing and coral gathering along the Atlantic and Mediterranean coasts of Portugal and received all fees paid by fishermen to fish in these areas. He was reputed to be the "richest man in Portugal" after the king, but he probably died in debt because of the money he spent on exploration. The Portuguese merchants supported Henry's work because of the potential profits to be gained from exploration and the slave trade. Even Portuguese pirates were pleased by the opportunity his work gave them to raid and plunder under the cover of "exploring." The Catholic Church supported Henry's missionary efforts to convert the heathen and fight the infidel, and the aristocracy generally liked both the idea of crusading and the idea of increasing Portuguese power. The loyal peasants, we must assume, enjoyed Portuguese greatness vicariously, as most peasants in most places enjoy most forms of greatness.

Because of the broad-based support for Henry's work that existed within Portuguese society, he did not need to be a navigator. One modern historian, critical of the myth of Henry as a nautical genius who ran a "school" for geographers and sailors at Sagres, put the matter quite simply: "Henry harnessed his own talents and energies to those of his family and country. He did not need to invent ships, train sailors, educate pilots or give courage to his men. He found all these at his command. What he needed to do, and what he did, was to give focus to Portuguese energies."[7]

It was this focusing of energies already there by Prince Henry of Portugal that began the "age of discovery and exploration" that we read about in our texts, while the voyages of Zheng He, the Ming admiral, remained "mere exploits."[8] We should not forget the interesting similarities between Henry and Zheng He. Both sought power for their respective rulers, though in different ways. While neither favored outright conquest of the lands he explored, both found the idea of economic domination by the "mother country" acceptable. Both had sailing vessels suitable for long ocean voyages. Yet Henry's voyages marked a beginning and those of Zheng He an ending of maritime activity. Why?

One reason this question is so intriguing is that we have the benefit of hindsight. We know what came of the voyages of Prince Henry. We know how, in the words of one of his biographers, "he set a nation's steps upon a path that led to the world's end."[9] And we know as well what happened to China—and we wonder what might have happened. Chinese vessels were not only larger but also technically superior to Western ones. Chinese sailors had the magnetic compass in the eleventh century, perhaps two centuries before their European counterparts. They also had watertight storage compartments and a "balanced rudder" that could be raised and lowered, creating greater stability. Europeans had neither of these until the late eighteenth century.[10] Given all this, it would not have been difficult for the Chinese to have dominated all of Southeast Asia, portions of India, and perhaps even the east coast of Africa.[11] There was already a substantial overseas Chinese population in Southeast Asia, and it showed every prospect of growing when the voyages were ended. If the Chinese had followed up on the voyages of Zheng He, what would the world be like today?

They did not do this, of course. Instead, China began to suffer from the intrusions of European sailors as early as the sixteenth century, just a century after Zheng He's voyages. China became prey to the West by 1850; it might have been Europe's strongest competitor. So much for speculation. What is certain is that the very structure of Chinese society in the fifteenth century made it difficult for Zheng He to be the pioneer that Henry was, even assuming that he wanted to be such a pioneer. Zheng He was a skilled administrator, diplomat, and seaman, but he was, above all, a servant of his emperor. His advancement in society depended on the emperor, not on any skills he might possess. There was little place in Ming society for a private or an independent entrepreneur [risk-taking capitalist]. Trade was a government monopoly. The Son of Heaven employed servants such as Zheng He to do his will; he would never "contract out" exploration, as the Portuguese king did.

There were also clear anti-commercial and anti-foreign biases in Chinese society during this time. The government got its money from taxes on land, not from taxing private traders and merchants. In addition, farming was considered more virtuous than business (as it was in medieval Europe until about this same time). Both Confucian and Christian ideologies glorified those who worked the land over those who soiled their hands with money. In the West, however, the diversity of states and their competition with each other, as well as the perceived need for outside goods "from the East," stimulated the rise of capitalist towns and trade after 1150. The crusades of this century also helped break down traditional biases against commerce in Europe. China was more self-sufficient and, thus, faced no real pressure to change the traditional attitude toward either trade or outsiders. Besides, some Confucian scholars felt that the very idea that China needed anything that was elsewhere, even medicinal herbs from Sumatra or Arabia, was itself demeaning.[12] The inhabitants of the Middle Kingdom (Ma Huan's translator calls it "the Central Country") did not look down upon outsiders because they were genetically programmed to do so; they did it because they could afford to; they did have a more prosperous country than their neighbors in the fifteenth century. Therefore, it is logical that the Chinese would simply view sea power as less important than maintaining a strong land army. It was. The chief threat to fifteenth-century China came from the northern barbarians; they, not Japanese or Malayan pirates, were to overrun the country in the seventeenth century. All this means that both the Chinese and the Portuguese were quite sensible in choosing the course of action they did.

Yet, given the wonderful benefit of hindsight available to historians, we can see clearly that the desire for riches of the European entrepreneurs meant that their voyages would have a much greater economic and political impact on the world than those of the Chinese, who were driven not so much by profit but by the will of one man and the immense resources of a large state. The story of these mariners and their respective countries did not play out the way anyone living in 1430 might have predicted.

Notes

1. B. Martin and S. Chien-lung, "Cheng Ho: Explorer and Navigator," in *Makers of China: Confucius to Mao* (New York: Halstead Press, 1972), 112; Louise Levathes, *When China Ruled the Seas: The Treasure Fleet of the Dragon Throne, 1405–1433* (Oxford: Oxford University Press, 1994), 64. Cheng, although his surname, is placed first in Chinese. (The new spelling of Zheng He [pronounced "Jung Huh"] used here represents the Pinyin system of transliteration adopted by scholars only in recent years.)

2. Ma Huan, *Overall Survey of the Ocean's Shores Annotated*, edited and introduced by J. V. G. Mills (Cambridge: Cambridge University Press, 1970).

3. Jung-pang Lo, "Cheng Ho," in *Encyclopedia Britannica*, 15th ed. *Macropedia*, vol. 4 (Chicago: Macmillan, 1974), 193–194.

4. Nora C. Buckley, "The Extraordinary Voyages of Admiral Cheng Ho," *History Today* (July 1975): 468.

5. Ma Huan, *Overall Survey of the Ocean's Shores*, editor's introduction, 7.

6. Levathes, *When China Ruled the Seas*, 174–175.

7. Bailey W. Diffie and George D. Winius, *Foundations of the Portuguese Empire 1415–1580* (Minneapolis: University of Minnesota Press, 1977), 122.

8. Ma Huan, *Overall Survey of the Ocean's Shores*, editor's introduction, 34.

9. Elaine Sanceau, *Henry the Navigator: The Story of a Great Prince and His Times* (New York: Norton, 1947), 247.

10. Levathes, *When China Ruled the Seas*, 81–82.

11. Fernand Braudel, *Capitalism and Material Life, 1400–1800* (New York: Harper, 1973), 308, says that a Japanese junk, constructed much like those of Cheng Ho, traveled from Japan to Acapulco in 1610.

12. See Lynda Schaffer, "China, Technology, and Change," *World History Bulletin*, vol. IV (Fall, Winter 1986–1987), 1, 4–6; also Levathes, *When China Ruled the Seas*, 179–180. Paul Kennedy, *The Rise and Fall of the Great Powers: Economic Change and Military Conflict from 1500–2000* (New York: Random House, 1987), 8, notes that members of the Confucian ruling class (mandarins) distrusted merchants because they had less control over them. The mandarins hindered foreign trade by confiscating the property of merchants or banning their businesses on occasion.

Further Reading

LEVATHES, LOUISE. *When China Ruled the Seas: The Treasure Fleet of the Dragon Throne, 1405–1433.* (Oxford: Oxford University Press, 1994). This readable explanation of the career of Zheng He and his times also includes fascinating information on earlier seafaring exploits of the Chinese people.

MA HUAN. *Overall Survey of the Ocean's Shores Annotated*, edited and introduced by J. V. G. Mills. Cambridge: Cambridge University Press, 1970. This is an interesting look at what fifteenth-century Chinese thought important.

SANCEAU, ELAINE. *Henry the Navigator: The Story of a Great Prince and His Times.* New York: Norton, 1947. Flowery hero worship in places but still useful and interesting reading.

CHAPTER 2

Elizabeth and Akbar: The Religion of the Ruler?

Can a ruler use religious conflict to strengthen his or her own rule? Can a ruler's religious preference be the basis of unity in a religiously divided state?

It seemed like a great idea at the time. In 1530 Catholic and Lutheran negotiators in Germany devised what they thought was a simple plan to end the first of many European religious wars that accompanied the Reformation begun by Martin Luther. It was the Latin phrase "cuius regio, eius religio" ("the religion of the prince is the religion of the people") that became the key words of the peace treaty of Augsburg. This meant that the religion of the ruler would be the only official religion in the ruler's land: if your prince was Lutheran, all churches in your state became Lutheran, and any who wished to remain Catholic had to pack up and move to the nearest state with a Catholic ruler. The reverse was true, of course, if your ruler was Catholic and you were Lutheran.

While this political response to religious conflict was seriously flawed (what if you were neither a Lutheran nor a Catholic but a follower of John Calvin?), it did illustrate the problems faced by rulers in religiously divided states in the sixteenth century. And the political problems posed by religious divisions were not limited to Europe. Muslim armies had swept as far east as western China and south into northwestern India as early as the eighth century. By the late twelfth century, central Asian Turks had established the Delhi Sultanate, a Muslim-dominated state in the northern heartland of the Hindu subcontinent of India, and one in which the native Hindus faced much discrimination.

How important, then, was "the religion of the prince" in the tumultuous sixteenth century? Two major rulers, Queen Elizabeth I of England (1533–1603) and Emperor Abu-ul-Fath Jalal-ud-Din Muhammad Akbar of Mughal India (1534–1606), give us the opportunity to answer this question. Both consciously tried to create what we might call a hybrid religion as a way of promoting social stability and loyalty to the ruler in their divided states. Elizabeth, daughter of King Henry VIII and Anne Boleyn, came to the throne determined to bring religious peace to a country that had experienced years of sometimes violent changes. Although Henry VIII broke with the Roman church in 1532 in order to divorce Queen Catherine and marry Elizabeth's mother, he did not become a Lutheran. Henry wanted England to remain Catholic, with himself in charge instead of the pope. He persecuted Lutherans and other Protestants until his death in 1547. For the next ten years, Elizabeth's half-brother, Edward VI (reigned 1547–1553), and half-sister, Mary (r. 1553–1558), took England on a dizzying religious ride. Edward and his advisors wanted the Church of England to be as much like Protestant churches as possible, while Mary (daughter of Henry's first wife, Catholic Queen Catherine of Aragon) officially returned England to the Catholic fold, executing some 300 Protestants as heretics in the process. Akbar (the name means "Great") faced the task of consolidating and expanding the Mughal Empire, which his father, Humayun, had lost and only partially regained before his untimely death. Unlike other Muslim rulers of India who looked down upon most non-Muslims as pagans or infidels, Akbar came to believe that a state policy of "universal peace," which accepted and appreciated the many different faiths of India (Hindus, Jains, Shia and Sunni Muslims, Zoroastrians [called Parsees in India] and Christians), was the best way to promote loyalty to the ruler.

Both Elizabeth and Akbar had weapons other than religion to control their subjects. Akbar's military skills were considerable and his conquest and rule of northern India from coast to coast was aided by an elaborate system of administration and revenue collection. Elizabeth used her cunning, energy, and intelligence to control friends and enemies alike. She also had a strong base of popular support, which she manipulated to her advantage. Both Elizabeth and Akbar were successful leaders who laid the foundation for the greatness of their respective states. They are generally seen by historians as having that special "something extra, that flash of the eye or turn of the head, which marks the crossing of the gulf between ability and genius."[1] The extent to which the religious policies of

Elizabeth and Akbar promoted unity in their respective states is a complicated question. Historians disagree, especially in their evaluation of the policy of Akbar, and it is clear that neither ruler got exactly what he or she wanted. A look at the careers of these colorful and powerful sixteenth-century leaders can help us better understand their strengths and weaknesses as we attempt to answer the questions posed at the beginning of this essay.

Religion was an issue for Elizabeth from the moment of her birth, which made her the Protestant heir to the throne in place of her Catholic sister, Mary. Her position changed suddenly when she was three; her mother, Anne, was declared a traitor and sent to the block [beheaded], and Elizabeth joined her sister, Mary, in being officially declared a bastard by a law of 1536. Despite this turn of events, Elizabeth was taught to love and honor her father as the king. She spent her early years pleasantly enough with Katherine Parr, Henry's last wife. Katherine brought all of Henry's children together as a family and saw to their education. Elizabeth received a classical education and could read Greek and Latin and speak French, Italian, and Spanish well enough to conduct business with ambassadors from those countries in their own languages. In 1547, shortly after Henry's death, Katherine married Thomas Seymour, and Elizabeth lived with them, experiencing some unwelcome sexual advances from Seymour when she was fourteen. When Katherine died in childbirth in 1548, Seymour wished to marry Elizabeth—by then living elsewhere— but she "replied evasively," a skill she refined in future years.[2] Because of Seymour's intrigues against the government of Edward VI, Elizabeth was briefly viewed with suspicion. She was in much greater danger after 1553 when her sister, Mary, became queen and some members of Elizabeth's household implicated her in some Protestant plots against the new Catholic monarch. Elizabeth responded by meeting with Mary, declaring her wish to become Catholic, and asking her sister to send her some vestments, crucifixes, and other Mass "gear" to use in her private chapel. Elizabeth was placed under guard in the Tower of London prison for a time, and many of Mary's advisors wanted her put to death as an enemy of the state. Interestingly, it was Mary's husband, Spanish King Philip II, who protected Elizabeth, something she always remembered, even years later when their countries were at war.[3]

Mary, like her half-brother, Edward, died after a short reign, and Elizabeth became queen on November 17, 1558. Even though her background as the "bastard" daughter of Anne Boleyn seemed to make it a foregone conclusion that she would restore Protestant Christianity as the official religion of England, one of Elizabeth's biographers points out that she could have left England a Catholic country. After all, many English subjects accepted Mary's return to the Catholic fold, and Elizabeth had professed to be a Roman Catholic for five years. Nevertheless, Elizabeth created a "Religious Settlement" in 1559 that made England a Protestant country because (1) she had been raised as a Protestant and was a sincere believer and (2) she would be accepted as the legitimate monarch by Catholics but would be supported more fervently as the "only hope" of the many Protestants, since the next in line to be ruler was Roman Catholic Mary Stuart, Queen of the Scots and Elizabeth's cousin.[4]

Elizabeth's "Religious Settlement," approved by the English Parliament within six months of her coronation, created what we know today as the "Church of England" or (outside of England today) the "Protestant Episcopal" Church. Like the Lutheran Churches in Germany, it was a state church and Elizabeth was declared the "Supreme Governor" of the church.[5] All clergy had to take an oath recognizing the queen's position and promising to "renounce and forsake all foreign jurisdiction . . . and authorities [the pope] and bear true faith and allegiance to the queen's highness" and to her successors. Parliament also passed, in addition to this "Act of Supremacy," an important "Act of Uniformity." This restored Protestant forms of worship, ratified Elizabeth's earlier decision to put most of the worship service in English, and provided penalties for churchmen who refused to accept these measures and fines for laypeople who refused to attend Sunday services.[6]

Elizabeth's church still looked like the "Catholic" Church of her father's day. It had bishops and priests instead of the ministers and elders used by Calvinists, and they were required by law to wear clerical garb at church services. Churches still had crucifixes, the queen kept candles in her private chapel, and she issued orders retaining stained glass windows and other "popish" elements in churches, even though these were hated by the Calvinists, or "Puritans." The Puritans not only wished a church "purified" of all Roman Catholic ritual and theology but they also wanted a state church which would control, with firm punishments, what people believed, how they worshipped, and all forms of "manners and moral." Elizabeth believed this strict of a policy could lead to a religious civil war in England.[7] Instead, the queen tried to create a church that had, both in appearance and doctrine, "a distinctive character of its own—neither Lutheran, Roman Catholic, nor Reformed [Calvinist or Presbyterian]." In 1563, she supported a group of moderate bishops who drew up a statement of beliefs, the Thirty-nine Articles. This contained many beliefs Catholics could have accepted, some which Lutherans and Calvinists could accept; it remained deliberately ambiguous on controversial issues such as the exact nature of Predestination and the question of whether or not Christ was really present in the Sacrament of the Eucharist.[8] Elizabeth was a sincere Protestant but not a person given to deep theological reflection. She once told the Catholic French ambassador that "there was only one Jesus Christ and one faith, all the rest they disputed about were trifles."[9] Her main concern was religious peace and the unity of her kingdom, not theological subtleties. If English subjects would show their loyalty to God and country by attending church on Sunday, and thereby accept the queen as "the only regulator of public worship and church government,"[10] she did not care much what people said or did in the privacy of their homes.

Elizabeth was not mistaken in fearing the political divisiveness of religion. During her reign, the neighboring country of France was torn apart by religious wars between Catholics and Protestants (Huguenots). The German states and the Netherlands remained divided religiously, and Catholic Spanish King Philip II, her former brother-in-law, was being urged by the pope to undertake a crusade against Protestant England. Elizabeth herself was officially "excommunicated" by the pope in 1570 during one of the several unsuccessful plots against her throne by those who wished to make her cousin, Mary Queen of Scots, the next queen of England.

Given these foreign and domestic threats, it was understandable that Elizabeth would follow a religious policy designed to prevent persecution of Catholics by zealous Protestants, in part because she did not want to give Catholic Spain an excuse to attack her. Unlike her sister, Mary, she went out of her way to avoid sending people to the stake for their religious views, even though she was quite firm with any person or group that questioned her royal authority. When Parliament (which contained many members favorable to Puritanism) passed a law in 1563 stating that any person who twice refused to take the oath recognizing the queen's supremacy over the church was to be executed, Elizabeth instructed Matthew Parker, the Archbishop of Canterbury, to be sure that no one was asked to take the oath more than once.[11] The wisdom of Elizabeth's policy was shown in 1588, when the Spanish sent a massive armada of ships to invade England in hopes of returning England to the Catholic fold. Catholics supported Elizabeth in this moment of national peril; there was no uprising of Catholics to overthrow their Protestant ruler. The Spanish were prevented from landing by the skillful work of English sailors and a timely storm that the English referred to as "a Protestant wind." Although Catholic priests were sent to England to secretly celebrate Mass and administer Sacraments to English Catholics and although over a hundred of these men were executed for treason, most English Catholics remained loyal to the queen, and the total number of Catholics declined during her reign. Elizabeth was also willing to deal harshly with Protestant critics of her policy. Two Dutch Anabaptists attending an illegal prayer meeting in 1575 were judged guilty of heresy for denying that a Christian could be a government official, and they were burned at the stake. And, in 1579, when a lawyer named John Stubbs wrote a work attacking the French royal family and the queen's proposed marriage to the French Catholic Duke of Anjou, she ordered that his right hand be cut off with a meat cleaver. It was said that, after his hand was severed at the wrist, he lifted his hat with his left hand and shouted, "God save the queen" before he fainted.[12] Elizabeth often used marriage negotiations as a diplomatic tool; some believed that she might have married the duke if there had not been such strong objections to this match with a Catholic foreigner.

Her religious policy was not the only reason Elizabeth is fondly remembered and has an era named after her. We speak of "Elizabethan England" because this queen ruled for forty-four years and was able to develop and use her skills as a ruler and a woman to create a strong sense of personal loyalty in her subjects. She had excellent advisors and adventuresome servants, such as Sir Walter Raleigh and Sir Francis Drake, who established England as a strong naval power. The queen also learned early in her reign that she could maintain her control by meeting with her councilors individually and by asking them for their individual views in writing. Hot-tempered at times, she was known to even slap her courtiers and order them out of her presence. Members of Parliament whose speeches displeased her were sent to prison. Yet she always released them, as she nearly always restored unlucky courtiers to "her favor" by inviting them back to court. This was a person "in which the spontaneous outburst of a high-tempered woman blended with the artifices of a calculating politician."[13] Although Elizabeth was doubtless difficult to work with, she certainly understood how to appeal to her subjects. Each year she moved her court around the country on her colorful "progresses," visiting the homes of her nobles, letting the people see her and entertain her with plays, speeches of praise, and poetry. These journeys allowed people to see their queen in person, as she gratefully acknowledged their devotion. She also used her position as a woman to strengthen this loyalty. Historians disagree on why Elizabeth never married, but, whatever her reason, she did deliberately create the impression among ordinary people that she cared more about them than about having a husband; she could be seen as "married" to England. On the eve of the anticipated Spanish invasion, when the armada had already entered the English channel, Elizabeth visited some of her troops and made one of the most famous speeches in English history, saying, "I know I have the body of a weak and feeble woman, but I have the heart and stomach of a king, and of a king of England too! And [I] think foul scorn that Parma [Spanish general] or Spain, or any prince of Europe, should dare to invade the borders of my realm!" The people loved it; perhaps in that moment she became the "good Queen Bess" remembered fondly by generations of English people.[14]

Since Mughal Emperor Akbar lived in a place so distant and different from Elizabeth's England, it is unusual to find any similarities between the two rulers beyond the dates of their reigns. Yet Akbar, like Elizabeth, experienced a troubled youth, marked by an awareness of religious differences. Descended from the great Mongol and Turkish conquerors Genghis Khan and Tamerlane, he was born in the house of a Hindu ruler, while his father was on the run, trying to recapture land in northeast India. Akbar's father was a Sunni Muslim, while his mother was a Shiite [two large, theologically different branches of Islam]. His tutor, Abul Latif, taught him the principle of "universal peace," which encouraged tolerance of all religions. While growing up, he was captured and rescued three times as his father and uncles fought for control of the empire. While these struggles were over family inheritance and not over religious issues, it was clear to the young prince that the support of Muslim scholars or holy men (ulema) could help a ruler gain popular support; it was also clear to the young Akbar that anyone who would successfully rule India would have to deal with the fact that most of his subjects would not be Muslims. When his father, Humayun, died in 1556, Akbar was only thirteen. The empire was ruled in Akbar's name by a regent, Bairam Khan, a Shiite Muslim who successfully completed the conquests of much of what is today Pakistan and Afghanistan. Bairam Khan's increasingly arrogant decisions and lavish living led Akbar to replace the regent and begin to rule in his own right in 1560.[15]

The young man who would expand the Mughal Empire to its greatest extent has been described as a broad-shouldered person of "uncommon dignity," with long hair, a loud voice of "peculiar richness," "bright and flashing eyes," and a "powerful, magnetic, and inspiring" personality.[16] Historians have also been impressed by the seeming contradictions in Akbar's personality. Akbar was a deeply spiritual man but also a brutal warrior. He said that "a monarch should be ever intent on conquest, otherwise his neighbors rise in arms against him," yet, when not fighting, he loved to engage in theological and philosophical discussions with learned men from many religions. He loved hunting but spent many years as a virtual vegetarian. He "spent whole nights repeating the name of the Almighty God," had mystical experiences, and went on pilgrimages. Yet this same man authorized the massacre of thousands of people, many of them women and children, after conquering the Hindu fortress of Chitor, and he ordered the building of a mound made from the heads of his fallen enemies after the battle of Panipat in 1556. Akbar could be extremely energetic, humane, and considerate, yet he also suffered from depression.[17] Clearly, this greatest ruler of the Mughal Empire was a complex man.

But Akbar was no more complex than the situation he inherited. Ethnically, the territory of the Mughal Empire contained Turks, Mongols, and Uzbeks (these three known collectively as Turanis), as well as hundreds of independent or semi-independent Hindu rulers (rajas). Some of these were territorial chieftains and others were the heads of large families, or clans. Those noblemen expected virtual independence and were reluctant to take orders from any central authority, while the Turks who had come from Persia, or Iran, were often skilled bureaucrats used to working in a strongly centralized administration. Both of these groups were composed of Muslims who viewed Hindus as polytheistic "idolaters."[18] When Akbar came to the throne, his territory was quite small; it consisted of a small crescent of land extending from central Afghanistan through the heart of modern Pakistan down to the north central Indian cities of Panipat and Delhi. By the end of his reign, Akbar's empire contained all of north and central India, including the Indus and Ganges river valleys.

Creating and maintaining a large empire inhabited by such varied ethnic groups required a variety of skills. Akbar needed large armies composed of artillery, archers mounted on horseback or elephants, and infantry with firearms. The young ruler spent most of the 1560s and 1570s subduing the Hindu (Rajput) kingdoms in central India from coast to coast. In 1580 and 1581, he put down revolts by family members seeking his throne and others in Kabul and elsewhere in the north taking advantage of Sunni Muslim discontent with his religious and administrative policies. Akbar was unable to finish his military consolidation of the empire until 1601, four years before his death.[19]

In the beginning of his career, Akbar was a skilled military leader intent on increasing his power by enlarging his empire. Until the mid-1570s, he was also a traditional Muslim ruler, subduing the armies of Hindu Rajputs in the name of Allah. However, even in his twenties he began to see both personal and political reasons for some changes in social and religious policy. In 1562, he married the daughter of the Rajput ruler of Jaipur after that kingdom submitted to Mughal overlordship. He was the first Mughal ruler to add Hindu princesses (he later married three more) to his harem and to allow them to maintain their religion. The following year, he dropped the Muhgal practice of enslaving the families of defeated enemies, and in 1563 he stopped taxing Hindu pilgrimages. Akbar also ended the traditional tax levied on non-Muslims in 1564, a more radical step, since this tax was levied in all Islamic countries.

Since Akbar remained a devout Muslim during these early years, these policy changes were made largely for political reasons, to win the support of the Rajput rulers. However, Akbar's own religious views and practices were beginning to change. In 1562, he became so impressed by the simple life and wisdom of Muslim mystic Shaikh Salim Chishti that he made a pilgrimage to his shrine each year for seventeen years and even built a new capital, Fatehpur-Sikri, near this site. Shaikh Salim correctly predicted that the emperor, who had difficulty having sons, would have three sons; when the first was born, Akbar named him Salim in honor of the Shaikh. In 1575, the emperor constructed a special building, the Ibadat Khana, in which he brought together thinkers from various religions to discuss the beliefs and practices of each. A Portuguese Jesuit priest, arriving at the court in 1580, recorded this speech by Akbar:

> I perceive that there are varying customs and beliefs of varying religious paths. . . . But the followers of each religion regard the institution of their own religion as better than those of any other. Not only so, but they strive to convert the rest to their own way of belief. If these refuse to be converted, they not only despise them, but also regard them as . . . enemies. And this caused me to feel many serious doubts and scruples. Wherefore I desire that on appointed days the books of all the religious laws be brought forward, and the doctors meet and hold discussions, so that I may hear them, and that each one may determine which is the truest and mightiest religion.[20]

Muslim historians were critical of Akbar's religious policy, which had moved him away from traditional practices by the 1580s, but they admit that he was "deeply religious by nature" and had a soul that "longed for direct spiritual experience." In 1578, Akbar had what has been described as a mystical experience, or "ecstasy," during a royal hunt. He freed all the animals that had been rounded up for him to kill, distributed a large sum of gold to the poor, and cut off his long hair.[21] By 1579, discouraged by Muslim clerical intolerance, Akbar issued a decree that gave him the authority to resolve religious disputes; his decisions would be "binding upon all the people, provided always that such an order is not opposed to the . . . explicit injunction of the Qur'an."[22]

Akbar's beliefs matured quickly. In 1582 he established the *Din-i-Ilahi,* usually translated as "Divine Faith." Its members vowed to dedicate their property, life, and honor to Akbar, espoused a simple monotheism, and renounced "traditional and imitative" Islam. Akbar borrowed rituals from those of the Parsees, Christians, and Hindus. There were initiation ceremonies, feasts on members' birthdays, and a form of bowing to the emperor previously reserved for prayer in the mosque.[23]

Historians disagree on whether or not *Din-i-Ilahi* was a "new" religion (something assumed by many history textbooks) or a way to appeal to non-Muslims and to focus loyalty on the emperor. Many traditional Muslims, led by court scholar Abdul Qadir Badauni, were bitterly critical of the "Divine Faith," which was supported and directed by Abul Fazl, Akbar's chief counselor, famous flatterer, and court historian. Some Muslim historians today see *Din-i-Ilahi* as a superficial form of emperor worship, forbidden by the Qur'an, which undermined the Muslim character of Akbar's state. More "secular" historians praise the emperor for a religious and social policy which, because it was accepting of many traditions, was far ahead of its time. It did not make loyalty to the state dependent on being a member of any official state religion, including Islam; membership in *Din-i-Ilahi* itself was voluntary and somewhere between two dozen and two thousand (sources vary significantly) noblemen joined.[24]

To better evaluate Akbar's religious policy, we need to understand that his administrative system combined features of the personal relations between rulers and their chief nobles found in early feudalism with the practices of a modern government that employs paid officials who feel more of an obligation to the institutions of government than they do to the ruler. Akbar chose his leading civil and military appointees, known as *mansabdars* [Persian for "officeholder"; *mansab* is an "office"], on the basis of their loyalty to him. They were organized into grades, based on how many troops and horses they were expected to supply to Akbar in time of war. To provide the *mansabdars* with money to help them meet this demand, they were assigned revenue from land *(jagirs)*. The emperor retained control of all land and could "fire" *mansabdars* and promote or demote them to higher or lower ranks. Akbar divided his empire into twelve large provinces, each led by a governor, who, aided by other officials, administered justice, collected revenue, recruited troops, and kept order. The whole system was reinforced by spies who reported to the court.[25] In 1572–1573 Akbar introduced "branding regulations" *(dagh)* requiring *mansabdars* to present their troops and horses for muster (only the horses were branded) to prove that they were using their money to actually pay troops and not for other, nonmilitary, purposes. By the end of the decade, strict implementation of the *dagh*—along with Akbar's *mahzar* and other religious changes—led some of the Turani *mansabdars* to revolt. After that, he eased the enforcement of the branding regulation.[26]

Some scholars see no connection between Akbar's religious policies (his ending of religious taxes and promoting of "universal peace" and the "Divine Faith") and the loyalty of his military and civilian officials. Others disagree and say that the emperor's "liberal religious ideas" were linked to his imperial system of administration. Akbar changed an empire that had been previously ruled by and for Muslims into one in which Hindu Rajputs could and did play a major role. He favored Hindus as much as he could because he could not always depend upon the loyalty of the Turkish and Mongol nobility. Also, by respecting non-Muslim religions, praising the ideal of "universal peace," and marrying Hindu princesses, Akbar, some say, "transformed" the nobility "into a constructive force" and helped erase the "foreign character of the Mughal Empire." From Akbar's time, the Mughal ruling class no longer saw theirs as *only* a Muslim Empire. Muslims continued to hold the majority of the *mansabs,* but the holders of power in the provinces defined themselves as Mughal *mansabdars,* not as mere servants of a Muslim ruling class. Akbar's court rituals, his use of Hindu *mansabdars,* and the *Din-i-Ilahi* created the impression "not [of] Muslims ruling over Hindus but [of] Muslims and Hindus together, serving a ruler who, whatever his personal beliefs, was not merely a Muslim or Hindu." The empire lasted as long as this practice.[27]

Both Elizabeth I of England and Akbar, the "greatest" Mughal, used a hybrid, or "mixed," religion to try to unify their divided states and promote loyalty to the ruler, and each had personal as well as political motives. Elizabeth's personal religious views, considered "heretical" by Catholics and too "Papist" by the Puritans, were nevertheless those of a sincere Protestant Christian; Akbar's personal views, to the extent that we can determine, given the controversy that surrounds them, were those of a sincere seeker after religious truth who clearly disliked the claims to exclusive truth advanced by Muslim theologians.

In both sixteenth-century England and India, the religion of the ruler did matter. Elizabeth's attempt to create a distinctive "Church of England" that was neither Catholic nor Calvinist suffered a severe setback forty-six years after her death, when the English beheaded Charles I in 1649 and established a Puritan commonwealth under Oliver Cromwell. Akbar's *Din-i-Ilahi* disappeared soon after his death, but his mixed Muslim and Hindu Mughal Empire survived much longer. Religion could be a unifying as well as a divisive force in this period. Perhaps "the religion of the ruler" can only truly become "the religion of the people" in situations in which the ruler's beliefs are only slightly out of step with the beliefs of the majority of his or her subjects. The "Church of England" still exists because Elizabeth did not overreach herself; she was in touch with the sentiment of her people, who would tolerate only a limited amount of religious regulation. The Puritans offered more of this than the English, in the final analysis, would tolerate. Akbar's *Din-i-Ilahi* evaporated after his death because an attempt to join an "inclusive" faith such as Hinduism with an "exclusive" one such as Islam has never succeeded, at least not for long. Akbar's failure perhaps foreshadows that of twentieth-century Indian leader, Mohandas Gandhi, who wished for Hindus and Muslims to live in peace after gaining independence from the British. Gandhi was assassinated in 1947 by a Hindu fanatic. Akbar was spared this fate; only his bones were dug up and burned by an angry mob some fifty years after his death.

Notes

1. Percival Spear, *India: A Modern History*, New Edition, revised and enlarged (Ann Arbor: University of Michigan Press, 1972), 128. Though included in a chapter on Akbar, Spear's statement also specifically refers to Elizabeth as having this quality.
2. Wallace MacCaffrey, *Elizabeth I* (London: Edward Arnold, 1993), 9–10.
3. Jasper Ridley, *Elizabeth I: The Shrewdness of Virtue* (New York: Viking Penguin, 1988), 41, 47–59, 66–67.
4. MaCaffrey, *Elizabeth I*, 48–51; see also Ridley, *Elizabeth*, 33, on her "sincere devotion to the Protestant religion."
5. Carole Levin, *The Heart and Stomach of a King: Elizabeth I and the Politics of Sex and Power* (Philadelphia: University of Pennsylvania Press, 1994), 14.
6. Carl S. Meyer, *Elizabeth I and the Religious Settlement of 1559* (St. Louis: Concordia, 1960), 39, 45–48.
7. See William Haller, *Elizabeth I and the Puritans* (Ithaca, NY: Cornell University Press, 1964), 1–2, 9–10, 21.
8. William P. Haugaard, *Elizabeth and the English Reformation: The Struggle for a Stable Settlement of Religion* (Cambridge: Cambridge University

Press, 1968), 78, 248–252; Susan Doran, *Elizabeth I and Religion* (London: Routledge, 1994), 18–19; Meyer, *Religious Settlement,* 149–167.

9. Haugaard, *Elizabeth and the English Reformation,* 25.

10. MacCaffrey, *Elizabeth I,* 300.

11. Joel Hurtsfield, *Elizabeth I and the Unity of England* (London: English Universities Press, 1960), 57.

12. Ridley, *Elizabeth I: Shrewdness of Virtue,* 119–123, 206–214; MacCaffrey, *Elizabeth I,* 202–205; Hurtsfield, *Elizabeth I and Unity of England,* 103.

13. MacCaffrey, *Elizabeth I,* 360–362; Carolly Erickson, *The First Elizabeth* (New York: Summit Books, 1983), 172–173, 313–314.

14. MacCaffrey, *Elizabeth I,* 376–377; Hurstfield, *Elizabeth and Unity of England,* 157. On the reasons Elizabeth may not have married, see Susan Bassnett, *Elizabeth I: A Feminist Perspective* (New York: Berg, 1988), 2–11, which contains a good summary of the speculation and theories of various historians.

15. S. M. Burke, *Akbar. The Greatest Mogul* (New Delhi: Munshiram Monoharlal Publishers, 1989), 17–25, 39–42, contains a clear account of Akbar's youth and the period of Bairam Khan's regency. See also Ashirbadilal Srivastava, *The History of India (1000 AD–1707 AD)* (Agra: Shiva Lal Agarwala, 1964), 469.

16. Burke, *Akbar,* 32; Khaliq Ahmed Nizami, *Akbar and Religion* (Delhi: Idarah-i-Adabiyat, 1989), 1.

17. Burke, *Akbar,* 58, 104–105; Srivastava, *History of India,* 447; Athar Abbas Rizvi, *Religious and Intellectual History of the Muslims in Akbar's Reign* (New Delhi: Munshiram Manoharlal Publishers, 1975), 110; Nizami, *Akbar and Religion,* 2, 165; Muni Lal, *Akbar* (New Delhi: Vikas, 1980), 64, 94, 128, 144–145.

18. Ahsan Raza Khan, *Chieftains in the Mughal Empire* (Simla; Indian Institute Of Advanced Study, 1977), 1–5; Douglas E. Streusand, *The Formation of the Mughal Empire* (Delhi: Oxford University Press, 1989), 23, 26–32.

19. The most convenient summary of Akbar's conquests is in Srivastava, *History of India,* 447–464.

20. Rizvi, *Religious and Intellectual History,* 126–131; Burke, *Akbar,* 102–103. The Ibadat Khana was misnamed the "House of Worship" by earlier historians. It was not a place of worship but a debating hall. For the attitude of the Jesuit missionaries toward Akbar, and their expectations that he would become a Christian, see the fascinating *Letters from the Mughal Court: The First Jesuit Mission to Akbar (1580–83),* ed. John Corveia-Afonso (St. Louis: Institute of Jesuit Sources, 1981).

21. Nizami, *Akbar and Religion,* is the modern historian most critical of Akbar's religious experiments, believing they constituted an unnecessary departure from traditional Islam that separated him from the

"Muslim masses"; see pp. 2, 159–160, 232, 245–246. See also the similar views of Ishtiaq H. Qureshi, in *Akbar: Architect of the Mughal Empire* (Karachi: Ma'aref Ltd., 1978), 165–166. See Burke, *Akbar*, 104, on Akbar's "ecstasy."

22. Rizvi, *Religious and Intellectual History*, 147.

23. Spear, *India: A Modern History*, 135; Burke, *Akbar*, 122–125.

24. Srivastava, *Akbar the Great*, vol. II (Agra: Shiva Lal Agarwala Publishers, 1967), 313–315, sees *Din-i-Ilahi* as "not a religion" but "a common religious bond for at least the elite of the various sections of India's population"; it was designed to promote imperial unity. See also his *History of India*, 474–475, 526–529; Burke, *Akbar*, 122–129, agrees with Srivastava that "Divine Faith" was not a religion but a Sufi brotherhood; it had no scripture, places of worship, or organization of clergy and was not promulgated among the population at large. Nizami, *Akbar and Religion*, 133, 191–193, 215–216, 243–245, 339–340, sees *Din-i-Ilahi* as a new religion, if a weak one, based on a "haphazard agglomeration of certain rituals, whimsically visualized and pompously demonstrated," and designed to improperly make Akbar a "prophet-king." Qureshi, *Akbar: Architect*, 166, agrees with Nizami that *Din-i-Ilahi* was an ill-conceived attempt to promote loyalty to the ruler; it only alienated the "natural [Muslim] supporters of the Empire." Badauni's attack on Akbar, written in 1595–1596, just before his death, is entitled *Muntakhab-ut-Tawarikh* ("History with a Vengeance"); see Harbans Mukhia, *Historians and Historiography During the Reign of Akbar* (New Delhi: Vikas, 1976) for a thorough analysis of Badauni.

25. See Stephen P. Blake, "The Patrimonial-Bureaucratic Empire of the Mughals," in *The State in India*, ed. Hermann Kulke (Delhi: Oxford University Press, 1995), 278–303; for a description of Akbar's military and the *mansabdari* system, see Srivastava, *Akbar the Great*, II, 217–247; Streusand, *Formation of the Mughal Empire*, 139–148.

26. See Streusand, *Formation of the Mughal Empire*, 154–172, on Akbar's "crisis and compromise."

27. Among those who see little connection between Akbar's religious policy and his success as an imperial ruler is Khan, *Chieftains in the Mughal Empire*, 222–23, who says that Akbar's military "striking capacity" and ability to punish rebels, and not his "liberal religious ideas," kept people loyal; see also Iqtidar Alam Khan, "The Nobility Under Akbar and the Development of His Religious Policy, 1560–80" *Journal of the Royal Asiatic Society of Great Britain and Ireland* (1968; parts I & II): 29–36, who believes that Akbar's religious concessions to non-Muslims were tactical devices in response to the hostility of the conservative Muslims, and not part of a broader vision of a multireligious Mughal Empire. The more common view, that his religious policy did matter,

is expressed by P. S. Bedi, *The Mughal Nobility Under Akbar* (Jalandhar: ABS Publications, 1985), vii, 22, and in Streusand, *Formation of the Mughal Empire,* 123–153.

Further Reading

BURKE, S. M. *Akbar, the Greatest Mogul.* New Delhi: Munshiram Monoharlal Publishers, 1989. This brief biography of the ruler tries to strike a balance between Hindu and Muslim historians and is written from a modern Western perspective.

DORAN, SUSAN. *Elizabeth I and Religion.* London: Routledge, 1994. A clear, brief account which summarizes much of the research of the past thirty years.

MACCAFFREY, WALLACE. *Elizabeth I.* London: Edward Arnold, 1993. Thoughtful, readable biography.

NIZAMI, KHALIQ AHMED. *Akbar and Religion.* Delhi: Idarah-i-Adabiyat-i-Delhi, 1989. Written by a Muslin scholar hostile to the *Din-i-Ilahi* who offers some good reasons this faith did not last.

CHAPTER 3

Kangxi and Louis XIV: Dynastic Rulers, East and West

To what extent can dynastic rulers control their own fate? What is the key to successful "absolutism"?

In the world of the late seventeenth century, a comparison between Kangxi and Louis XIV is an obvious one. At opposite ends of the Eurasian land mass, these two rulers clearly stand out. In western Europe, Louis XIV (1638–1715), a member of France's Bourbon dynasty, ruled that continent's most powerful nation. In the Far East, Kangxi (1654–1722), a member of the Qing [pronounced "ching"] dynasty, was emperor of China.[1] Both rulers had equally long reigns. Kangxi's years of personal rule lasted from 1669 to 1722 (fifty-three years and four major wars), while those of Louis XIV extended from 1661 to 1715 (fifty-four years and the same number of wars).

Given their longevity, it is not surprising that each man experienced personal tragedies. Son and grandsons preceded Louis XIV in death, so that a five-year-old great-grandson, Louis XV, was left as successor in 1715. Kangxi's oldest son and "heir apparent," Yinreng, was infamous for his acts of sexual depravity, sadism, and irresponsibility. After years of fatherly patience, sorrow, and cover-ups, Kangxi declared him mad and then deposed and arrested him in 1712.[2] These family problems were also political ones, for the success of dynastic government depends upon the quality of the ruler. In the Chinese case, Kangxi's fourth son, Yinzhen, proved to be a far more capable ruler than the original heir apparent would have been. The French were less fortunate; Louis XV proved to be a lazy and mistress-ridden monarch. The Qing dynasty lasted until

1911; the Bourbon dynasty collapsed in the storm of the French Revolution (1789–1799).

The great energy and determination that both Kangxi and Louis XIV displayed clearly distinguish them from their successors. Kangxi's writings frequently note the importance of hard work and attention to detail. "This is what we have to do," he wrote, "apply ourselves to human affairs to the utmost, while remaining responsive to the dictates of Heaven. In agriculture, one must work hard in the fields *and* hope for fair weather." Louis also relished the hard work necessary to run a large state. In notes he wrote for his successor, he warned against "prolonged idleness" and advised that a regular work schedule was good for the spirit: "No satisfaction can equal that of following each day the progress of glorious and lofty undertakings and of the happiness of the people, when one has planned it all himself."[3] Both rulers felt personally responsible for the welfare of their subjects, yet both fought major wars to extend their lands and their power. Since warfare was expensive in money and lives, it was not always easy for these men to balance their desire for power with their desire to improve the lives of their subjects.

This very tension between war and peace helps illuminate some of the problems facing even a conscientious autocratic, or "absolute," ruler during these last few centuries before the world was transformed forever by the Industrial Revolution. Neither Louis XIV nor Kangxi had to please voters or make decisions about social and economic programs, with one ear cocked to a national stock market or an international monetary system. Their job was simpler—in theory, anyway. It was to strengthen the power of their dynasty by maintaining the military and economic strength of their country. The precise way in which each ruler pursued this goal tells us something about China and western Europe and something of the pitfalls facing an "absolute" ruler in the days before telephones, fax machines, and computers.

Kangxi was a Manchu. That fact defined his political task. The warlike Manchu nomads, who lived northeast of China, had gradually increased their territory and power at the expense of the Ming dynasty, which ruled China from 1368 to 1644. In the early seventeenth century, Manchu leader Nurhaci (1559–1626) began to transform the Manchu tribes into a modern state by curbing the power of local chiefs and by centralizing the government. His sons continued this process of consolidation, and the Manchus thus were able to conquer Beijing easily in 1644, once the last Ming emperor was defeated and committed suicide. Kangxi's father, the first Qing emperor, needed to win support from native Chinese leaders, especially the Confucian scholars. To accomplish this, he appointed two men to all top-level government positions, one a Manchu and the other a native [or Han] Chinese. Throughout his long reign, Kangxi continued his father's balance in making all major appointments so that native Chinese would not unduly resent their foreign leaders. This proved wise, since the Manchus, while militarily superior to the Chinese in the beginning of the reign, were vastly outnumbered. To govern China successfully, a foreign dynasty had to have so much native help in ruling that it became virtually Chinese.[4]

Kangxi was only seven years old in 1661 when his father died, leaving the government to four noblemen assigned to govern on his behalf. Although Kangxi ended this regency in 1667, it was two years later before he was able to break the power of one particularly powerful regent. When the fifteen-year-old ruler acted, he did so decisively, throwing the offending overmighty subject, Oboi, into prison, where he died five years later.[5]

By acting decisively and wisely and appearing strong, Kangxi strengthened his own personal power and that of his empire. He increased the army's size from one hundred eighty-five thousand men in 1661 to three hundred fifteen thousand in 1684. He also took up to seventy thousand of them north of the Great Wall two or three times a year on hunting trips (really military maneuvers) so that they might keep their archery and riding sharp. He appointed former Manchu army leaders as provincial governors. In 1667, such appointees governed twenty-eight of the twenty-nine provinces. Kangxi also shrewdly conducted frequent audiences with military leaders; he believed that a general who occasionally bowed to the emperor remained humble and "properly fearful."[6]

By the middle of his reign, Kangxi's wise choice of subordinates, realistic understanding of people, and close attention to detail reduced the danger of rebellion by unhappy Chinese subjects or discontented Manchu clan leaders. Before this happened, however, the emperor had to fight a bloody and prolonged war against three rebel leaders in the south. This war began in 1673 and lasted until 1682, in part because the emperor had trouble finding good generals. After defeating the three rebel states, Kangxi was able to add the island of Taiwan to his empire in 1684. It was more difficult to establish Chinese power firmly in the north. This took major campaigns against the Russians and against the Mongol chieftain, Galdan.

Before moving to dislodge the Russians from Chinese territory along the Amur River, where they had been settling since the 1650s, Kangxi made his usual careful preparations. He collected enough military supplies for a three-year war and moved Dutch-designed cannons and men trained to use them to the front. In 1685, he captured the Russian fortress at Albazin, and in 1689 the Treaty of Nerchinsk restored Chinese control in the area.[7] It took eight more years for Kangxi to defeat the western Mongol tribes led by Galdan. "Now my purpose is accomplished, my wishes fulfilled," the elated emperor wrote when a defeated Galdan committed suicide in 1697. "Isn't this the will of Heaven? I am so extremely happy!" These western victories set the stage for Chinese domination of Tibet, which began in the final years of Kangxi's reign and has lasted intermittently to our own day.[8]

Of course, external security was not enough. Dynastic rulers were obliged to keep constant and careful watch over subjects and subordinates. Kangxi did this by devising a system of palace memorials. These secret reports from agents of unquestioned loyalty to the ruler and the dynasty contained detailed information and comments, sent directly to the emperor and viewed by him alone. Their use allowed him to bypass official channels, to learn of official incompetence and would-be plots, and to quickly acquire more accurate information than that provided by the Grand Secretariat.

One of the emperor's most trusted agents was a Manchu bondservant named Cao Yin (1658–1712). This competent administrator had a classical Confucian education and wrote poetry with his Chinese friends in his spare time; he was an ideal informant for Kangxi, who sent him to the city of Nanjing as textile commissioner in 1692. In his role as manager of imperial textile factories, Cao Yin supervised twenty-five hundred artisans and 664 looms, and he shipped quotas of silk to Beijing. In secret palace memorials written between 1697 and his death, he gave the emperor detailed information on the local harvest, problems faced by the local governor, and the "condition of the common people." Another secret memorialist sent reports to the emperor on the movements of 5,923 grain boats that left Yangzhou for Beijing each year. Such information helped the emperor keep his officials honest and stop trouble before it started.[9]

Such close supervision of foodstuffs and silk production was important to a ruler who relied on a closely regulated economy. The textile factories at Nanjing, Hangzhou, and Suzhou were monopolies run by the government, which provided funds and established production quotas. During his reign, Kangxi tried to strengthen these government controls over trade. In 1699, for example, a statute ended private rights to purchase copper and gave the copper monopoly to merchants from the imperial household in Peking.[10] Neither Kangxi nor his French counterpart favored "free enterprise," which they considered inefficient and foolish. In their opinion, the state alone had sufficient wealth to underwrite large commercial projects. These mercantilist rulers also asked why private citizens should enrich themselves with money that could be going to the state and ruler. They also worried that overly rich subjects might be more likely to rebel against their rule.

One of the central features of absolutist government was the clear tendency to link the welfare of a country with the power of its ruler. If this was the case in China, which enjoyed two thousand years of unified government, it was even more true in France. There, in the absence of a long tradition of dynastic government, it was often only the strength of the ruler that prevented the kingdom from breaking into the separate provinces from which it had been created. Louis XIV early learned the need for a strong monarchy; his lesson was as important in shaping French absolutism as was Kangxi's Manchu heritage in shaping Chinese government policies.

In 1648, when Louis was ten, an uprising known as the Fronde forced his mother and her chief minister, Cardinal Mazarin, to flee Paris to avoid capture by hostile armies. Although this uprising was poorly organized and sputtered within a few years, the revolt had impressed the young monarch (as had Kangxi's battle with the too powerful regent Oboi) with the need to create both the image and the reality of a strong monarchy. When Louis assumed personal rule in 1661 after the death of Mazarin, he quickly established his authority by refusing to appoint a new chief minister and by arresting Nicholas Fouquet, his extremely wealthy and corrupt finance minister. By hard work, Louis soon convinced others he was the "Sun King"; his palace at Versailles was soon the envy of other European monarchs.

The challenge Louis faced was greater than that which confronted Kangxi, since the former had to create a new tradition; the

Manchu ruler, on the other hand, had only to prove that his new dynasty fit into existing Chinese traditions. For centuries the French nobility had seen the king as only "first among equals." Louis had to change all that, and he did, using some of the same methods as his Chinese contemporary, as well as some unique ones.

Like Kangxi, Louis employed officials loyal to him alone. But these differed from those in China, who were members of an ancient bureaucracy. Since France lacked a traditional bureaucracy, Louis had to build a new bureaucracy on the foundation laid by his father. His objective was to create an administration that allowed him to undercut the power of the old nobility while he strengthened his power at home and abroad. In selecting officials, the young king chose people from France's middle-class—men of dedication and ability, such as Michel Le Tellier as secretary of state for war and Jean-Baptiste Colbert as controller-general of finance. These commoners, like the Manchu bondservants used by Kangxi, had no social or political status other than that conferred on them by their employer; they were loyal servants because they owed everything to the king.

By employing them, the king was able to create a civil and military organization that freed his dynasty from dependence on the old noble families of the realm. Louis's appointment of Colbert, in particular, proved judicious and shows some of the similarities between economic developments in Europe and China. As chief financial official, Colbert attempted to create a strong, state-directed economy designed to make the king strong in France and France strong in Europe. His international goal was a favorable balance of trade. So, while the Chinese were using state factories in Nanjing to produce silk for export to Europe via the Philippine Islands, Colbert was making France as self-sufficient as possible and generating income for the king by exports abroad from government-subsidized silk works at Lyons, linen factories at Arras, and pottery works at Nevers. To curb the import of foreign products into France, Colbert convinced the king to raise tariffs [taxes on foreign goods] in 1664 and 1667.[11] France's adoption of this mercantilist economic system was based on the belief that there was only a limited amount of wealth in the world, and the country that got to it first would prosper the most. Naturally, Colbert encouraged Frenchmen to establish trading colonies overseas, and he strengthened the royal navy and merchant marine in order to make this sort of expansion more attractive. The limited success of Colbert's policies was due to their expense. The tax structure and its collection system could not generate enough revenue to meet military and civilian needs. The French farmed out tax collection to private citizens, or tax farmers, who had to turn in a fixed amount of money to the king but could keep for themselves anything collected beyond that amount. Such a system encouraged graft and placed a great burden on the poor. The fact that Louis was unable to scrap this system in favor of one able to produce more revenue and greater fairness, and the fact that the nobility remained exempt from taxation, show some of the limitations on absolute monarchs in the seventeenth century.

That Louis used Le Tellier's professional army to engage in dynastic wars rather than using his limited funds to promote greater domestic prosperity shows another flaw in the system of absolutism. Dynastic wars reflected the will of a single person, and they served as the quickest path to necessary short-term prestige. Louis chose war, at first to secure glory and territory, and finally in self-defense. The War of Devolution, 1667–1668, was fought to get territory in the Spanish Netherlands [modern Belgium]. It was a limited success but led to the less successful Dutch War of 1672–1678; the Dutch prevented a decisive French victory when they opened the dikes and flooded the territory around Amsterdam. The French did expand their frontiers in both wars, and they used dubious legal claims after 1678 to continue annexations along their eastern border, taking the important fortress city of Strasbourg (then in the Holy Roman Empire) in 1681.

All this, especially when combined with Louis' insufferable vanity (he offered to settle with the Dutch in 1672 if they would strike a gold medal in his honor, thanking him for giving them peace),[12] naturally alarmed Louis' neighbors. When the king moved troops into Germany in 1688, he soon found himself facing a coalition of Germans, Dutch, and English. The War of the League of Augsburg lasted until 1697 and ended in a stalemate. Louis' last war, also fought against many enemies, was the War of the Spanish Succession, 1701–1713. The decision of the French king to place his grandson on the vacant Spanish throne threatened the "balance of power" in Europe by giving the Bourbon dynasty control of two major states. Louis made matters worse by refusing to promise that the two thrones would never be united. The "Sun King" was partly defeated this time. Like the earlier contests, this was a battle for overseas markets as well as political power, with the English fighting to capture French territories across the Atlantic as well as in Europe. The French lost Nova Scotia and Newfoundland to the British in 1713 at the Peace of Utrecht. It was the prelude to further French defeats in the Americas later in that century.

In the final analysis, the wars of Louis XIV damaged his country and his dynasty as much as the wars of Kangxi had strengthened his. In Louis' defense, we should note that neither his armies nor his territorial gains were any greater than those of the Chinese emperor. His pursuit of glory and prestige was probably not as determined as that of Kangxi. The reasons Louis's absolutism was less successful than that of Kangxi are twofold: the Chinese absolutist system was much older and more firmly established than that of France; second, in the absence of strong neighbors, the Chinese did not have to conduct foreign policy (the very term would have seemed strange to Kangxi) in the midst of a system of rival states, each one concerned that none of the others becomes too strong. Kangxi did not have to establish a tradition of strong central government in the face of a hostile aristocracy. He had only to show that he, a Manchu, was fit to sit on the throne of the "Son of Heaven." In addition, Kangxi's foreign enemies were all inferior to him in strength. Finally, there was no "balance of power" in east Asia that the Chinese emperor was expected to maintain; China was the "central country" in east Asia in fact as well as in name.

All this is not to excuse Louis XIV's arrogance or errors of judgment. It was not a good idea, either politically or economically, for Louis to achieve religious unity by allowing his officials to persecute Huguenots [French Protestants] and in 1685 to revoke the Edict of Nantes, which had given them limited religious freedom. As a consequence, a significant number of Louis' most productive subjects fled to other countries, giving the king a bad image. Louis' splendid palace at Versailles did help him control the nobility by skillfully keeping them there in attendance on him. It also awed foreign monarchs and visitors. However, the "splendid isolation" of the dynasty outside of Paris alienated later Bourbon monarchs from their subjects and contributed to the collapse of the monarchy during the French Revolution. While the Chinese emperors might also be accused of "arrogance" by a Westerner (their court ceremonial, for example, was much more elaborate than that of Louis), their "arrogance" was sanctioned by centuries-long traditions. It was, we might say, an institutional rather than a personal arrogance.

It is impossible, then, to evaluate the success or failure of either of these dynasts without taking into account their cultural and historical setting. For the Chinese, Kangxi proved a blessing. After fifty years of turmoil and inefficiency, he brought his subjects a long period of decisive, sensible, efficient rule. In short, he proved himself a conservative restorer of the old.[13] Louis, on the other hand, while considered a conservative by modern standards (how else could a modern student of government view an advocate of one-man rule, sanctioned by God?), was revolutionary in the context of seventeenth-century French and European history. By identifying himself with the state, he helped to shift people's attention to the state as a focus for their primary loyalty.[14] His bureaucratic innovations, and even his wars, helped the French to see their country as more than a collection of provinces. Louis may not get the credit for this, but he did help pave the way for the day when the French would die for "la patrie," the "fatherland." It is one of the ironies of French history that a chief victim of that new spirit of national unity Louis helped create was the Bourbon dynasty that he had worked so hard to strengthen.

Notes

1. Kangxi (spelled K'ang-hsi in older works) was his title, not his personal name. Chinese rulers, much like Roman Catholic popes, took a new name when they began their rule, and so Xuan Ye (this ruler's personal name) became *the* Kangxi emperor. Many historians simplify matters and avoid confusion by using the reign title or name as if it were a personal one. We do the same in this chapter.
2. Silas H. L. Wu, *Passage to Power: K'ang-hsi and His Heir Apparent, 1661–1722* (Cambridge, MA: Harvard University Press, 1979) is an excellent study of the "murderous power struggle" between K'ang-hsi and his son; see a good short summary in Jonathan D. Spence, *The Search for Modern China* (New York: Norton, 1990), 69–71.
3. Jonathan D. Spence, *Emperor of China: Self-Portrait of K'ang-hsi* (New York: Random House 1974), 57; see also 11, 12–13, 47, 58–59, 147; Louis XIV, King of France, *Memoires for the Instruction of the Dauphin*, translated with an introduction by Paul Sonnino (New York: Free Press, 1970), 29–30.

4. This process by which the Manchu dynasty became both powerful and Chinese is discussed in the first fifty pages of Lawrence D. Kessler, *K'ang-hsi and the Consolidation of Ch'ing Rule, 1661–1684* (Chicago: University of Chicago Press, 1976).

5. Ibid., 65–73.

6. Ibid., 105, 116–118; Spence, *Emperor of China*, 42–43. Governor-generals were military leaders who controlled more than one province.

7. Kessler, *K'ang-hsi*, 100–101.

8. Wu, *Passage to Power*, 65; Spence, *Search for Modern China*, 68.

9. Jonathan D. Spence, *Ts'ao Yin and the K'ang-hsi Emperor, Bondservant and Master* (New Haven: Yale University Press, 1966), 213–254.

10. Ibid., 109–110.

11. Vincent Buranelli, *Louis XIV* (New York: Twayne Publishers, 1966), 72–78.

12. John B. Wolf, *Louis XIV* (New York: Norton, 1968), 224.

13. See Jonathan D. Spence, "The Seven Ages of K'ang-hsi (1654–1722)," *Journal of Asian Studies*, XXVI (February 1967): 205–211.

14. See Roland Mousnier, *Louis XIV*, trans. J. W. Hunt (London: The Historical Association, 1973), 18–25.

Further Reading

LOUIS XIV, KING OF FRANCE, *Memoires for the Instruction of the Dauphin*. Trans. PAUL SONNINO. New York: Free Press, 1970. Louis speaks for himself. Read with care.

SPENCE, JONATHAN D. *Emperor of China: Self-Portrait of K'ang-hsi*. New York: Alfred A. Knopf, 1974. Excellent. Brings this ruler to life.

WOLF, JOHN B. *Louis XIV*. New York: Norton, 1968. Long but readable.

CHAPTER 4

Bacon and Galileo: The New Science

What did each of these men contribute to the creation of the scientific method? How did their approaches to science differ?

Why does an arrow shot in the air fall back to earth? Is it because it is seeking its "natural place"? Or is it because gravity pulls the arrow down? The different answers to this question explain in a nutshell the difference between pre-modern and modern physical science. Our understanding of the force of gravity and many other scientific laws is due in part to the pioneering work of Francis Bacon (1561–1626) and Galileo Galilei (1564–1642).

Bacon was born in the Protestant England of Elizabeth I and Galileo in Pisa, Italy, at a time when the Catholic Church was struggling to defend its position after the Reformation sparked by Martin Luther. It was a time of religious and political turmoil, and this is reflected in the lives of these two men. Each was egotistical and made enemies. Each was also high-strung, suffered from a variety of minor illnesses, and ended life in partial disgrace. Bacon lost favor with King James I after being convicted for taking bribes while serving as Lord Chancellor, the king's chief legal officer. Galileo died under house arrest after challenging the authority of the Catholic Church (and making fun of the pope) in his book defending the heliocentric theory of Copernicus.

While these two geniuses had colorful and dramatic lives, their fundamental importance is the challenge each offered to the philosophy of nature associated with ancient Greek philosopher Aristotle (384–322 B.C.E.). Aristotle, so highly regarded in medieval Europe that he was referred to as "the Philosopher," believed that everything on earth was composed of four elements: earth, air, fire, and water. Everything above the earth was composed of a fifth, unnamed element. Aristotle also believed that all natural laws were subordinate to unchanging, Divine principles. Thus, the planets had to move in perfect circles because the circle was a perfect figure which reflected the Divine order in nature. In sum, physical laws were only important as *illustrations* of Divine Truth. It was important to understand the essence of objects in nature, but not their mechanism. It was important to understand how the body affected the soul but not the physical mechanisms of the body itself. Humans should study how motion on earth, for example, revealed Divine principles, but it was not important to have accurate theories of *why* arrows fell to earth. Science was far less important than philosophy or theology. That, of course, is why the ideas of Aristotle appealed to the religious thinkers of medieval Europe, the "Schoolmen" or "Scholastics" found in the medieval universities.

Though they were not the very first to make this point, both Bacon and Galileo argued that true knowledge of physical nature required experiments to discover just how and why nature acted as it did. Bacon promoted a method of logical reasoning known as inductive thinking, which requires us to collect specific examples before drawing general conclusions. This was the opposite of Aristotelian deductive logic, which used general theological or philosophical principles to explain particular events. Galileo accepted general or abstract principles, but wanted these based on geometry at a time when mathematics was considered of little value. He also wanted to test the truth of these principles with experiments. Both men wanted to know God through a study of nature, but, as Galileo put it, nature "is written in the language of mathematics, and its characters are triangles, circles, and other geometrical figures, without which it is humanly impossible to understand a single word of it. . . ."[1] Bacon and Galileo's studies in what they called "natural philosophy" became the basis of the modern scientific method.

Francis Bacon grew up in the highest circles of Elizabethan England. His father held office under Henry VIII and Elizabeth I; his mother had served as a tutor to Elizabeth's brother, King Edward VI, and his cousin Robert Cecil was a chief minister at the end of Elizabeth's reign. The Bacon family property bordered that of the queen, and it was said that young Francis amused the queen by giving his age as "I am two years younger than Her Majesty's happy reign."[2] His association with the "rich and famous" of his day caused some inner conflict for Bacon. He claimed that he wanted nothing more than the life of a quiet scholar, yet he spent a great deal of time seeking important political positions or other forms of "royal preferment," as it was called. Bacon was a man of wide-ranging intellectual ability who once said, "I take all knowledge as my province," without realizing how arrogant that might sound to others. He is one of the few Western thinkers whose books are found in today's library listed under both humanities and science. He wrote plays, literary essays, and legal, philosophical, and political treatises while leading an active political life.

As a teenager, Bacon spent two years at Cambridge University, where he "fell into dislike of the philosophy of Aristotle" because of its "unfruitfulness." After serving briefly as a lower-level diplomatic official in Paris for several years, Bacon returned to England, became a lawyer at twenty-one and a member of Parliament two years later. During the rest of Elizabeth's reign, he sought royal appointments without much success. Bacon was refused the job of attorney-general, which was given to his rival, Sir Edward Coke, who also married a girl Bacon had been courting. His friendship with Robert Dudley, the Earl of Essex, a close friend of the queen's, proved unfortunate when Essex fell out of Elizabeth's favor, was convicted of treason, and was executed.[3] It was not until the reign of Elizabeth's successor, James I, that Bacon's fortunes improved. He flattered the new monarch in the introduction to his *Advancement of Learning* (1605) by saying that "there has not been since Christ's time any king . . . so learned in all literature and erudition, divine and human."[4] Such language may have helped Bacon finally achieve high office, culminating in his appointment as Lord Chancellor, the chief legal official, in 1618. Bacon, however, soon had a falling-out with the Duke of Buckingham, one of the king's favorites, and the king did not save him when Bacon's enemies in Parliament convicted him of bribery in 1621. He was fined heavily, temporarily jailed, and forbidden to hold public office or even come within thirty miles of the court for the rest of his life. Bacon died in debt in 1626, his public service soon forgotten, his philosophical writings long remembered.

Much of Bacon's importance as a pioneer of modern science stems from his analysis of how humans think, found in his *Novum Organum* [*New Instrument of Reasoning*], published in 1620. In this work, Bacon described certain prejudices, or "Idols," which cause

us to make errors in reasoning and keep us from discovering useful, practical knowledge. Here he also made his famous distinction
between deductive and inductive reasoning. Before we could begin
to think clearly about nature, Bacon was convinced, we had to rid
ourselves of the four "Idols of the Mind," prejudices that keep us
from seeing the world as it really exists. These idols include those
common to all humans (Idols of the Tribe) and those peculiar to individuals (Idols of the Cave). The third group (Idols of the Market-
place) developed through contact with others, and the fourth (Idols
of the Theater) were found in false philosophies [thinking here especially of Aristotle], "founded on too narrow a basis of experience
and natural history."[5] After abandoning idols, humans had to learn
a new form of logic, or reasoning. In the deductive reasoning favored by the Aristotelians, Bacon wrote, we start "with axioms of
the most general kind, and from these principles . . . proceed to
judgement and to the discovery of intermediate axioms." The better, inductive way of reasoning "calls forth axioms from the senses
and . . . by a gradual and continuous ascent . . . arrive[s] at the
most general axioms last of all."[6] This second form of reasoning
from specific instances to a general conclusion, when combined
with empirical knowledge [derived from the senses] would become
one of the foundations of the scientific method. Bacon knew that we
could never really understand nature without precise examination
of the physical world. What process of abstract thought could have
led us to believe, he wrote, that silk could come from a worm spinning? We had to see it. At the same time, he realized that the senses
often deceive us. We need a combination of observation and rational calculation. Bacon dismissed *both* the mere fact collectors *and*
the rationalists who ignored empirical observation:

> The Empirics are like ants; they gather and consume. The Ratio-
> nalists are spiders spinning webs out of themselves. But the bee
> combines both functions. It gathers its material from flowers of
> garden and field, and digests and transforms them by a faculty of
> its own. This is the only true philosophy.[7]

Bacon wanted us all to imitate the bees, not only because they
combined collection of material with adequate processing of it, but
also because they produced something useful. Bacon is famous for
saying that "knowledge is power" and because of that phrase he
has been accused of promoting the human exploitation of the

natural environment. That is a misreading. Bacon said we should seek knowledge, not so we could dominate others or nature, "nor for reward, or fame, or power," but "to direct and bring it to perfection in charity, for the benefit and use of life." Science, like religion, Bacon believed, should be judged by its fruits.[8] However, to use science to help humans, we need the accurate knowledge of nature that could only be acquired through careful experimentation.

Scientific experiments cost money. Bacon has been called the "first great statesman of science" because, even as a young man, he promoted government support of scientific research. In 1591 he proposed to Queen Elizabeth that she establish a group of councilors to advise her on scientific matters. He also recommended a government-sponsored research library, a botanical garden and zoo, a museum of inventions, and a research laboratory.[9] Years later, in *New Atlantis,* Bacon described an imaginary utopian community where scientists rode in fancy carriages and the government, among other things, sponsored experiments in refrigeration and horticulture and built laboratories for the study of optics and acoustics.[10]

When we combine Bacon's political career with his philosophical writings, we see a man who propagandized mightily on behalf of the importance of correct reasoning and experimentation in science, yet he was less a scientist than a "man of letters." Over a century after Bacon's death, two famous European thinkers, Voltaire and David Hume, acclaimed Bacon as the man whose ideas pointed out the road to true science. Both said, however, that Galileo was the one who actually began to travel that road. Hume noted that Bacon was ignorant of geometry, while Galileo excelled in it. Later historians of science have echoed this view, applauding Bacon for promoting science but valuing Galileo for *doing* science.[11] On those relatively few occasions when Bacon did write scientific treatises, he accepted some silly ideas such as the belief that drinking gunpowder mixed in water before a battle could give a soldier courage.[12] By modern standards, Galileo was certainly the better scientist of the two.

Like Bacon, Galileo was born into a noble family, although a poorer one. His father was a musician—and Galileo was the oldest of seven children. He received his early education at a monastery near Florence but entered the University of Pisa in 1581 to study medicine. While there he had his first doubts about Aristotle's natural philosophy, finding it hard to believe that the speed of falling bodies was proportional to their size, as Aristotle said.[13] He became so fascinated by geometry that he changed his major (as we would say) from medicine to mathematics. Although he left the university in 1585 without a degree, he completed several early studies, one showing that the amount of water displaced by an object was determined by its density. These earned him a position teaching mathematics at the University of Pisa in 1589. Three years later, after showing that light and heavy bodies fall to earth at the same rate (and that their shape has nothing to do with their rate of fall, as the Aristotelian philosophers argued), Galileo secured a new mathematics position at the University of Padua in the Republic of Venice. There he earned three times the salary he was paid at Pisa,[14] and he stayed there for eighteen years before returning in 1610 to spend the rest of his life in his home state of Tuscany.

Galileo's first and most important scientific work involved the study of terrestrial [earthly] motion. His later, more dramatic defense of the Copernican, or heliocentric, theory led to his trial and condemnation by the Catholic Church. However, this more famous part of his life was less important in the history of science than his studies of gravity and the motion of objects. He demonstrated mathematically in 1604 not only that bodies of different weight fall at the same speed but that their rate of fall increases uniformly, at the rate of 32 feet per second. (The story that he dropped weights from the leaning tower of Pisa is a later invention.) He also used geometry to develop the "law of parabolic fall," demonstrating that a ball thrown will follow a semi-parabolic, or curved, path as gravity pulls it to earth. His demonstration of the laws of inertia proved that an object will keep moving if there is no friction to stop it, and it doesn't need a force pushing it, as the Aristotelians argued. These laws of gravity and motion are taught as basic principles in introductory physics courses today.[15]

Galileo was also important in the history of science because he was one of the first people to combine mathematical analysis with a study of the physical properties of objects. He also emphasized the testing of a hypothesis with experiments and tried to predict what would happen in a scientific experiment. One example of how his method challenged the Aristotelians concerned the volume of water in a bottle. The Aristotelian university professors said that water decreased in volume as it froze because there was an empty space between the surface of the water and the layer of frozen ice in a bottle. Galileo said that frozen water could also break a bottle. Did that prove that the volume increased? He suggested placing ice cubes in water to see if the water level rose when they melted, as Aristotelian theory predicted. Since the water remains level when the ice melts, Galileo was proved correct and the Aristotelians wrong.[16]

In 1609, while still working for the doge [ruler] of Venice, Galileo heard about the recent Dutch invention of a telescope; he immediately built one powerful enough to see ships in the harbor two hours before they could be seen by the naked eye.[17] This impressed the doge, who tried unsuccessfully to keep Galileo from leaving the Venetian Republic by increasing his salary. This invention shows that Galileo understood the connection between science and technology and, like Bacon, wanted science to be directly useful to humans. Galileo also invented a thermometer and something he called a "geometric and military compass," or "sector." This was the remote ancestor of the modern slide rule, which has now been replaced by the indispensable pocket calculator.[18] Of course, the most important product of Galileo's technical expertise was the telescope, and the most dangerous thing he did with it was to point it toward the heavens.

Galileo's *Starry Messenger*, published in 1610, announced that the telescope revealed a rough surface on the moon, something which the Aristotelians did not think possible because the heavenly bodies were not supposed to be solid objects. In the same work, he announced that he had discovered four moons around Jupiter, and later that year he verified that the planet Venus had phases like the moon. All these discoveries supported the theory of Nicholas Copernicus (published in 1543) that the planets moved around the sun instead of the earth. Galileo announced his support for the Copernican theory in 1613. Since this theory was not supported by a literal reading of the Bible, and was not yet proven conclusively, the Catholic Church placed Copernicus' book on the Index of Forbidden Books in 1616. Galileo was told in 1616, in a meeting with the head of the Holy Office of the Inquisition [charged with protecting the faith and persecuting heretics] in Rome, that he could no longer publicly "defend or hold" the doctrine "that the earth moves around the Sun and that the Sun is stationary in the center of the world and does not move from east to west."[19] He could continue to discuss the ideas of Copernicus, but only as a hypothesis, not as the truth. While many churchmen accepted the ideas of Copernicus, the church as an institution could not yet bring itself to abandon older views. All went well until 1632, when Galileo published *Dialogue Concerning the Two Chief World Systems—Ptolemaic and Copernican.* Within weeks he was summoned to Rome to be put on trial for heresy. While his book had not said the heliocentric theory was correct in so many words, it was clear that Galileo's strongest arguments supported it. In Rome, the seventy-year-old Galileo was shown the instruments of torture which could be used on him if he refused to recant. He did, although a popular legend (colorful but untrue) has it that he whispered as he left the room, "but it still moves."

While it has often been said that the trial of Galileo was a clear case of narrow-minded religious leaders interfering with science, the story is more complicated. Some say that Galileo's abrasive personality was part of the problem. Galileo's supporter from Florence, Cardinal Maffeo Barberini, had been elected Pope VIII in 1623 and had welcomed Galileo to Rome, assuring him that he could continue to write about Copernicus but asking him to be discreet and not issue a frontal challenge to church authority. The pope was surely insulted when Galileo put some of Barberini's views in the mouth of the weakest character in his *Dialogue,* a man named Simplicio. Galileo was also undiplomatic in dealings with his Aristotelian enemies, some of whom were priests and scholars whom he angered by harsh verbal assaults on them. In a *Letter to Castelli,* in 1613, for example, he bluntly said that if science and Scripture disagreed, one should follow the dictates of science:

> I do not feel obliged to believe that the same God who has endowed us with senses, reason, and intellect has intended us to forgo their use and by some other means to give us knowledge which we can attain by them. He would not require us to deny sense and reason in physical matters which are set before our eyes and minds by direct experience or necessary demonstrations.[20]

On another occasion, Galileo wrote that theologians "should not arrogate to themselves the authority to decide on controversies in professions which they have neither studied nor practiced."[21] He said these things, knowing that he could not himself prove that Copernicus was correct. That proof would come only in 1687 when

Isaac Newton mathematically proved the law of universal gravitation. While Galileo's words read like a stirring declaration of intellectual freedom to people of our day, who value the separation of church and state, they might look differently if we put ourselves in the shoes of church officials. Galileo's work could seem to them an arrogant threat at a time when the church had lost half of its members as a consequence of the Protestant Reformation. Also, church leaders considered individual salvation more important than theories of how planets moved. "They feared," one modern scientist reminds us, "that the idea of a nongeocentric world might seem to undermine the supremacy of humans in God's plan, thereby confusing people and threatening their salvation." On the other hand, one scholar is convinced that Galileo was a devout Catholic who published the *Dialogue* precisely to prove that the church supported the new science. In his view, the church encouraged Galileo in this belief and then abandoned him when he was attacked. Galileo's judges did use a forged document, which said that Galileo had been told not only that he couldn't defend Copernicanism but also that he was not even to "discuss" it.[22] The conflict between Galileo and the church was clearly a complex one.

One of the most interesting aspects of the "Galileo controversy" was that Galileo himself, even while defending Copernicus, refused to accept the conclusion of Johannes Kepler (1571–1630) that the planets moved in elliptical orbits. Galileo rejected this belief, surprisingly, using the Aristotelian argument that orbits must be perfect circles. It is also interesting that Galileo supported the Copernican theory because the movement of the earth, he believed, was responsible for the ebb and flow of the tides.[23] He originally wanted to call his *Dialogue Concerning the Two Chief World Systems* a *Dialogue on the Tides*. He was wrong about the tides, which we know are caused by the gravitational pull of the moon, just as he was wrong about circular orbits of planets.

The errors of fact and the personal problems which beset Bacon and Galileo remind us of the importance of hindsight in understanding the past. Textbooks, and even essays such as this, can make it appear that Bacon and Galileo were aware that they were part of an intellectual and scientific revolution. Because we see them as two of the first "modern" thinkers in western Europe, it is easy to assume that they saw themselves that way as well. They may have, since each had a strong sense of his own self-importance.

On the other hand, they could not know how others would use their ideas. Bacon's emphasis on inductive reasoning certainly helped people understand nature better in the centuries to come. It was far more important than the political appointments he sought so diligently throughout his life. Had he actually been honored with high office by Elizabeth or earlier in the reign of James I, he might not have had the time to write the great works on which his fame rests today. Galileo's emphasis on experimentation and his linking of mathematics and physics were far more important than his defense of Copernicanism or his other work in astronomy.

In the final analysis, then, we write history, in part at least, by what we choose to remember about those who have gone before us. One of the things we choose to remember about Bacon and Galileo is that their work allowed us to view the natural world as predictable. Perhaps we should remember as well that they viewed the natural world with great respect and even humility. Galileo wrote in his *Dialogue* that "there is not a single effect in nature . . . such that the most ingenious theorists can arrive at a complete understanding of it." Bacon said that "we can only command nature by obeying her." More colorful, but expressing somewhat the same sentiment, are these words of twentieth-century science writer Loren Eiseley, who described Bacon in words which might also apply to Galileo: "he walked to the doorway of the future, flung it wide, and said to his trembling and laggard audience, 'Look. There is tomorrow. Take it with charity lest it destroy you.'"[24]

Notes

1. Galileo Galilei, *The Controversy of the Comets of 1618*, trans. Stillman Drake and C. D. O'Malley (Philadelphia: University of Pennsylvania Press, 1960), 183–184.
2. A. Wigfall Green, *Sir Francis Bacon* (New York: Twayne, 1966), 17–21.
3. Ibid., 25–35.
4. *Francis Bacon: A Critical Edition of His Major Works*, ed. Brian Vickers (New York: Oxford University Press, 1996), 121.
5. Francis Bacon, *Novum Organum*, trans. ed. Peter Urbach and John Gibson (Chicago: Open Court Press, 1994), 47–48.
6. Bacon, *Novum Organum*, 53–68.
7. Bacon, *Thoughts and Conclusions on The Interpretation of Nature or a Science Productive of Works* (written in 1607 as *Cogitata et Visa*), trans. Benjamin Farrington in Farrington, *The Philosophy of Francis Bacon: An Essay on Its Development from 1603 to 1609, with New Translations of Fun-*

damental Texts (Chicago: University of Chicago Press, 1966), 96–97; the ants-spiders-bees passage is also in *Novum Organum*, 105; on Bacon's distrust of sense knowledge by itself, see *Novum Organum*, 19–20, 22–23, 38, 128, and Steven Shapin, *The Scientific Revolution* (Chicago: University of Chicago Press, 1996), 92–93.

8. Bacon, *Novum Organum*, 15; *Critical Edition of Major Works*, 146; also see note on page 600, and Farrington, *Philosophy of Francis Bacon*, 28, 54–55.

9. Green, *Sir Francis Bacon*, 36; Farrington, *Philosophy of Francis Bacon*, 13.

10. *Bacon: Critical Edition of Major Works*, 479–485.

11. See. B. H. G. Wormald, *Francis Bacon: History, Politics, and Science, 1561–1626* (Cambridge: Cambridge University Press, 1993), 26; David Hume, *History of England*, vol. 4 (Philadelphia: E. Littell, 1828), 347; A. Ruppert Hall, *The Revolution in Science, 1500–1750*, (London: Longman's, 1983), 190–194; Herbert Butterfield, *The Origins of Modern Science, 1300–1800* (New York: Macmillan, 1959), 102–104.

12. Green, *Sir Francis Bacon*, 139.

13. Stillman Drake, *Galileo* (New York: Hill and Wang, 1980), 21

14. Drake, *Galileo*, 22–25.

15. Laura Fermi and Gilberto Bernardini, *Galileo and the Scientific Revolution* (New York: Basic Books, 1961), 112–123. Many of Galileo's studies of motion were summarized by Galileo in his *Two New Sciences*, written at the end of his life and first published in 1638. See Galileo Galilei, *Two New Sciences, Including Centers of Gravity and Force of Percussion*, trans. Stillman Drake (Madison: University of Wisconsin Press, 1974).

16. William R. Shea, *Galileo's Intellectual Revolution* (London: Macmillan, 1972), 42.

17. Drake, *Galileo*, 42.

18. Fermi and Bernardini, *Galileo and the Scientific Revolution*, 32.

19. Giorgio de Santillana, *The Crime of Galileo* (New York: Time, 1962), 140.

20. Fermi and Bernardini, *Galileo and the Scientific Revolution*, 80. For contrasting views of Galileo's trial, compare Santillana's *Crime of Galileo*, which supports the idea that Galileo was unfairly persecuted, and Arthur Koestler, *The Sleepwalkers* (New York: Universal Library, 1963), 425–496, which sees the trial as a result of Galileo's arrogance.

21. Arthur Koestler, *Sleepwalkers*, 436.

22. Karl Kuhn, *In Quest of the Universe*, 2d ed. (St. Paul: West Publishing Company, 1994), 69; Drake, *Galileo*, 2–5; Santillana, *Crime of Galileo*, 283–297.

23. Joseph Pitt, *Galileo, Human Nature, and the Book of Nature* (Dordrecht, Netherlands: Kluwer Academic Publishers, 1992), 104, 162.

24. Galileo Galilei, *Dialogue Concerning the Two Chief World Systems—Ptolemaic and Copernican*, trans. Stillman Drake (Berkeley: University of California Press, 1967), 101; Bacon, *Novum Organum*, 43; Loren Eiseley, *The Man Who Saw Through Time* (New York: Scribners' Sons, 1973), 20.

Further Reading

BACON, FRANCIS. *Novum Organum*. Trans. PETER URBACH and JOHN GIBSON. Chicago: Open Court Publishing Co., 1994. Very readable translation of what is perhaps Bacon's most important work.

DE SANTILLANA, GIORGIO. *The Crime of Galileo*. New York: Time, 1962. Readable yet detailed account of his trial. It is interesting to compare this with the very different but equally readable description of Galileo in ARTHUR KOESTLER, *The Sleepwalkers: A History of Man's Changing Vision of the Universe* New York: Universal Library, 1963.

EISELEY, LOREN. *The Man Who Saw Through Time*. New York: Scribners' Sons, 1973. A lively, well-written, essay that will introduce you to the spirit of Bacon and to excellent writing about science.

JARDINE, LISA, and ALAN STEWART. *Hostage to Fortune: The Troubled Life of Francis Bacon*. New York: Hill and Wang, 1999. Up-to-date full biography of Bacon by two Renaissance scholars

CHAPTER 5

Burke and Condorcet: Are People Perfectible?

Are human beings perfectible, or are they fallen creatures who need to be controlled by an elite? Can human nature and moral progress be understood through rational calculation?

It is a sign of the intellectual mood of the eighteenth century that this question, which most of us would consider private and religious, became public and political. After centuries, even millennia, in which the basic structure of government and society had been taken for granted, political thinkers such as Montesquieu (1689–1755), Voltaire (1694–1778), and Rousseau (1712–1778) began to earnestly and self-consciously wonder which form of government was best, and how to make governments more responsive to the needs of larger numbers of people.

However, the thinkers of the eighteenth century did more than wonder. The last years of the century gave both the English and the French the opportunity to implement some of their theories of government. In the 1770s, the transplanted English in the North American colonies complained about "taxation without representation" and fought a successful war to free themselves from England and what they called the "tyranny" of English King George III. In 1787, guided by the ideas of European thinkers, the Americans designed a new republic with elected lawmaking bodies and a "Bill of Rights" to protect its citizens. Political rights—the right to vote and hold office—were limited to adult white males, who elected George Washington first president of the new United States of America in 1789.

In that same year, a more radical experiment began in France, when inept monarch Louis XVI called together representatives of each of the three Estates of the Realm (Clergy, Nobility, and Commoners) to deal with the bankruptcy of the French government.

The Third Estate (Commoners) soon took over and declared themselves a National Assembly. Within four years, the French created first a constitutional monarchy and later a republic; the king was executed in January 1793.

These two revolutions—and particularly the one in France, which resulted in a series of wars, culminating with the defeat of Napoleon in 1815—led people to take more seriously words such as *liberty* and *equality*. A centuries-old social structure, marked by a distinct aristocratic ruling class and an equally distinct group of lower- and middle-class "subjects," was collapsing. At issue was not only which form of government was best but also how human nature should be understood.

The basic link between human nature and government was addressed most directly and dramatically at this time by two men, Edmund Burke (1729–1797) in England and Marie-Jean-Antoine-Nicolas Caritat, Marquis de Condorcet (1743–1794) in France. An English politician with nearly thirty years experience in Parliament, Burke expressed his anger at the French revolutionaries in *Reflections on the Revolution in France,* written in 1790. Condorcet, a social philosopher, expressed his optimism about the future in his *Sketch for a Historical Picture of the Progress of the Human Mind,* written in 1793.

Both Burke and Condorcet were men of letters as well as public men who served their respective states for many years. Each had a consistent view of how people ought to be governed. Each looked to history to justify his beliefs, and each wanted humans to be as free as possible. Both opposed the tyranny of an unthinking electorate and that of an unchecked, absolute monarch. The political and personal lives of both thinkers were marked by emotional struggle. Burke was a middle-class Irishman trying to succeed in the aristocratic political world of eighteenth-century England. Condorcet was an aristocrat who became a republican and voted to depose the king in 1792.

The central issue dividing these two passionate publicists is one which continues to intrigue many of us two centuries later: are human beings perfectible on this earth? To this question, the violently antireligious "liberal" Condorcet answered yes; the traditionally religious "conservative" Burke said no. The question is deceptive because, while it can be answered briefly, the implications of the answer are far-reaching, and very divisive. A look at the lives and thoughts of these two men can help us see why this is so.

Born on New Year's Day in 1729 in Dublin of a Protestant father and a Roman Catholic mother, Edmund Burke was "pure Irish," in the words of one biographer. Although raised as a Protestant, his later sympathy for the Catholics in Ireland [who were then denied all political rights] may have been stimulated by his closeness to his mother; also, between the ages of six and eleven he lived with his mother's relatives. Burke received his college degree in Dublin before going to London to study law in 1750. Despite his father's wishes, the young man found traveling, coffee-houses, and debating clubs more interesting than legal studies. He lived this carefree life for a half-dozen years until his father cut off his allowance. Burke settled down in 1757; in that year, he married Jane Nugent and published one of his first major literary works, an essay *On the Sublime and the Beautiful,* a philosophical study of what constitutes beauty.[1]

Burke's life-long interest in politics soon led him away from the literary career he had planned. From 1759 to 1765, he worked in London and Dublin for William Hamilton, chief secretary of the British government for Ireland. During this time, he wrote a tract against the "Popery Laws," which were used by the British to keep the Catholic Irish in the status of second-class citizens. After a disagreement with Hamilton in 1765, Burke became private secretary to the Marquis of Rockingham, leader of the mild opposition or Whig faction in the British Parliament. A seat in the House of Commons was arranged for Burke, and he remained a member for nearly thirty years, retiring in 1794.

It was in Parliament that Burke made his reputation as an orator and a supporter of limited government. In a 1770 essay on "Thoughts on the Cause of the Present Discontent," he argued against the attempt by George III to play a more active role in governing the country, and, in a famous speech in 1774 after the Boston Tea Party, he urged Parliament to remove the duty on tea for the sake of peace with America and the preservation of the empire. One can picture the intense Irishman (contemporaries said he spoke quickly and with an Irish brogue) addressing these words to his colleagues:

> Be content to bind America by laws of trade; you have always done it. . . . Do not burden them with taxes; you were not used to do so from the beginning. . . . When you drive him hard, the boar will surely turn upon the hunters.

Burke believed that the English government did have the *right* to tax the colonies; it was part of the crown's sovereignty [right to govern]. But he warned that, "if that sovereignty and their freedom cannot be reconciled, which will they take? They will cast your sovereignty in your face. Nobody will be argued into slavery."[2] Burke proved correct. The Americans put their practical needs ahead of their loyalty to the mother country. Because Burke had supported the Americans against George III's government and the Catholic Irish against the "Protestant Ascendancy," as the English rule in Ireland was known in those days, many were surprised when he argued so strongly in 1790 against the actions of the French revolutionaries. Had Burke lost his "liberal" spirit as he aged? Was he being inconsistent in supporting freedom for Americans but not for the French? Thomas Jefferson, for one, was "astonished" by Burke's views on the French Revolution and suggested that it was evidence of "the rottenness of his mind." Even a more conservative John Adams agreed.[3]

However, Edmund Burke had not become soft-headed in his old age, as these detractors thought. True, the language he used to describe the French revolutionaries in his *Reflections* was often intemperate, as when he described the revolution, then little more than a year old, as a "strange chaos of levity and ferocity . . . all sorts of crimes jumbled together with all sorts of follies."[4] Later in the book, he heaped exaggerated praise on the French queen, Marie-Antoinette, who had been forced by a mob to leave her palace at Versailles. Burke lamented that the age of chivalry was gone and had been succeeded by one "of sophisters, economists, and calculators . . . the glory of Europe is extinguished forever."[5] As dramatic and romantic as this language is, it does contain some insight. Early on, Burke understood that the French were doing more than just remodeling their government a bit.

They were, in fact, changing the very basis of government. One of the first articles of their "Declaration of the Rights of Man and the Citizen, "a bill of rights drawn up by the revolutionary National Assembly in the late summer of 1789, stated that "all sovereignty resides in the nation." This was a genuinely revolutionary statement, for it suggested that the right to govern came not from God but from the people, not from above but from below. Long before many of his contemporaries, Burke sensed—perhaps intuitively— what this would mean. Although the revolutionaries had not yet overthrown the monarchy when Burke wrote, their new abstract principles of government based upon popular sovereignty (or mob rule, as Burke called it) would allow them to make this change whenever they had the desire and the votes.

It also angered Burke that the French leaders were "atheists," a word he used frequently in the *Reflections*. They confiscated all church property in France in the fall of 1789 in order to provide security for the national debt. In Burke's view, this was immoral, illegal, and a bold attempt to destroy religion. Again, despite his strident language, he had a point. The ideals of the French revolutionaries were profoundly secular; they wished to free people from "the chains of superstition" so that they could guide their lives by the rules of reason. The revolutionaries saw reason as something opposed to religion. Burke did not. Twenty years earlier, in 1769, Burke had written that "politics ought to be adjusted not to human reasonings but to human nature; of which reason is but a part, and by no means the greatest part."[6]

Although a reformer in the context of English politics, Burke wanted to base change on tradition. "A disposition to preserve, and an ability to improve, taken together, would be my standard of a statesman," he told the French.[7] People's political rights, he argued, were established by long usage and custom. They could not be based upon some abstract rule of justice. Such changes as the French were making, and especially their replacement of aristocrats by middle-class commoners in the government, would subvert "the natural order of things."[8]

Burke's basic objections to the work and ideas of the French revolutionaries reveal more than his basic distrust of reason and abstractions. They show him to be a man with little faith in human ability to use reason. He admitted this at one point in the *Reflections,* when he wrote

> We are afraid to put men to life to trade each on his own private stock of reason, because we suspect that this stock in each man is small. . . .[9]

By the end of the eighteenth century, almost all political thinkers believed that people had certain rights. Burke and Condorcet, in fact, agreed that people had the right to justice, personal security, and protection of their property. It is interesting that Burke added to his particular list of rights, however, the people's right to have governments place "a sufficient restraint upon their passions."[10] Condorcet, while he agreed that people do not always act in their own interest, preferred to stress the duty of governments to enlighten rather than punish. Whereas Burke was a pessimistic Christian, Condorcet was an optimistic atheist. This is one of the unexpected twists we find when comparing the two men.

Another twist is that Nicolas Condorcet, an accomplished mathematician, was as "religious" in pursuit of his truth as Burke, the defender of tradition and history, was "empirical" [depending upon experience or observation alone] in pursuing his. Condorcet's intense hostility to religion is one of the most notable features of his political writings. This hostility may have been created in part by his very religious upbringing. A month after Condorcet's birth, his father died and his mother was widowed for the second time. She consoled herself by dedicating her young son to the Virgin Mary and dressing him in girl's clothes until he was eight. Condorcet was also educated by the Jesuits [a religious order whose priests had reputations as good teachers and as scheming politicians].[11]

Young Condorcet's dislike of religion may also have been due in part to his willingness to place his faith in mathematical reasoning. At age twenty-two, he had an "Essay on Integral Calculus" published by the prestigious French Academy of Science, a body that admitted him to membership several years later in 1769. During these years, Condorcet was also the protégé [under the care and protection] of famous French mathematician Jean d'Alembert. He showed great promise.

However, just as Burke was drawn from literature and philosophy into the world of politics, so, too, was Condorcet drawn from the study of mathematics into what one biographer has called "social mathematics." In the mid-1770s, Condorcet was becoming convinced that one could find the same kind of certainty in "the moral and political sciences" that one found in the physical sciences. After all, a century earlier Isaac Newton had discovered a mathematical formula that described the movement of the planets around the sun and the force of gravity. Was it not only a matter of time before we discovered laws which could make rational sense of the moral, social, and political behavior of people? To the quest for this "social science," Condorcet committed his life. He had faith that politics could be understood scientifically.

Since he believed that "to do good, one must have at least as much power as goodwill," Condorcet associated himself with Jacques Turgot (1727–1781), an economic and political reformer who attempted to strengthen the financial structure of the Old Regime government of Louis XVI during the mid-1770s. After Turgot was dismissed as controller-general of France in 1776, Condorcet continued his work, publishing an important "Essay on the Application of Mathematics to the Theory of Decision Making" in 1785. In this work he tried to show that one could use a calculus of probability to determine whether or not a given legislative body would produce what he called a "true" (i.e., enlightened) decision. Basically, his argument was that good people make good decisions; bad (i.e., unenlightened) people make bad ones. It is interesting that, either despite or because of his belief in the value of mathematical abstractions, Condorcet was just as emotional as Burke when it came to letting the uneducated mob rule. However, unlike Burke, Condorcet went out of his way to stress the importance of educating "the mob." He turned in a lengthy "Report on the General Organization of Public Instruction" to the French National Assembly in April 1792.[12]

After the French Revolution broke out, Condorcet's political activities became more direct. He was elected to the revolutionary legislative assembly in 1791 and was one of the first to declare himself in favor of a republic after he realized that King Louis XVI would not wish to cooperate with the revolutionaries. After the king was deposed in the fall of 1792, Condorcet soon found himself among the more conservative members of the new legislative body of the republic, called the Convention. He drew up a plan for a new constitution in February 1793. His plan, which would have provided for a system of representative government with universal male suffrage, was dismissed when his party (the Girondins) was replaced in mid-summer by the more radical Jacobins.[13]

When the Jacobins took over the Convention, not only was Condorcet's attempt to create a "rational politics" ended, but he was soon ordered arrested when he attacked the new Jacobin constitution. It was during those last months of 1793, while in hiding in order to avoid execution, that Condorcet wrote his most optimistic and most famous essay, his *Sketch for a Historical Picture of the Progress of the Human Mind.* It is in this work, which begins with the bold assertion "that nature has set no term to the perfection of human faculties . . . the perfectibility of man is truly indefinite," that the differences between Condorcet and Burke become most apparent.[14]

Condorcet's *Sketch* was really just the outline for a much longer work that he was unable to complete before he left his hiding place, was arrested, and died in prison in March 1794. In this work, he planned to trace human progress through nine stages, running from earliest times to the beginning of the French Revolution. A chapter on the "Tenth Stage" was to describe "the future progress of the human mind." In each of the earlier stages of history, human attempts to make progress—usually defined in scientific or materialistic terms—had been stymied by greedy priests and despotic rulers, who used elaborate religious systems and sheer force to keep most people ignorant. It was only in the last few centuries before his own, Condorcet believed, that men and women began to throw off their prejudices and superstitions and to become more rational, more willing to question authority and to think for themselves.[15]

Condorcet became the most lyrical in describing the future. "The time will therefore come when the sun will shine only on free men who know no other master but their reason; when tyrants and slaves, priests and their stupid or hypocritical instruments will exist only in works of history and on the stage," he wrote at the beginning of this chapter.[16] Condorcet expected that various kinds of inequality—in wealth, status, and education—would all be reduced if not eliminated. Medical discoveries would, he predicted correctly, lengthen human life. He also noted, again correctly, that the stock of human knowledge would increase, not because people would become more intelligent, but because they would learn how to measure and classify facts more carefully. Condorcet announced that the future would see greater equality for women, and even something like what we call social security: "guaranteeing people in old age a means of livelihood produced partly by their own savings and partly by the savings of others who make the same outlay, but who die before they need to reap the reward."[17]

All this would happen, Condorcet was convinced, because people would continue, despite occasional setbacks, to apply abstract reason to the solution of human problems. Of course, it was just that use of abstract reason, in Edmund Burke's view, that caused the problems associated with the French Revolution in the first place. If the revolutionaries had not turned politics into an ideology [set of ideas] but had left it the art of working with people, there would be less pain in the world. If people like Condorcet were less intent on removing "prejudices" such as religion and, instead, were willing to learn from them, changes might come slowly but be more lasting.

Burke had his point, even if he did underestimate the abuses and errors of the royal government in France before 1789, and even if he was unwilling to admit that a concerted effort at social and political change can sometimes change things for the better (e.g., the New Deal or the civil rights movement in the United States). But Condorcet also had a point, or rather a vision, which causes people to continue to read his *Sketch* to this day. If Burke anticipated the warnings issued by many twentieth-century political conservatives, Condorcet was an intellectual ancestor of many reforming liberals. If Condorcet was naive in believing that moral progress could be made the subject of a calculus of probabilities, or that moral progress would necessarily follow from material progress—and he was—at least he put the accent on the improvement of people rather than on their control. That idea, even if wrong, has something uplifting about it.

If to Burke must go the award for common sense, to Condorcet must go the prize for hope. In the two centuries since the deaths of these men, many statesmen have concluded that we need both of these virtues.

Notes

1. Philip Magnus, *Edmund Burke: A Life* (London: John Murray, 1939), Volume I, 6–12.
2. *The Works of Edmund Burke* (Boston: Little and Brown, 1839), vol. I, 489–490; see also Russell Kirk, *Edmund Burke: A Genius Reconsidered* (New Rochelle, NY: Arlington House, 1967), 62–65.
3. Isaac Kramnick, ed., *Edmund Burke* (Englewood Cliffs, NJ: Prentice-Hall, 1974), 125. The question of Burke's possible inconsistency in defending the Americans and not the French revolutionaries was raised again by the reviewer of a biography of Burke. "How could the Burke who defended the right of the American colonists to defend themselves against the British government complain when the French tried to defend themselves against their government . . . how could Burke spend years trying to teach George III the limits of royal authority and

now defend absolute monarchy in France?" See Alan Ryan, "Who Was Edmund Burke?" in the *New York Review of Books,* December 3, 1992, 40; the essay reviews Conor Cruise O'Brien, *The Great Melody: A Thematic Biography and Commented Anthology of Edmund Burke* (Chicago: University of Chicago Press, 1992).

4. *Works of Edmund Burke,* III, 28.
5. Ibid., 98.
6. Thomas H. D. Mahoney, ed., *Reflections on the Revolution in France* (Indianapolis: Bobbs-Merrill, 1955), xiii.
7. *Works of Edmund Burke,* III, 185.
8. Ibid., 69.
9. Ibid., 110.
10. Ibid., 81; Keith Michael Baker, ed., *Condorcet: Selected Writings* (Indianapolis: Bobbs-Merrill, 1976), 73.
11. Keith Michael Baker, *Condorcet: From Natural Philosophy to Social Mathematics* (Chicago: University of Chicago Press, 1975), 3–4; see also J. Salwyn Schapiro, *Condorcet and the Rise of Liberalism* (New York: Harcourt, Brace, 1934), 66–67.
12. Baker, *Condorcet: Selected Writings,* x, xviii–xxii, 33–68; see F. De la Fontainerie, trans. and ed., *French Liberalism and Education in the Eighteenth Century: The Writings of La Chalotais, Turgot, Diderot, and Condorcet on National Education* (New York: McGraw-Hill, 1932), 323–378.
13. Schapiro, *Condorcet,* 129–133; Baker, *Condorcet: Natural Philosophy to Social Mathematics,* 316–330.
14. Marie-Jean-Antoine-Nicolas Caritat, Marquis de Condorcet, *Sketch for a Historical Picture of the Progress of the Human Mind,* trans. June Barraclough (London: Weidenfeld and Nicolson, 1955), 4.
15. Ibid., 99–172. Condorcet's titles are interesting. His "Eighth Stage" runs "from the invention of printing to the time when philosophy and the sciences shook off the yoke of authority." His "Ninth Stage" begins with the philosophy of Descartes (seventeenth-century French rationalist) and ends with "the foundation of the French Republic."
16. Ibid., 179.
17. Ibid., 179–193, 199.

Further Reading

BAKER, KEITH MICHAEL, ed. *Condorcet: Selected Writings.* Indianapolis: Bobbs-Merrill, 1976. A good look at the variety of his work.

CONDORCET, MARIE-JEAN-ANTOINE-NICOLAS CARITAT, MARQUIS DE. *Sketch for a Historical Picture of the Progress of the Human Mind.* trans. June Barraclough. London: Weidenfeld and Nicolson, 1955.

KIRK, RUSSELL. *Edmund Burke: A Genius Reconsidered.* New Rochelle, NY: Arlington House, 1967. Sympathetic account by a modern conservative thinker.

KRAMNICK, ISAAC, ed. *Edmund Burke.* Englewood Cliffs, NJ: Prentice-Hall, 1974. Various views of Burke in his day—and later.

CHAPTER 6

Toussaint and Tecumseh: Resisting the Odds

Two leaders resist those who would enslave or exterminate them. Did either have a chance of succeeding? What legacy did they leave for us?

The nineteenth century was the great age of Western imperial expansion. Rich new lands had been discovered in Africa, Asia, and the Americas and partially explored by white Europeans. Bolstered by their superior technology and their belief in a "civilizing mission," Western countries extended and tightened their economic and political control over lands occupied by races they considered inferior. By the end of the century, the industrialized nations of the northern hemisphere dominated much of the rest of the world with a series of colonies, territories, and "spheres of influence."

However, the path of conquest and control was not always a smooth one. Despite inferior weapons and faint hopes of success, native leaders often resisted the white conquerors. Occasionally, a superior leader among the nonwhite peoples was even able to defeat or temporarily delay the conquerors. Toussaint L'Ouverture (1744–1803) and Tekamthi (1768–1813), whose name was later spelled Tecumseh by whites to make it easier to pronounce, were two such men.

Between 1792 and 1802, ex-slave Toussaint created an army of blacks and mulattos [persons of mixed race] that dominated Hispaniola, a Caribbean island with a French colony in its western half and a Spanish one in its eastern half. His defeat of English, Spanish, and French armies liberated the French colony of Santo Domingo. The independent black nation of Haiti emerged in 1804, a year after his death, and a year after that, the Shawnee Indian warrior Tecumseh began to unite the Indian tribes in the Ohio and Mississippi river valleys of North America. His seven-year effort to create an

Indian confederation to prevent further seizure of Indian lands ended with his death in 1813, during the War of 1812 between Britain and the United States. Both men are remembered as brilliant military leaders and humane statesmen. Both were seen as worthy opponents by those who fought against them. While neither was able to ensure the prosperity of his people, each proved to be a shrewd political leader. Toussaint and Tecumseh left to their respective peoples a legacy of achievement and hope; each had a vision of freedom and racial harmony which transcended his place and time.

Visions of freedom were in short supply among the slaves of Santo Domingo when the great French Revolution broke out in the mother country in 1789. By that date, nearly 1 million Africans had arrived, imported to labor on the 800 sugar plantations. Although the slaves outnumbered the white masters ten to one and the mulattos seventeen to one, their death rate was much higher. Since many slaves were killed for sport or worked to death, the colony had to import large numbers of Africans (forty thousand in 1787, for example) to keep the slave population at full strength.[1]

Despite the fact that his mother was a slave, Toussaint was better off than most members of his race. His father was a free man, educated by Christian missionaries, who gave Toussaint the opportunity to learn to read and write; he also mastered a few Latin phrases, which he later repeated to the amazement of his troops. His education allowed him to become a house slave, which guaranteed him better treatment than that given field hands.[2]

It was the reaction by the white planters to the French Revolution's extension of political rights that gave the oppressed blacks their opportunity for revolt and Toussaint his chance for leadership. In 1790, the colonial planters were given the right to govern themselves through a colonial assembly. The planters sought to deny political rights to mulattos, although the mulattos owned about a third of the land and a quarter of the colony's slaves. In response to their protests, the French National Assembly in May 1791 confirmed the rights of male mulattos in the colony to vote and hold political office, but the French planters suspended that decree. As a result, the mulattos organized their own army and began a civil war. Both sides in this struggle ignored the blacks until a major slave revolt broke out on August 22, 1791, near the city of Le Cap François in the northern part of the island. When the white planters persisted in their refusal to grant limited rights to both blacks and mulattos, they lost their chance to control their fate; their world "collapsed under the weight of their own vengeance."[3]

The new Republican French government then attempted to salvage the situation in this economically important Caribbean colony by appointing a new governor and sending three commissioners from France to assist him in 1792. The most powerful of the three, Leger Felicite Sonthonax, was as hostile to the objectives of the pro-monarchist planters as the planters were to the objectives of the colony's blacks and mulattos. Unlike Toussaint would later, he failed to realize that he needed planter support to avoid the total collapse of the island's economy. Sonthonax supported first the mulattos, then the blacks; the state of near-anarchy worsened in 1793, when Spanish and British troops invaded the colony as part of their war against revolutionary France. Many white planters cast their lot with the British as a means of opposing Commissioner Sonthonax. Desperate for black assistance against the Spanish and British, Sonthonax abolished slavery on August 29, 1793.[4] This measure set the stage for Toussaint L'Ouverture, a shrewder and more racially tolerant man than either Sonthonax or the white planters, to play a major role in the Haitian Revolution.

Earlier, in 1791, the gray-haired Toussaint had abandoned his position as a steward of livestock at the Breda plantation after having first helped his master's family find safety in Le Cap. He then joined the black rebels. Because he had organizational skill and could correctly assess the motives and abilities of others, Toussaint soon became a leader among the black insurgents and created a strong, disciplined army.[5]

In 1793, Toussaint and other black leaders joined the Spanish side in order to fight against their former French masters. But, in May 1794, Toussaint made a crucial decision to defect to the French side. Some historians believe that he did this for both practical and idealistic reasons. Once the French National Assembly approved Sonthonax's abolition of slavery by its decree of February 4, 1794, it seemed logical to join the former enemy, especially since by this time virtually all the pro-slavery white planters had allied with the British. In addition, Toussaint realized he had little chance to rise to the top level of leadership with the Spanish because his way was blocked by two other black leaders, Biassou and Jean François.[6] Toussaint's decision proved a wise one. Within two years, his troops controlled most of the colony, and his territory was more unified than that controlled by mulatto leader André Rigaud. Limited to territory in the southern part of the colony, Rigaud "kept whites in rigid subjection," whereas "for Toussaint, all colors were part of Saint-Domingue." By April 1796, Toussaint had been appointed lieutenant governor by French governor Etienne Laveaux, whom Toussaint had previously saved during a mulatto mutiny. By 1797, the black leader had a well-trained army of 20,000, the most powerful military force on the island.[7]

Once Toussaint defeated the British and Spanish and forced Sonthonax to sail for France in August 1797, he began to consolidate his personal power and to secure the political independence of the island. Although still technically subordinate to the French governor, Toussaint signed a treaty in May 1799 with the United States and the British, who controlled the nearby island of Jamaica. In this treaty, Toussaint guaranteed Jamaica and the southern United States against attack (U.S. officials feared the slave revolt would spread) and received protection for his small navy. Armed with this new international respectability, he defeated the mulatto forces of Rigaud in August 1799. By summer 1801, Toussaint had merged the former Spanish colony on the island with his new country, had issued a new constitution, and had made himself governor-general for life. All this he did without permission from the French government, yet he claimed to remain a loyal subject. He did so in fear that revolutionary France would try to reimpose slavery when it had the chance.[8]

Toussaint's brilliant tactics were one reason for his great military and political successes. He was able to inspire his troops to march nearly 100 miles in a single day over mountainous terrain. As a master of guerrilla warfare, he was able to strike without warning and then to disappear quickly into the mountains. But Toussaint L'Ouverture (his last name, added in 1791, meant "the opener") was also a clever judge of both his enemies and of what we call today "public opinion." He anticipated Sonthonax's proclamation to abolish slavery four days in advance and issued his own proclamation. In it he reminded slaves that freedom was not a gift confirmed by whites but, rather, a status which had to be earned with his help. In late 1796, when Sonthonax proposed to Toussaint that they establish an independent state, kill all whites, and make Sonthonax dictator, Toussaint responded with a grin: "And when I have declared my independence of France and have massacred the whites, what would the Commissioner advise me to do with him?" Several years later, Toussaint told a friend that he was glad to have the emotional and vengeful Rigaud as his mulatto opponent. "Monsieur Rigaud," observed Toussaint, "lets go the bridle when he gallops. He shows his hand when he is about to strike. I gallop too, but I know how to curb. And when I strike people feel the blow, but do not see it coming."[9]

Toussaint's wisdom is also confirmed by his plans for the social and economic reconstruction of the colony. Toussaint astutely realized that many ex-slaves would seek to avoid field work if allowed and that the economy of the island would disintegrate if all the skilled white planters and mulattos left. To avoid this, he used military force to keep field hands on the plantations but guaranteed them collectively one-quarter of the income from the plantations. The government also took over abandoned plantations and kept half of the proceeds, but it made sure that the absentee proprietors received 25 percent of the profits. Toussaint also tried to maintain cordial relations with Britain and the United States, for he realized how important foreign trade was to the welfare of his people.[10] All of Toussaint's policies, however, required two things which he knew he could not guarantee: racial peace at home and the absence of foreign interference from abroad. That he was aware of these social and political realities is revealed in a comment Toussaint made to a white woman, who wanted him to grant her husband an official position and be godfather to her son:

> Madam, God alone is immortal. When I am dead, who knows if my people will not again . . . pass under the yoke of slavery? . . . Man's work does not endure. . . . You wish me to appoint your husband? So be it! Let him be an honest man and remember that even if I can't see everything, wrong does not remain unpunished. As for becoming your son's godfather, I can't grant that request. The whites would blame you, and the time might come when your son would blame you too.[11]

Toussaint realized his achievements might be short-lived. Once Napoleon Bonaparte assumed control of France in November 1799, he decided to restore authority over France's colonial empire in the West Indies and reimpose slavery in Santo Domingo. Toussaint's power forced Bonaparte to move slowly, and it was not until 1802 that the first installment of twenty thousand French troops arrived on the island. Jealousy among his military subordinates stymied Toussaint's plan to draw the French troops into the mountainous interior, where they could be more easily defeated. Nevertheless, the French lost many troops to battle and yellow fever. For reasons which are still disputed, Toussaint agreed to a truce with the French in May 1802. He was then lured into a trap and arrested by the French General Charles-Victor Leclerc on June 7, 1802. Toussaint was imprisoned in France where he died less than a year later.[12]

Shortly after Toussaint's death in 1803, the French were defeated and Haiti became an independent state. However, it did not become the country Toussaint wished it to be. His successors, Jean Jacques Dessalines and Henri Christophe, threw out the French and avenged Toussaint's death at the price of an anti-white policy which turned Haiti into one of the most impoverished states in the Western hemisphere. This social and racial policy was a betrayal of Toussaint's vision. At best, it enabled them to stir up the blacks to the extent necessary to obtain their personal and national freedom.[13]

In 1805, two years after Toussaint's death in prison, his Shawnee contemporary, Tecumseh, began his effort to unite North American Indians as Toussaint had attempted to unite blacks, whites, and mulattoes in Haiti. Tecumseh's effort was as determined as that of the black leader; it was also, in the last analysis, as unsuccessful.

Tecumseh, or "shooting star," was born in March 1768 in the Shawnee village of Piqua, situated in what is now southern Ohio. The youth witnessed constant conflict between Indians and white settlers, and he developed a keen hatred for whites. When he was six, Tecumseh's father was killed fighting against Virginians. Two of his brothers were also killed by American settlers and, in 1780, an American army commanded by George Rogers Clark wiped out his native village and destroyed the crops. Two years later, a village of peaceful, Christianized Delaware Indians in eastern Ohio was destroyed and the people massacred in cold blood by frontiersmen. In response to these offensive acts, some sources say, Tecumseh's mother stirred him to take vengeance against the "enemies of his race," people whose "souls are dark in treachery and their hands red in blood."[14]

Like Toussaint, Tecumseh learned early that no single race had a monopoly on cruelty or virtue. Tecumseh befriended several white "foster brothers," children captured and raised by the Indians; he even lived with Daniel Boone when the famous Kentuckian was a captive of the Shawnee from April to June 1778. As a teenage member of a Shawnee war party, Tecumseh became angry when his comrades tortured and killed an innocent white captive along the Ohio River. Throughout his life, he maintained that mistreatment and murder of captives were unworthy of a warrior. Tecumseh's biographers also generally note his kindhearted treatment of the elderly, the poor, and the weak among his own people and among whites. His Indian and white contemporaries were impressed with his forcefulness and nobility. Some reported that he had "a marked sense of personal dignity" combined with "a hot temper and strong self-control." Tecumseh could command respect and could use his anger effectively.[15] One American trader described Tecumseh as a man "fluent in conversation and a great public speaker [who] was hospitable, generous and humane—the resolute and indefatigable advocate of the rights and independence of the Indians."[16]

Despite his natural leadership abilities, Tecumseh did not begin his organization of the Northwest Indians until his early thirties. By that time, it had become clear that the whites would slowly push the Indians ever further west unless the Indians organized across tribal lines to stop them. A 1795 treaty with some tribes gave the United States government two-thirds of Ohio and a portion of southeastern Indiana. By that date, Indian leaders had been forced to abandon their hunting grounds in Kentucky, and settlements in the rest of Indiana were obviously the next goal of the whites. President Thomas Jefferson's administrative policy from 1801 to 1808 encouraged the Indians to farm rather than hunt (which required much more land), and those who refused or took up arms were forced across the Mississippi River. Meanwhile, the supply of game animals in this area dwindled, and many Indians, unable to supply their families with game and unwilling to take up farming, faced serious food shortages. The situation was worsened when whole tribes took to drink, imbibing large quantities of rum willingly supplied by white traders.

Aided by his brother Lalawethika, Tecumseh tried to halt this decline. In 1805, Lalawethika experienced a mystical religious conversion that turned this formerly lazy drunkard into the "Prophet." Changing his name to Tenskwatawa ("the open door"), Tecumseh's brother appealed to the Shawnees and to Indians of other tribes to stop drinking, stop marrying whites and wearing white people's clothing, and return to the traditional Indian ways of life. The Prophet claimed to have supernatural powers given him by "the Master of Life" [God] which could help his followers defeat the whites in battle. Tecumseh hoped this religious revival could inspire his people to halt the white advances. He had long believed that Indian land belonged to all tribes and that individual Indian leaders had no right to sell parcels piecemeal to the American government. Tenskwatawa's appeal as a powerful holy man gave him a new weapon to use in his effort to unify the Indians of the northwest and Ohio River valley against the Americans. In the following years, Tecumseh made a series of journeys through Indian territories from Wisconsin to Florida and as far west as Missouri and Arkansas to organize an Indian confederation. To help focus their movement, Tecumseh and the Prophet moved with many supporters to Greenville, Indiana, and, in 1808, to a new village along the Tippecanoe River in western Indiana. Alarmed by this Indian political and religious revival, William Henry Harrison, territorial governor of Indiana, countered it by poking fun at the new prophet and his followers. If Tenskwatawa was really a prophet with supernatural powers, Harrison scoffed, let him "cause the sun to stand still, the moon to alter its course, the rivers to cease to flow. . . . If he does these things," he told the Indians, "you may then believe that he has been sent by God." When he discovered that there was to be an eclipse of the sun on June 16, 1806, Tenskwatawa accepted Harrison's challenge and said he would make the sun darken on that day. Following appropriate ceremonies and before a large audience, the Prophet prayed and ordered the sun to disappear. The eclipse won many converts for Tenskwatawa that day.[17]

However, the American settlers continued to flock west, despite Tecumseh and Tenskwatawa's best efforts to promote Indian unity. "These lands are ours; no one has a right to remove us, because we were the first owners," Tecumseh told an Indian council in 1807. "As to boundaries, the Great Spirit above knows no boundaries, nor will his red people know any."[18] However, in the Treaty of Fort Wayne, signed in 1809 while Tecumseh was away on one of his recruiting trips, Harrison secured tribal agreement to abandon further territory to the United States. The new treaty helped Tecumseh recruit more Indians to his confederation during the coming year, but a face-to-face meeting between Harrison and the Indian leader in 1810 resulted in brave and angry words by Tecumseh but no political concessions by the governor. Late in 1811, while Tecumseh was again away seeking allies among the Choctaws and Creeks in the south, Harrison, fearing Tecumseh's growing power, defeated the Prophet's forces and destroyed the village at Tippecanoe.[19]

The battle of Tippecanoe was a turning point in Tecumseh's career. The "strong medicine" of the Prophet failed to work against Harrison's troops. Tecumseh was angry with his brother because he had wanted to avoid conflict until the confederation was fully organized. When he returned to stand upon the ashes of his former home, Tecumseh publicly humiliated Tenskwatawa, grabbing him by his hair and threatening to cut his throat. Then he vowed vengeance against the "long knives" for the attack.[20]

That vow of vengeance forced Tecumseh to lead his band of a thousand warriors to ally with the British in the War of 1812 against the Americans. Despite the fall of Detroit to the British in that year, the Americans greatly outnumbered their protagonists. Once Oliver Hazard Perry had defeated the British on Lake Erie in September 1813, final American victory was certain. Tecumseh was angered at the British retreat east into Ontario after Perry's victory, but he followed, leading his braves into and dying in his final battle against his old enemy, Harrison, at the Thames River on October 5, 1813. The fact that neither his body nor his secret grave has ever been positively identified only adds mystique to the legend of the Shawnee who dreamed of an independent Indian nation in North America.[21]

Tecumseh lived on in the imagination of the American people. Even Harrison saw fit to report to Washington that, if Tecumseh had not had to fight the United States, he might have created an Indian empire that would have rivaled that of the Aztecs in Mexico or that of the Incas in Peru. One biographer called him "a man of extraordinary abilities and possibilities"; another called him "the greatest Indian."[22] Such praise should not obscure the fact that Tecumseh's dream of Indian unity was, in fact, impossible from the beginning. Many tribal leaders opposed his confederation because of jealousy or simply because such an idea was alien to their traditional ideas of tribal autonomy. Such opposition was apparent on his recruiting trip south in 1811. On that trip, Tecumseh spoke to leaders of six great tribes, yet only the Muskogee and the Seminole leaders paid much attention to his pleas—and they promised only to consider his request for warriors. He had no firm commitments from the southern tribes at the time of the battle of Tippecanoe.[23] Even if Indians had joined him in large numbers, American settlers eventually would have used their numerical superiority to occupy the valuable agricultural lands of the Midwest. Any victories the outnumbered Indians would have won on the battlefield would have been only temporary. Even these Indians who did turn to agricultural pursuits were believed to be racially inferior by whites and were soon pushed onto the least arable lands—eventually, to Indian reservations in the western United States.

Although both Tecumseh and Toussaint relied on outside forces in an effort to achieve their goals, Toussaint achieved greater success in playing off the white nations against each other in Haiti than Tecumseh did by relying upon the British to defeat the Americans. Toussaint was at least able to end slavery in his homeland.

Given the uneven mix of failure and limited successes achieved by these men, what is their legacy? In the first place, both Toussaint and Tecumseh were heroes to their people. One modern author sees the struggle by Tecumseh and the Prophet as the antecedent of the twentieth-century "Red Power" movement by Native Americans. Their noble pan-Indian effort failed, but it could be recalled with pride by their descendants.[24] In addition, Tecumseh's Indians, by joining the British in the War of 1812, may have played a crucial role in keeping the Americans from capturing Upper Canada [the area directly north of the Great Lakes] during the war. This could have resulted in permanent U.S. control of part of Canada.[25] Toussaint's struggle had a more direct effect on American territorial expansion. When the French lost the colony of Santo Domingo, the French ruler gave up his hope of creating a western empire and on "May 3, 1803, exactly one week after the death of Toussaint in one of Napoleon's dungeons, Louisiana was sold by treaty to the Americans."[26] Thomas Jefferson's Louisiana Purchase virtually guaranteed that the new United States of America would become a continental nation.

Another reason for choosing to remember these men today, in a much "smaller" but still hostile world, is the vision of racial harmony which each man tried unsuccessfully to impart to his followers. While it was certainly "good politics" for Toussaint and Tecumseh to promote harmony between the races, it is important that they opposed torture, murder, and mistreatment of captives and other innocent people of other races at a time when most people were willing to accept such things. In promoting racial harmony, as in their broader political struggles, Toussaint and Tecumseh resisted the odds against them, even among their own followers.

Any attempt to evaluate the achievement of these men, then, must take into account the way we choose to define greatness in history. "Great men make history," one historian wrote in evaluating Toussaint, "but only such history as it is possible for them to make. Their freedom of achievement is limited by the necessities of their environment."[27] A true test of historical greatness might require us to ask not only what a person has done but also how successfully a person was able to resist the odds against success. By that test, both Toussaint L'Ouverture and Tecumseh have more than earned the few words they usually are given in most textbooks.

Notes

1. Ralph Korngold, *Citizen Toussaint* (New York: Hill and Wang, 1965; original, 1944), 11, 15, 33–34, 105–106.
2. Ibid., 55–57.
3. Ibid., 20, 55–57; Thomas O. Ott, *The Haitian Revolution, 1789–1804* (Knoxville: University of Tennessee Press, 1973), 48–55.
4. Ott, *Haitian Revolution*, 65–72; Korngold, *Citizen Toussaint*, 103.
5. Ott, *Haitian Revolution*, 57–58; Korngold, *Citizen Toussaint*, 77–78; C. L. R. James, *The Black Jacobins: Toussaint L'Ouverture and the San Domingo Revolution*, 2d ed., (New York: Vintage Books, 1963), 90–93.
6. Ott, *Haitian Revolution*, 82–83; Korngold, *Citizen Toussaint*, 105–106; Martin Ros, *Night of Fire: The Black Napoleon and the Battle for Haiti* (New York: Sarpedon, 1994), 71.
7. Ott, *Haitian Revolution*, 85–88; James, *Black Jacobins*, 181.
8. Ott, *Haitian Revolution*, 110; Korngold, *Citizen Toussaint*, 89, 118–119, 139.
9. Korngold, *Citizen Toussaint*, 99–101, 110–111, 129, 160.
10. Ott, *Haitian Revolution*, 130–134; Korngold, *Citizen Toussaint*, 130–131, 205–208.
11. Korngold, *Citizen Toussaint*, 150.
12. See Korngold, *Citizen Toussaint*, 284–297; Ott, *Haitian Revolution*, 160–161; "Memoir of Toussaint L'Ouverture," in *Toussaint L'Ouverture: Biography and Autobiography* (Boston: James Redpath, 1863; reprinted by Books for Libraries Press, Freeport, NY, 1971), 295–328.

13. Ott, *Haitian Revolution*, 189–191; Franklin W. Knight, *The Caribbean: The Genesis of a Fragmented Nationalism* (Oxford: Oxford University Press, 1978), 156–157; Ros, *Night of Fire*, ix, 180–185.

14. Glenn Tucker, *Tecumseh: Vision of Glory* (Indianapolis: Bobbs-Merrill, 1956), 26–27, 46; Benjamin Drake, *Life of Tecumseh and His Brother The Prophet* (Cincinnati: Anderson, Gates and Wright, 1858; reprinted by Kraus Reprint, New York, 1969), 66–71; Alvin Josephy, Jr., "Tecumseh, The Greatest Indian," in *The Patriot Chiefs: A Chronicle of American Indian Resistance* (New York: Penguin Books, 1976), 137–141.

15. Albert Britt, "Tecumseh, the Shawnee Who Dreamed of Empire," in *Great Indian Chiefs* (Freeport, NY: Books for Libraries Press, 1969), 136–137; Tucker, *Tecumseh*, 30–32, 36–40, 67; R. David Edmunds, *Tecumseh and the Quest for Indian Leadership* (Boston: Little, Brown, 1984), 44.

16. Bil Gilbert, *God Gave Us This Country: Tekamthi and the First American Civil War* (New York: Doubleday, 1990), 194.

17. Tucker, *Tecumseh: Vision of Glory*, 99–101.

18. Drake, *Life of Tecumseh*, 93.

19. Josephy, "Tecumseh, the Greatest Indian," 160–161.

20. Tucker, *Tecumseh: Vision of Glory*, 230.

21. See Klinck, *Tecumseh: Fact and Fiction*, 200–230, for conflicting accounts of Tecumseh's death.

22. Gilbert, *God Gave Us This Country*, 5; Josephy, "Tecumseh, the Greatest Indian," 131–132.

23. Tucker, *Tecumseh: Vision of Glory*, 214–217.

24. Arrell Morgan Gibson, *The American Indian: Prehistory to the Present* (Lexington, MA: D.C. Heath and Company, 1980), 284–286.

25. For a look at the numerical weakness of the British and the strength of the Americans, see James W. Hammack, Jr., *Kentucky and the Second American Revolution: The War of 1812* (Lexington: University Press of Kentucky, 1976), 25, 32, 109–111. See also Gilbert, *God Gave Us This Country*, 329.

26. Ros, *Night of Fire*, 124.

27. James, *The Black Jacobins*, x.

Further Reading

GILBERT, BIL. *God Gave Us This Country.* New York: Doubleday, 1990. Excellent study of Tecumseh in context of U.S. history in this period.

JOSEPHY, ALVIN, JR. "Tecumseh, The Greatest Indian." In *The Patriot Chiefs: A Chronicle of American Indian Resistance.* New York: Penguin Books, 1976. Good short biography.

KORNGOLD, RALPH. *Citizen Toussaint.* New York: Hill & Wang, 1965. Most readable biography.

ROS, MARTIN. *Night of Fire: The Black Napoleon and the Battle for Haiti.* New York: Sarpedon, 1994. Shows how Toussaint was betrayed by his chief general Dessalines, a brutal man whose effect on the future of Haiti was very negative.

CHAPTER 7

George Sand and Harriet Beecher Stowe: Exploring "Woman's Sphere"

What did these two popular nineteenth-century female authors see as the problems facing women? What did each see as the best sort of equality for women? What impact did each have on her society?

In the famous American anti-slavery novel, Uncle Tom's Cabin, author Harriet Beecher Stowe (1811–1896) has the slave, Eliza, one of her main characters, dress in boy's clothing so she can cross Lake Erie with her husband and find freedom in Canada.[1] About the same time as this novel was written, a French author, Aurore Dudevant (1804–1876), adopted occasional use of men's clothing and a male pseudonym, George Sand, in order to achieve greater freedom as a person and writer.

The fact that both of these female writers and reformers saw that appearing male gave women greater freedom only hints at the difficulties facing creative women in the nineteenth century. Such women lived complex lives and faced serious legal and emotional problems.

Industrializing nations such as the United States and France in the middle of the nineteenth century were patriarchal societies where most political, social, and economic rights were reserved for males and few women then sought or claimed a limited equality. Those who did argue for woman's rights stressed the differences between the sexes to make their point, as the lives and careers of George Sand and Harriet Beecher Stowe illustrate.

"It will be in the female heart . . . as it always has been, that love and devotion, patience and pity, will find their true home. On woman falls the duty, in a world of brute passions, of preserving the virtues of charity and the Christian spirit." This statement may strike you as arrogant, sentimental, wrong-headed, or correct. What is interesting is that these words on the character of women were written, not by the profoundly religious Harriet Beecher Stowe, but by George Sand, the scandalous Frenchwoman who took so many lovers that she was once called "the most obscene of women."[2]

Stowe would have fully agreed with Sand for, despite their quite different lifestyles, these two writers had much in common. Their lives spanned turbulent years of social and civil strife in France and the United States. And each woman played an active public role, Sand by writing revolutionary articles in Paris in 1848 and Stowe with her dramatic, history-making *Uncle Tom's Cabin*, published in 1852.

In their novels, both writers addressed controversial social issues, although Sand generally focused on the injustices facing women and the lower classes in France, while Stowe became famous for describing the plight of slaves in the American South. Neither would qualify as a modern feminist, but each advocated the value of a woman's way of looking at things, and each felt that society could be improved if men understood and valued this viewpoint as well. Each wanted to see women gain substantial control over their personal lives and property. It was Sand, however, who engaged in serial monogamy [living with a series of men, one at a time], who made this point much more directly than did the more traditional Stowe. Each woman believed that virtues taught at home, often called "woman's sphere" in the United States, were the foundation of civilization, though Stowe made this point far more powerfully than did Sand. By examining the lives and works of these authors, we can better understand both the difficulties facing women in the nineteenth century and the debates over the role of women in our own time.

George Sand was born Amandine Aurore Lucie Dupin. Her father, an officer in Napoleon's army, traced his ancestry back to a king of Poland, while her mother, Sophie Delaborde, was a dancer and the daughter of a Parisian bird seller. In later life, after Aurore had taken the name George Sand as a way of earning respect in a profession dominated by males, she would make much of her working-class background: "I was born . . . and started life in poverty, in the harsh, vagabond life of military camps. . . . I never forget that the blood of the [common] people ran in my veins."[3]

From her father's death in 1808, when Aurore was only four, until she married in 1822, her life was an emotional tug-of-war between her unstable mother and her paternal grandmother, Madame Dupin de Francueil. Sophie could not afford to support her daughter, and young Aurore felt abandoned when her mother left her at Madame Dupin's estate at Nohant in return for financial support from her mother-in-law. A cultured musician and friend of eighteenth-century "romantic" thinker Jean-Jacques Rousseau, Dupin de Francueil gave Aurore a good education and tried to train her in the ways of the aristocracy to better inoculate her against her "low-born" mother. However, the sensitive Aurore continued to crave her mother's love. When Aurore was nine, Sophie foolishly promised her that she would "rescue" her from the discipline of her grandmother and take her to Orléans, where they would open a hat shop to support themselves. Aurore was crushed when her mother failed to follow through on this promise, and her grandmother made her feel worse by cruelly telling her that her mother's early sexual indiscretions made her "a lost woman."[4] Later she recalled feeling that her parents had left her "a poor waif marked out for slavery, injustice, tedium, and eternal unrequited longing."[5] Beginning at age thirteen, she spent several years in a convent school in Paris, where she had a mystical "conversion experience" which left her with the feeling that God could (and would) communicate directly with her, something Harriet Beecher Stowe also believed. What one biographer has called Sand's "desperate search for parental affection" may account for her religious experience. This desire for acceptance would haunt George Sand the rest of her life; it helps explain the way she lived, and it gave great power to her fiction.[6]

At age eighteen, Aurore entered what proved to be an unhappy marriage with Baron Casimir Dudevant. Although they soon had a child, Maurice (named for Aurore's father), Casimir proved resistant to Aurore's attempts to "improve" his mind, to get him to spend less time drinking and hunting and more time reading. Within three years, Aurore had formed a platonic [non-sexual] relationship with a "witty, elegant" young lawyer named Aurélien de Sèze. Although she tried to work out an agreement that would allow her to stay married to Casimir while continuing to visit and receive letters from Aurélien, by 1828 her marriage was clearly "on the rocks." In September of that year, Aurore had a daughter,

Solange, fathered by a young friend in Paris, Stéphane Ajasson. While Madame Dudevant was giving birth to Solange, she could hear Casimir in another room making love to a female servant.[7] In 1831, she moved to Paris, initially leaving the children with Casimir. Although not legally separated from Casimir until 1836, she immediately began living with a series of younger men, most of them artists. Jules Sandeau was the first, and it was his name which she modified for her masculine pseudonym when she published her first novel, *Indiana*, in 1832. A succession of men—composer Frédéric Chopin being the most famous—would follow in the coming years.

Indiana, like other Sand novels, was partly autobiographical. The heroine, Indiana, like Sand, is a young woman unhappily married to an older man, the jealous Colonel Delmare. The novel opens with Delmare wounding a presumed thief, Raymon de Ramière, whom he finds breaking into his house. Raymon, however, was really sneaking in to continue his affair with Noun, Indiana's foster sister and servant. Once he realizes this, Delmare forgives him, even becoming his friend, for such behavior is almost expected of such high-born noblemen. As Sand remarks cynically: "The lady of quality sacrifices twenty previous lovers to you; the lady's maid sacrifices only a husband that she might have had."[8] Later, Indiana falls in love with Raymon, and Noun commits suicide when she discovers that she is pregnant and that Raymon will not marry or love her. Indiana's cousin Ralph tries to protect her from the insincere Raymon by telling her why Noun committed suicide. Meanwhile, Colonel Delmare beats Indiana after discovering her letters to Raymon; Indiana leaves Delmare but finally discovers that Raymon does not really love her. At the end of the novel, Ralph and Indiana fail in a suicide attempt and finally decide to live out their days together in seclusion on a small island.

As her first and perhaps most "romantic" novel, *Indiana* tells us much about how Sand viewed women's roles and rights. The novel portrays women as the victim of both suppressed passions and legal injustice. Indiana, Sand tells us, "is love dashing her head blindly against all the obstacles of civilization." In a preface to the 1842 edition, Sand, aware that French laws treated women as children with few rights, said she "wrote *Indiana* with a feeling . . . that the laws which govern woman's existence in wedlock, in the family and in society are unjust and barbarous." She appeals to public opinion to change them, adding that she is not advocating revolution but only trying to "reconcile the welfare and the dignity of oppressed individuals . . . without modifying society itself." In the novel, Sand satirizes Colonel Delmare (modeled after her husband, Casimir) as an "honest man" who does not steal from his neighbors or "ravish maidens in the public road" but who "may beat his wife, maltreat his servants, ruin his children and it is nobody's business," since "society punishes only those acts which are injurious to it; private life is beyond its jurisdiction." Later, Indiana attacks Raymon's patriarchal notion of God:

> Yours is the God of men, the king, the founder and upholder of your race; mine is the God of the universe, the creator, the preserver and the hope of all creatures. Yours made everything for you alone; mine made all created things for one another. . . . You think that God . . . authorizes you to possess the empire of the earth; I think that . . . the day will come when His breath will scatter you like grains of sand. . . . All your morality, all your principles, are simply the interests of your social class which you have raised to the dignity of laws. . . . I tell you, it ill becomes you to invoke His name to crush the resistance of a poor, weak woman, to stifle the lamentations of a broken heart.[9]

Indiana shows us Sand's conviction that neither women's passions nor their legal rights are taken seriously by her society; it also shows us Sand's romantic idealism, her search for an impossibly perfect love and lover. At one point in the novel, Indiana is "terrified" by her awareness "that she was of so little account in his [Raymon's] life while he was everything in hers." She wonders "in dismay if this man, for whom life had so many different aspects . . . could devote his whole mind to her, sacrifice all his ambitions to her."[10] In a later novel, *Lélia,* Sand's main character becomes depressed because she intellectualizes love, calling it "the aspiration of our most ethereal part for the unknown." Her sister, a prostitute, tells her: "You should have applied your superior intellect to enjoy, not to deny, because if you don't, what good is intelligence?"[11]

Sand's biographers highlight her tendency to take as lovers younger men who were sensitive but frail artists, often afflicted with consumption [tuberculosis]. They suggest she selected men she could nurse and mother. One biographer found Sand "a man in her insistence on freedom, but a woman, too, craving the shelter of a 'home' with her children about her" and with "a passion for tending the sick."[12] Perhaps this was her way of compensating for her weak relationship with her own parents.

If Sand's childhood and early adult experiences drove her to be motherly and denied her stable long-term relationships with men, they also made her more tolerant of the poor and of women trapped in unhappy marriages. Many of her sixty novels and hundreds of essays and articles deal with the plight of the poor. Her novel *Horace*, for example, contrasts the middle-class life of a flighty law student with that of a hard-working artisan. In the late 1830s and through the 1840s, she was attracted to the ideas of Pierre Leroux, who invented the word *socialism (socialisme)* and who felt that poverty was un-Christian and led people to a life of vice.[13] Her defense of women's rights, then, was not only an outgrowth of her own experience with Casimir; it was also set in this broader social-political context. In her second novel, *Valentine*, the heroine is a "naturally amiable and sweet" aristocrat who is in love with a peasant (Benedict) but is forced to marry an insensitive nobleman who cares only about money. Sand's belief in Rousseau's idea that people are born good but are corrupted by society is expressed in her judgment that marriage between Valentine and Benedict is impossible because they come from different social classes: "society stood between them and made their mutual choice absurd. . . . Providence created the admirable order of nature, men have destroyed it; whose is the fault?" At the end of the novel, Valentine and Benedict die tragically, as did Romeo and Juliet in Shakespeare's play.[14]

As Sand grew older, she turned from writing novels with romantic or social messages to more pastoral themes, exalting the simplicity of peasant life in her beloved province of Berry. Yet, during the Revolution of 1848, she took time to defend the workers and promote her vague ideas of "socialism"—meaning for her little more than social and economic equality for the poor and a dislike for the lazy arrogance of the rich, who "are not used to working."[15] George Sand's sympathy for the lower classes of France was recognized in 1870, when, during the Franco-Prussian War, one of the balloons used to help French leaders escape from the besieged city of Paris was named the *George Sand*.

It is interesting that despite her radical lifestyle and the many anti-male statements in her works, Sand specifically opposed political rights, even suffrage, for women. She said that women needed civil equality in marriage and "equality before God," but, in the words of Sand's chief biographer, she "had . . . too low an opinion of the political intelligence of most members of her sex to be a suffragette." Besides, involvement in politics would undermine confidence in women's role as mothers. She wrote:

> How could even honest judges have confidence in women who, coming forward to claim the dignity now refused them in the family home, especially the sacred authority over children which they are denied, demand . . . not peace in the household or freedom for their motherly affections, but the right to take part in the political struggle, a sword and a helmet, the right to condemn to death?[16]

Statements such as this, stressing the importance of social rather than political equality for women, show Sand to be more politically conservative than her American counterpart. Harriet Beecher Stowe favored women's suffrage as a way to advance those special virtues of domesticity ("peace in the household . . . freedom for motherly affections") that both she and Sand thought important.

However, despite her advocacy of women's suffrage, Stowe was fundamentally a conservative person who, ironically, helped bring about a radical change—the end of slavery in the United States. Her emphasis on home as the appropriate sphere for female activity was an idea that both aided and restricted women in nineteenth-century America. On the one hand, it made women powerful judges of all issues related to home and family, especially the education and religious upbringing of children. But where women governed the domestic sphere without male interference, the world beyond the home—the world of business, industry, and government—belonged solely to men.

The genius of Stowe's *Uncle Tom's Cabin,* then, was that it appealed to Northern readers to end slavery, not because it was a political evil, but because of the devastating effect it had on the Christian family. Slavery was, in effect, a threat to the "woman's sphere." This conviction and Stowe's sense of missionary idealism developed out of her childhood experiences, which were as challenging as those of George Sand, but very different. Harriet Beecher was the daughter of one of America's most famous Calvinist clergymen, Lyman Beecher. If George Sand had roots in the French aristocracy,

Harriet Beecher was a member of the New England "nobility." The first Beechers arrived in New Haven, Connecticut, in 1638, just eighteen years after the *Mayflower,* and the family had remained important since that time. Lyman Beecher was such a powerful evangelical preacher and patriarch that all four of his sons became ministers and two of his three daughters—Catharine and Harriet—turned their religious zeal in the direction of social reform. Harriet would, in fact, "outpreach her father and all her gifted brothers combined"; if *Uncle Tom's Cabin* was a sermon (and it was), she would "count into her flock the peoples of the earth."[17]

However, "Hattie" Beecher's religious vision would be notably different from that of her father, who believed in Predestination and a stern God. Especially after the death of her mother when she was four, Harriet tried hard to please her father, a difficult task, since Lyman could be a fiery preacher and strict disciplinarian one minute and a man in the depths of emotional despair and hypochondria [imaginary ill health] the next.

As a child, Harriet was convinced of her depravity. She did not escape this religious depression until her late teens, when she decided to believe in a compassionate Christ instead of the judgmental, monarchical Old Testament God of her father. Her decision would help change American history, for, without it, *Uncle Tom's Cabin* would never have been written. Some historians have argued that Harriet's personal decision was part of a much greater change she helped inspire in American religious history during the mid-nineteenth century. She kept the revivalistic spirit and moral tone of traditional Calvinism but softened, or "feminized," its message in her novels by emphasizing the power of love over judgment. Her approach to Christianity also stressed the equality of all people in the eyes of God, relied on spreading the gospel through action (especially informal "peer counseling" among women) instead of preaching, and looked for God in everyday experience rather than in the thunderings of authority figures. Because of this, the type of Christianity found in Harriet Beecher Stowe's novels was an "explicit challenge [to] the male clerical establishment."[18] It would be many years, however, before Harriet's fictional "ministry of the word" would begin in earnest. During her twenties, she helped her sister Catharine set up a school for young women in Hartford. When Lyman took a position as director of the Lane Theological Seminary in Cincinnati in 1832, Harriet and Catharine moved to this western frontier town, and there Harriet married Calvin Stowe, a Lane professor. Between her wedding in 1836 (which she told her best friend she was "dreading" as an "overwhelming crisis") and the birth of her last child in Maine in 1850, she wrote only a few short stories and magazine pieces. She was devoted to her family and believed (as most of the female characters in her novels did) that the well-regulated home was one of women's greatest contributions to the world.

However, like Sand, she was not able to be only a homemaker. In one letter, she told her friend Mary Dutton that she earned enough money from her "sketches" that she could hire an extra servant and have more time to write. Later, she accepted Calvin's insistence that she "must be a literary woman" and then asked him for "a room to myself, if I am to write." There was an undercurrent of half-suppressed discontent in comments she wrote during this period. In an 1845 letter, she complained: "I am sick of the smell of sour milk, and sour meat, and sour everything, and then the clothes will not dry. . . . When the brain gives out . . . and one cannot think or remember anything, then what is to be done?" Other letters reveal some marital tensions; she and Calvin spent five of the first fifteen years of their married life apart—each in turn taking "rest cures" in Vermont. Calvin had, in the words of one modern historian, "intense and unremitting" sexual needs and, like Harriet's father, suffered from what she called "hypochondriac morbid instability."[19] One biographer claims that difficulties Harriet Beecher Stowe faced in her married life contributed to her passionate first novel.[20] Whether or not this was true, Stowe had learned to appreciate the sufferings of women and mothers, and *Uncle Tom's Cabin* was her first and most powerful statement of her belief in the importance of the "woman's sphere."

When President Abraham Lincoln met Stowe in the fall of 1862 and greeted her with the comment "So this is the little lady who made this big war," he was referring not only to her size but also to the impact of *Uncle Tom's Cabin*, a book which sold three hundred thousand copies the year it was published (1852) and over half a million copies during the next five years. This work has been called "the most powerful and influential book of the nineteenth century" and "one of the most famous novels ever written."[21]

What made *Uncle Tom's Cabin* so popular and powerful was the way it personalized and even feminized the issue of slavery, stressing that this institution tore mothers from their children in a manner that was both inhuman and, more important, un-Christian. In literary terms, *Uncle Tom's Cabin* may have been too sentimental (though the public liked sentimental novels), but it was "a great revival sermon, aimed directly at the conversion of its hearers."[22]

Tom, the novel's main character, lives successively with three masters. The first, kind Mr. Shelby in Kentucky, is forced to sell Tom because of hard times. Tom's second master, Augustine St. Clare, has mixed feelings about slavery and decides to free Tom, but fails to do so before he is unexpectedly killed. The infamous Simon Legree, Tom's last master, is a slaveowner so wicked that he even refuses to let his slaves sing religious hymns. He beats Tom fatally after Tom refuses to tell Legree the whereabouts of two slaves planning to escape. Other famous characters include Eliza, who makes a daring escape with her son across the Ohio River by jumping from one ice floe to the next, and her husband, George, who is finally able to lead his family to freedom in Canada.

While sharing the journeys of these characters, we meet others whose actions reinforce the negative effect of slavery on Christian family life. There is the fictional Senator Bird of Ohio, who voted for the 1850 Fugitive Slave Law that required Northerners to assist in returning runaway slaves to their owners, yet, when Eliza shows up at his door and his wife admonishes him to put the Biblical injunction to "feed the hungry, clothe the naked, and comfort the desolate" ahead of politics, he provides help.[23] It was significant that Mary Bird, like Harriet herself, had recently lost a son the same age as Eliza's boy, Harry. Mothers, Stowe was saying, understand other mothers.[24] Elsewhere in the novel, a slave mother leaps overboard and drowns herself in the Ohio after discovering that her baby has been sold away from her during the night, and the Louisiana slave, Cassy, kills her newborn with opium after having two older children sold away from her. Ophelia, Augustine St. Clare's Vermont cousin, helps him care for his invalid wife and angelic child, Eva. Ophelia represents, among other things, the virtues of a neat, well-organized kitchen (also found in the Quaker settlement where the Birds take Eliza).[25]

One of the criticisms made of Stowe's novel is its lack of subtlety; this is also the reason for its appeal. Uncle Tom and Eva St. Clare are exaggerated Christ-figures. Tom helps St. Clare find faith and then dies to save others; Eva, as she nears death, asks her father to free Tom and reminds him, "Papa, these poor creatures love their children as much as you do me." And, just in case anyone missed the point, Stowe ends her novel with an appeal to northern mothers to end slavery:

> Mothers of America,—you who have learned, by the cradles of your own children, to love and feel for all mankind. . . . I beseech you, pity those mothers that are constantly made childless by the American slave trade! . . . The people of the free states . . . are more guilty for it, before God, than the South, in that they have not the apology of education or custom."[26]

Aside from Tom himself, the strongest characters in *Uncle Tom's Cabin* tend to be female. Some are white women, such as Mrs. Shelby, Mrs. Bird, and Ophelia, who deplore the evils of slavery and the domestic disorder it brings but leave the final decisions to men. Eva represents women of strong character who seek the reward for their suffering in Heaven, while black slave women, such as Eliza and Cassy, have the strength to rebel and escape to a better life in Canada.

Uncle Tom's Cabin appealed to a wide readership not only because it was a powerful, sentimental novel but also because it was as much about the role of women in American society as it was about slavery. Two years after *Uncle Tom's Cabin* was published, Stowe wrote an "Appeal to the Women of the Free States," urging them to petition Congress to prevent the extension of slavery. Her language was powerful and direct: "However ambition and love of political power may blind the stronger sex, God has given to woman a deeper and more immovable knowledge, in those holier feelings, which are peculiar to womanhood, and which guard the sacredness of the family." By seeing slavery as a threat to the sanctity of "woman's sphere," Stowe, says one critic, "designates slavery as a domestic issue for American women to adjudicate and manage . . . abolishing slavery means . . . erasing [a] reminder of the precariousness of the feminine sphere."[27]

For Stowe and other nineteenth-century American female reformers, especially in the post-Civil War generation, the virtues found in the "feminine sphere" of the home stood in opposition to the spirit of greedy capitalism that dominated the world of business in this "Gilded Age." "Our men are sufficiently money-making," Sarah Josepha Hale wrote in the *Ladies Magazine*. "Let us keep our women and children from the contagion as long as possible."[28] In Stowe's later "social novels," *Pink and White Tyranny, My Wife and I* (both 1871), and *We and Our Neighbors* (1873), she addresses more explicitly the question of women's roles. Here Stowe's male characters are in charge of business, while "the woman and her educated daughters [are] in charge of Culture." Stowe believed women had the right to own property, and the right to work and be paid equally with men, things George Sand would have applauded. But the case for women's rights, she argued, rested on women's moral superiority. Women's votes, for example, "would close grogshops [taverns], . . . stop the traffic in spirits" and improve society, as women were already working to improve the family.[29]

Stowe wanted a world in which women's work would be recognized as equally important as that of men. Like George Sand, she did not want to challenge the fundamental patriarchal structure of society. In fact, in *My Wife and I* she pointedly attacked the radical feminists of her day, such as Victoria Woodhull, satirizing them in the person of a loose-living character named Audacia Dangyereyes, whom she called an advocate of "the wildest principles of modern French communism." By modern feminist standards, of course, keeping women in the home—even as domestic dictators—is the best way to thwart equality for women and to preserve the patriarchal society. Less than a century later, Betty Friedan's *Feminine Mystique* would find oppressive the very "domesticity" which Stowe extolled.[30]

George Sand and Harriet Beecher Stowe never met. After *Uncle Tom's Cabin* was published in France, Sand offered Stowe the following backhanded compliment: "I cannot say she has talent as one understands it in the world of letters, but she has . . . the genius of goodness, not that of a man of letters, but of the saint." For her part, Harriet "read everything that George Sand wrote"; after reading one of Sand's novels, she found it remarkable "that so corrupt a woman could describe so beautiful a character."[31] When Stowe went to Europe in 1853 and visited Paris, she wanted to meet Sand but was told that her reputation would suffer if she did so.[32] Had they met, perhaps they would have found more in common than either might have thought.

Both women had a stronger spirit of independence than most of their contemporaries, male or female. Both were determined to be writers, and each wanted her writing to make a difference. Both succeeded admirably though they shared an exaggerated belief in the ability of a woman's love and virtue to change the world. Sand's fiction is attractive to feminists today because it conveys the anguish that this sensitive woman felt as she struggled to find her ideal lover. Sand is also better than Stowe at identifying problems facing women; Stowe—despite the ultimate failure of her "domesticity" strategy—is better at suggesting solutions. However, they both *did* change the world. Sand was one of the first modern women to demand sexual equality with men and live as if she had it. Her novels are still read by those interested in how women *felt* about life in the mid-nineteenth century. Harriet Beecher Stowe's *Uncle Tom's Cabin* did contribute to the coming of the American Civil War. Lincoln was right, at least in part.

Did either contribute significantly to women's equality? Here the jury is still out—evaluations of their contributions to modern feminism are mixed. Neither would be troubled by this, for each lived life to a fuller extent than generally thought possible in her day. And, although both would have specific disagreements with modern women's rights activists, their aim—to speak as women and be heard—would be shared by these writers and by most women today.

Notes

1. Harriet Beecher Stowe, *Uncle Tom's Cabin* (New York: Bantam Books, 1981; original 1851–1852), 381–382; Stowe also used the male pseudonym "Franklin" when writing an anti-slavery letter to a Cincinnati newspaper in 1836—see Forrest Wilson, *Crusader in Crinoline: The Life of Harriet Beecher Stowe* (Westport, CT: Greenwood Press, 1972; original, 1941), 179.

2. Andre Maurois, *Lelia: The Life of George Sand,* trans. Gerard Hopkins (New York: Harper and Brothers, 1954), 324; J. M. Quadrado, "To George Sand: A Refutation," in George Sand, *Winter in Majorca* (Chicago: Academy Press, Ltd., 1978), 200.

3. From a letter to Charles Poncy (December 1843), in *George Sand in Her Own Words,* trans. and ed. Joseph Barry (Garden City, NY: Doubleday Anchor, 1979), 287–288.

4. Curtis Cate, *George Sand: A Biography* (Boston: Houghton Mifflin, 1975), 35–39, 52–54.

5. George Sand, *My Life,* trans. and adapted by Dan Hofstadter (New York: Harper and Row, 1979), 123.

6. Cate, *Sand*, 62–66; Sand, *My Life*, 145–150; Maurois, *Lelia*, 324; Renee Winegarten, *The Double Life of George Sand: Woman and Writer* (New York: Basic Books, 1978), 33–34.

7. Samuel Edwards, *George Sand* (New York: David McKay Co., 1972), 50; see also Cate, *Sand*, 112–126.

8. George Sand, *Indiana*, trans. George Burnham Ives (Chicago: Academy Press Ltd., 1978), 31.

9. Sand, *Indiana*, xxiv, xxviii, xxxii, 96, 224.

10. Ibid., 115.

11. George Sand, *Lelia*, trans. Maria Espinosa (Bloomington: Indiana University Press, 1978; original, 1833), 36, 106.

12. See Maurois, *Lelia*, 92, 140; see also 103, 140, 173, 261; Cate, *Sand*, 321–322; Winegarten, *Double Life*, 186–187; Joseph Barry, *Infamous Woman: The Life of George Sand* (Garden City, NY: Doubleday, 1976), 34–35, 67–68, 73.

13. See Cate, *Sand*, 493–497.

14. George Sand, *Valentine*, trans. George Burnham Ives (Chicago: Cassandra Editions, 1978; original 1832), see especially pp. 108–113, 137, 326–333.

15. Sand, *In Her Own Words*, 355–390.

16. Cate, *Sand*, xxx–xxxi; Sand, *In Her Own Words*, 404–405; see also 411–413. For some of Sand's strongest anti-male statements, see 339–340 of this work.

17. Wilson, *Crusader*, 21.

18. Ann Douglas, *The Feminization of American Culture* (Garden City, NY: Doubleday, 1988; original, 1977), 4–12, 244–256; Joan D. Hedrick, *Harriet Beecher Stowe: A Life* (New York: Oxford University Press 1994), 39, 155–157; see also Dorothy Berkson, "Millennial Politics and the Feminine Fiction of Harriet Beecher Stowe," in Elizabeth Ammons, *Critical Essays on Harriet Beecher Stowe* (Boston: G. K. Hall, 1980), 246–249.

19. Mary Kelley, "Harriet Beecher Stowe: 'Changing to Nobody Knows Who,' " in Jeanne Boydston, Mary Kelley, and Anne Margolis, *The Limits of Sisterhood: The Beecher Sisters on Women's Rights and Woman's Sphere* (Chapel Hill: University of North Carolina Press, 1988), 52, 62, 67–70, 73; Mary Kelley, "At War with Herself: Harriet Beecher Stowe as Woman in Conflict Within the Home," *American Studies*, vol. 19 (1978): 31.

20. John R. Adams, *Harriet Beecher Stowe* (New York: Twayne Publishers, 1963), 19, 27.

21. Wilson, *Crusader*, 484; Robert F. Lucid, "Harriet Beecher Stowe," *McGraw-Hill Encyclopedia of World Biography* (New York: McGraw-Hill, 1973), 240; Winifred E. Wise, *Harriet Beecher Stowe: Woman with a Cause* (New York: Putnam's Sons, 1965), 10, 165.

22. Douglas, *Feminization*, 244.

23. Stowe, *Uncle Tom's Cabin*, 77.
24. In a letter to abolitionist Eliza Cabot Follen (December 1852), Stowe wrote that it was at her son's deathbed and grave in 1849 "that I learned what a poor slave mother may feel when her child is torn away from her." After *Uncle Tom's Cabin* was finished (it began as a magazine serial), Harriet said on several occasions that "The Lord Himself wrote it. I was but an instrument in His hand." Whether or not *Uncle Tom's Cabin* was so "inspired," the story clearly conveyed the personal passion that she felt on this subject (see Wilson, *Crusader*, 270ff.).
25. Stowe, *Uncle Tom's Cabin*, 129, 131, 154ff., 365.
26. Ibid., 276, 301, 441.
27. Boydston et al., *Limits of Sisterhood*, 180–181; Gillian Brown, "Getting in the Kitchen with Dinah: Domestic Politics in *Uncle Tom's Cabin*," *American Quarterly*, vol. 36 (Fall 1984): 506. It is interesting that none of the blacks in *Uncle Tom's Cabin* are weak, despite later use of the term "Uncle Tom" by modern blacks to describe someone who is too passive and accepting of white leadership. See Beatrice A. Anderson, "Uncle Tom: A Hero at Last," *American Transcendental Quarterly* (June 1991): 95–108.
28. Quoted in Brown, "Getting in the Kitchen with Dinah," 505.
29. Alice C. Crozier, *The Novels of Harriet Beecher Stowe* (New York: Oxford, 1969), 157; Stowe, "The Woman Question," *Atlantic Monthly* (December 1865): 672–683, quoted in Boydston et al., *Limits of Sisterhood*, 266–269.
30. Harriet Beecher Stowe, *My Wife and I* (Boston: Houghton Mifflin, 1896; original, 1871), 268–283; Douglas, *Feminization*, 11–12. See Betty Friedan, *The Feminine Mystique* (New York: W. W. Norton, 1963).
31. Hedrick, *Harriet Beecher Stowe: A Life*, 266; see also 371–372.
32. Cate, *Sand*, 329, 429–430.

Further Reading

CATE, CURTIS. *George Sand: A Biography*. Boston: Houghton Mifflin, 1975. Comprehensive, readable, and fair presentation of life of Sand.

HEDRICK, JOAN D. *Harriet Beecher Stowe: A Life*. New York: Oxford University Press, 1994. Comprehensive biography of Stowe, emphasizing her role as a reformer for women's rights, as well as an opponent of slavery.

SAND, GEORGE. *George Sand in Her Own Words*. Trans. and ed. Joseph Barry. Garden City, NY: Doubleday Anchor, 1979. Good sampling of her fiction and essays; contains lengthy portions of early novels.

STOWE, HARRIET BEECHER. *Uncle Tom's Cabin*. Many editions. A must reading for understanding of Stowe, slavery, and "domesticity" in the 1850s.

CHAPTER 8

Bismarck and Ito: Conservatives and Constitutions

Why do conservative aristocrats want or need quasi-democratic [democratic appearing] constitutions? What is the connection between such constitutions and nation-building?

Modern constitutions are, for most of us, dull but necessary documents. Following the examples drawn up by the United States or by the French revolutionaries more than 200 years ago, these documents usually list the rights of citizens and spell out the powers of government. While such documents are not exactly bedtime reading, they are important in the process of modern nation-building. Constitutions presuppose but also help build a consensus about what the people in a particular state consider important; they also help people distinguish themselves from their neighbors. Perhaps most important, such documents give most groups in the state a sense of security. By usually guaranteeing some civil and political rights, they give the people a feeling of participation and a sense of belonging. By defining the powers and limits of government, they reassure business people and help promote economic development. They even aid rulers by giving them the comfort of knowing that the people have agreed, by adopting or accepting the constitution, not to overthrow the existing government—unless absolutely necessary.

The nineteenth century was a time when being modern meant having a constitution, when the terms *nationalism* and *constitutionalism* were almost synonymous. The most important nation-state created in nineteenth-century Europe was the German empire, founded in 1871 after three wars presided over by the Prussian chancellor, Otto von Bismarck (1815–1898). Certainly the most dynamic nation-state in eastern Asia during the past century has been Japan. Japan began the process of nation-building in 1868 with the Meiji Restoration, but its constitution was not promulgated [presented to the people] until 1889. This document, adapted from Bismarck's Prussian constitution, was largely the work of Ito Hirobumi (1841–1909).

Today, the very words *Germany* and *Japan* cause Americans to think immediately of economic competition and World War II. A century ago both were equally dynamic states. Bismarck's Prussia, the largest state in north Germany, had a reputation for military strength until it was humiliated by the armies of French emperor Napoleon in 1806. Ito was thirteen in 1853, when Commodore Matthew Perry arrived in Japan to demand political and economic privileges for the Americans. He could do this because the Western nations possessed superior weapons and advanced industrial technology. Their desire to compete on equal terms in the world drove both Bismarck and Ito to create strong, centralized nation-states. Both realized that new political structures were necessary before this could happen. Each wanted to preserve as much of the conservatives' political power as possible while adopting only as much political modernization as was necessary to create a strong nation-state. Although each succeeded in maintaining the power of the ruling class, neither man was able to limit the growth of popular anti-government parties as much as he had hoped. Both tried to limit popular sovereignty [rule by the people]. Both left a flawed nation as a legacy to later leaders. The wars fought by Germany and Japan during the twentieth century were, in part, a consequence of their constitutions and the nationalisms of the late nineteenth century.

Otto von Bismarck's life and career were marked by a tension between his conservative political goals and the sometimes radical methods he used to pursue them. This tension was foreshadowed in his parentage. His father was a Prussian nobleman, a "Junker" [pronounced "yoongker"], whose family had owned land in Brandenburg for five centuries. His mother (with no "von" before her name to indicate nobility) was simply Wilhelmine Mencken, a middle-class descendant of civil servants and academicians. From his father, Bismarck learned to love the land and respect the values of the agricultural classes. From his more cosmopolitan and ambitious mother, Bismarck acquired cleverness, sophistication, and an urban education not common among his Junker neighbors. Some historians believe that Bismarck's attempt to imitate both of his very different parents made him a neurotic genius.[1]

Genius or not, Bismarck's early years were unproductive. As a student at the University of Göttingen, he spent much time drinking, falling in love, and delighting in duels (he fought twenty-five of them). His less than brilliant university career ended in Berlin, where he crammed to pass his law exam in 1834–1835. Bismarck's aggressive tendencies were diminished somewhat by a religious experience in 1846 and by his marriage to Johanna von Puttkamer in 1847, yet the "natural lust for combat" that led Bismarck to duel appeared later in struggles against political opponents and foreign rulers. Sometimes he expressed it more directly. In 1866, after Bismarck had become Prussian chancellor, a would-be assassin fired upon him five times on a Berlin street. As the man finished firing, the tall Junker turned upon him and seized him by the throat.[2]

Although he spent the seven years before his wedding managing his family's estates, Bismarck's real loves were diplomacy and statecraft. He was able to pursue these after his king appointed him Prussian representative to the Diet of the German Confederation at Frankfurt in May 1851. During the 1850s, the Prussians and Austrians were struggling for control of the other German states after a group of middle-class revolutionaries had failed to unify Germany in 1848. In his role as Prussian ambassador to the Diet [where representatives from each German state met periodically to discuss common problems], Bismarck tried to promote Prussian domination of a new German national state, which would exclude Austria. The Austrian empire at this time was ruled by Germans but included many non-German peoples living in southeastern Europe. During this decade, Bismarck also pursued his goal of Prussian leadership in Germany when he served for a time as the Prussian ambassador to Russia.

Bismarck's chief advantage was that he knew precisely what he wanted: He favored not only Prussian domination of Germany but also a Prussia in which the Junker nobility, and not the middle-class liberals or (worse yet) democrats and socialists, would dominate the government and the army. He got his chance to work directly to create such a state in the fall of 1862, when the Prussian king asked him to become chancellor [like a prime minister] and help the monarch win a political conflict in which he had become embroiled.

King William and his war minister wanted to modernize the Prussian army by drafting more men and keeping them in active service for three years instead of two. They also wanted to do away with the reserve, or *Landwehr*, with its supposedly less professional middle-class officers. Since this reform would mean a 50 percent increase in the military budget and a 25 percent tax increase, the king was required to ask the Prussian Parliament, or Diet, to approve the expense. In order to maintain some middle-class influence over the military, the members of the Prussian Diet wanted to keep both the *Landwehr* and the two-year period of service. This would give the Junker officers less time to indoctrinate new conscripts. For two years, the king was unable to get the Diet to approve the army bill. By 1862, when Bismarck was made chancellor, the two sides had become deadlocked.

Bismarck showed both determination and shrewdness in solving the king's problem. First, he told the members of the Diet that the German people preferred a strong army and national unification to liberal constitutional limits on the power of the government. Then he proved he was right and called the bluff of the liberals by telling the Prussian bureaucrats to collect the taxes to pay for the army reform, even though the Diet had not approved them. They did, and the people paid. Bismarck put the capstone on the liberal defeat in 1866. After the Seven Weeks' War, in which the newly strengthened Prussian army decisively defeated Austria, Bismarck offered the Prussian Diet an Indemnity Bill. He would admit the government had been wrong in illegally collecting taxes if the Diet would retroactively approve the collection of those taxes. The bill passed 230 to 75. Forced to choose between liberal restraints on government and national power, the liberals chose power. Bismarck sensed they would.

After defeating Austria, Prussia was free to organize the North German Confederation, a union of all German states except Austria, Bavaria, Württemberg, and Baden, in 1867. In 1871, after a war with France that Bismarck helped provoke and that resulted in another quick Prussian victory, the south German states (except Austria) joined in creating the German Empire. The Prussian king became Kaiser (Emperor) William I. Bismarck created the constitution for the new state, and this document shows how the "iron chancellor," as he was later known, was able to combine modern political forms with careful protection of traditional aristocratic values.

Perhaps the most modern feature of Bismarck's constitution was the election of the lower house of the legislature (Reichstag) by universal male suffrage. A man did not even have to own property in order to vote. Bismarck's fellow Prussian conservatives were shocked at such radicalism. However, the appearance of popular government was deceptive. In the first place, the Reichstag had little real governing power. Representatives could not introduce, or "initiate," legislation but could only discuss and vote on what was brought to them by the government. All members of the "executive branch" of the government were appointed by the emperor and did not have to "respond" to the Reichstag. That body could not vote "no-confidence" in the chancellor, or chief minister, and thus force a change in the government, as the British Parliament could do.

In the upper chamber of the legislature, the Federal Council or Bundesrat, conservative forces clearly dominated. Like the United States Senate, the Bundesrat had to approve all treaties and other legislation. However, members were not elected but appointed by the various state governments. They voted as instructed. Prussia, the largest state in the new empire, controlled three-fifths of the territory and seventeen of fifty-eight seats in the Bundesrat. Although the Reichstag did have to approve military spending, control of the army and the entire civil administration remained in the hands of the emperor. The entire constitution was seen as a *gift from* the princes to the German people rather than as a *right of* the people.[3] The federal constitution contained no bill of rights; civil liberties and social services were left to the individual states.

Bismarck's government was designed to be authoritarian with some democratic window dressing. Popular elections to the Reichstag would mobilize national sentiment and give people a feeling of participation in the government, while real power would remain in the hands of the aristocracy and upper-middle-class business interests. But it did not work out that way. First, to be a genuine national symbol, the *Reichstag* had to be used; besides, the government was required to seek approval for legislation, especially that which involved spending money. Second, from 1871 to 1890, when Bismarck was forced to resign, the growing working-class electorate sent increasing numbers of socialist delegates to the Reichstag. Bismarck and the emperor refused to work with the socialists, whom they considered radical. This would eventually bring legislative business to a standstill. Third, the constitution did not work as designed. Although the emperor himself had absolute authority over both the army and the civil administration, including the appointment of the chancellor and final decision on Reichstag measures, in practice Emperor William I generally took advice from Bismarck, whose skillful manipulation of the various political constituencies was needed to keep the system working reasonably well. When William I's grandson, William II, took over in 1890, he wanted the constitution to work as it had been designed on paper, with himself in charge. Bismarck was dismissed, and William's attempts to use the constitution as written soon led to disaster.

As perhaps the most skillful politician of his century, Bismarck was able to maintain political equilibrium both at home and in Europe, like a man standing at the center of a seesaw, applying weight as needed to keep his potential enemies in the air. During the 1870s, he allied himself with the liberals in the Reichstag to establish laws (such as those removing trade barriers among German states and setting up a common coinage) which would promote industrialization. During the 1880s, Bismarck allied himself with the Catholic Center Party (which he had attacked in the 1870s) and the conservatives while attacking the liberals and the socialists. This policy of unifying people by creating common enemies was also pursued in European diplomacy. Bismarck tied both Russia and Austria to Germany with alliances in which he promised to help either country if the other attacked. He also tied himself to Russia in the Reinsurance Treaty of 1887 in order to forestall any alliance between France and Russia which would encircle Germany. At the Berlin Conference in 1878, he prevented Russia from taking too much territory in the Balkans, thus disturbing the balance between Russia and Austria in that area. In 1885, at another Berlin Conference, he helped provide for a friendly division of European territory in Africa. Bismarck clearly wished to keep peace at home and abroad, yet he could do this only by a delicate balancing of forces, which his successors were not able to continue. Their attempts to imitate him, in a world of changing economic and political conditions, degenerated into bluster and bullying. After 1890, Germany's alliances led to war instead of peace.

Over a decade after Bismarck's forced retirement in 1890 and just a few years before his own death, Japanese statesman Ito Hirobumi wrote "Some Reminiscences of the Grant of the New Constitution." In this essay, Ito summarized the policy of the Japanese government in 1868 after the Meiji Restoration, a coup led by young aristocratic warrior-bureaucrats [samurai] from several of the major domains [large feudal estates]. These Meiji bureaucrats, or oligarchs, as they came to be known, abolished the Tokugawa Shogunate [a form of government in which a military leader, or shogun, ruled in the name of the emperor] and proclaimed the young emperor the power center of a new Japanese government. These men wished to modernize the country and were determined to meet the threat posed by the Western powers. In words which might have been used by a German statesman at the same time, the emperor, as Ito remembered, swore

> to educate the people to the requirements of a constitutional state, to fortify the nation with the best results and resources of modern civilization, and thus to secure for the country prosperity, strength, and . . . the . . . recognized status of membership upon an equal footing in the family of the most powerful and civilized nations of the world.[4]

To seek a place in the sun, among the great powers, was as important to late-nineteenth-century Japanese as it was to their German counterparts. From 1868, when he was made an Imperial councilor, to his death in 1909, Ito was a part of a process of modernization which sought to combine Western economic and military power with the social and political stability of traditional Japan. The results of this attempt, as in Germany, were mixed.

Ito hailed from the village of Tsukari in the domain of Choshu in southern Japan. His father, Hayashi Juzo, though a farmer, was descended from the samurai warrior class, the rough equivalent of medieval European knights, and traced his family back to the third son of Emperor Kiorei (290–214 B.C.).[5] Ito received the education of a samurai and grew up sharing this group's dislike for foreigners who demanded special commercial and legal rights such as extraterritoriality [being subject to their own laws rather than those of the country in which they resided]. Many Japanese warriors, especially those in the western domains of Choshu, Satysuma, Tosa, and Hizen, wished to overthrow the shogun because he had made deals with the foreigners. Leaders in the western domains wished to restore the power of the emperor—in whose name the shogun's family had ruled Japan for more than two centuries—*and* to fight to throw out the foreigners. By 1864, as a result of a unique journey,

Ito had become one of the first young samurai to suggest restoring the emperor, as well as making temporary peace with the foreigners.

In May 1863, Ito and four other young samurai secretly boarded a freighter to sneak to Shanghai and then England in order to learn Western sea-faring techniques. Ito returned to Japan six months later with some knowledge of English and the conviction that Japan must become a modern nation. The way to do this was to learn from the foreigners rather than expel them. This was a more mature Ito than the young man who, several years earlier, had helped burn down the house of the British diplomatic representative in Yedo because it had been built on sacred ground.[6]

After the Meiji Restoration, Ito and his fellow oligarchs faced the task of building a modern nation-state in Japan. Their job was to create a truly central administration to replace the old domains. Japan also needed a national army, modern communications, a common currency, and national laws. The difficulty of this task of modernization is illustrated by the story of how peasants cut telegraph wires because they believed the wires would be used to transmit their blood to quench the thirst of the foreigners. Other, less fearful peasants decided that, if the wires could carry thoughts, they ought to be able to carry packages. Riders had to be hired to keep the lines free and uncut.[7]

Ito and his colleagues proceeded slowly and carefully in devising a political system. It took them more than twenty years to promulgate a constitution designed to strengthen the state and the allegiance of the people. Ito was sent on three missions abroad during his career, and the second of these, in 1882–1883 took him to Bismarck's Germany, whose constitution the Japanese used as a model for their own. A Prussian, Carl Friedrich Hermann Roessler, was even a member of the five-man committee that wrote the Japanese document.[8] Ito himself shared the Prussian belief that a legislature dominated by political parties should not control the Imperial government. When one of his colleagues proposed an English-style constitution with an executive responsible to a parliament, or diet, Ito strongly opposed him, writing, "Your memorial calls for selecting the heads of ministries and imperial household officials from political parties. In the final analysis this is equivalent to transferring the imperial prerogatives to the people. Such heretical views should not be held by any subject."[9]

When finally written and presented as "a voluntary gift of the Emperor to his subjects," the Japanese constitution continued the broad powers of the emperor over the military and civil adminis- tration. Civil rights were guaranteed to the people "only within the limits of the law." The Japanese authors thought they had solved the problems of getting money for the budget from the lower house, or Diet. If the Diet could not agree on a budget, the budget from the previous year would automatically come into force. While a clever idea in theory, in practice the lower house attained control over the budget, since the Japanese government, and especially the military, was expanding throughout the late nineteenth century and needed increases every year.[10]

During his long career, Ito served his emperor in many ways. He was the chief minister, or premier, on four separate occasions and at other times was minister for finance and "home affairs" and presiding officer of the House of Peers, or upper chamber of the legislature. At one point in the mid-1880s, Ito's positions as pre- mier, head of the staff of the imperial household, and chairman of the commission to draw up the constitution gave him powers com- parable to those of Bismarck.[11] When it became clear that political parties were going to remain a force in Japan, despite the dislike of the oligarchs for party government, Ito responded by organizing his own party in 1900. The Seiyukai, or [literally] "friends of the Constitution," party won the Diet elections in 1900. Ito became pre- mier again, and set a healthy example of working within the politi- cal process rather than just manipulating the existing parties, as Bis- marck had done. Ito spent the last years of his life attempting to moderate the influence of the military in foreign policy, but he was unable to avoid a war with Russia over Korea, which the Japanese won. In 1905, he became the first "resident general" for Japan in Korea and four years later was assassinated by a Korean national- ist. With Ito's moderating influence gone, and using his death as a pretext, the Japanese annexed the peninsula outright in 1910.

Increasing domination of Japanese politics by the military led to more wars, culminating in World War II. As in Germany, the civilians supported these wars as long as the army was successful. Also as in Germany, political parties increased their influence in the generation after Ito's death, despite the authoritarian system of government envisioned in the original constitution. Of course, in

Japan loyalty to the semi-divine emperor was a more important nation-building force than were popular elections to the Diet. This and as the more limited suffrage in Japan (only slightly more than 1 percent of the populace could vote in 1889) were important differences in the politics of the two new states. Another cultural difference between the two nations was the more dominant position of the male in Japanese society. Twenty-five years after his death, Ito's biographer wrote, with only a hint of apology, that his subject, "like all privileged men of his race, . . . made the rounds of the various inns where wine, women, and the noisy twang of the shamisen [musical instrument] served to conjure up that delectable freedom of oblivion for one brief night."[12] If Bismarck enjoyed such pleasures, the customs of his society required that he do so less publicly.

In neither of these two modern nations did the authoritarian groups lose their ability to shape the destiny of the country until the middle of the twentieth century. Ironically, Adolf Hitler did more to destroy the old Prussian Junker class than did Germany's enemies in World War II after members of this group helped organize a plot to kill him in 1944. In Japan, while members of the old oligarchic families continued to influence national life in the years after World War II, the military clique lost its power and the post-World War II constitution clearly announced "that sovereign power resides with the people."

We can say, then, that the attempts by Bismarck and Ito to combine the social and political values of an agrarian warrior aristocracy with the industrial and military power of a dynamic modern state had only limited success. In both cases, the new nations were flawed. On the one hand, liberal capitalists wished to use government to create a new industrial society. A move in this direction would necessarily require giving some power to the working class, however much the industrialists resented doing so. On the other hand, the more conservative rulers distrusted both the upstart businesspeople and industrialists and the working masses. These rulers, however, did value the ability of the industrialists to make guns and the ability of the men of the lower classes to use them in war.

Perhaps the best example of these rulers' desire to keep their power while pretending to share it was the constitutions they devised. When a government issues a constitution, it is saying that people are governed by laws that will be fairly enforced. It is also saying that people have a right to know what the rules of government are. These points, of course, both the Prussian Junkers and the Japanese oligarchs would concede. But it is only a short step from having clear rules to saying that the people who have the right to these rules also have the right to change them. This is the principle of popular sovereignty, one which the conservative Bismarck and Ito would not accept but, in the final analysis, could not deny.

Notes

1. Theodore S. Hamerow, ed., *Otto von Bismarck: A Historical Assessment* (Boston: D.C. Heath, 1962), 13–14; see Otto Pflanze, "Toward a Psycho-analytic Interpretation of Bismarck," *American Historical Review* (April 1972): 419–444.
2. Otto Pflanze, *Bismarck and the Development of Germany. The Period of Unification, 1815–1871* (Princeton: Princeton University Press, 1963), 59.
3. Gordon A. Craig, *Germany, 1866–1945* (Oxford: Oxford University Press, 1978), 42–44.
4. Hirobumi, Ito, "Some Reminiscences of the Grant of the New Constitution," in *Fifty Years of New Japan*, compiled by Count Shigenobu Okuma; English version edited by Marcus B. Huish, Vol. I, 2nd ed. (London: Smith, Elder and Company, 1910), 125–126.
5. Kengi Hamada, *Prince Ito* (Tokyo: The Sanseido Company, Ltd., 1936), 5–6. East Asians typically place the surname last in English. Hirobumi's last name is Ito rather than Hayashi because his father, in financial difficulty, had himself adopted by a samurai, Ito Buhei. This practice was common in pre-Meiji Japan.
6. Ibid., 34–40.
7. Hugh Borton, *Japan's Modern Century* (New York: Ronald Press, 1955, 69–71, 79, 173.
8. George Akita, *Foundations of Constitutional Government in Modern Japan, 1868–1900* (Cambridge, MA: Harvard University Press, 1967), 60–63.
9. Ibid., 36–38.
10. Hamada, *Prince Ito*, 96; see Borton, *Japan's Modern Century*, 126, 145, and the entire constitution in Appendix IV, 490–507.
11. Borton, *Japan's Modern Century*, 137.
12. Hamada, *Prince Ito*, 211–212.

Further Reading

AKITA, GEORGE. *Foundations of Constitutional Government in Modern Japan, 1868–1900*. Cambridge, MA: Harvard University Press, 1967. Scholarly, clear account of the change of government.

HAMADA, KENGI. *Prince Ito*. Tokyo: The Sanseido Company, Ltd., 1936. Flowery but entertaining biography by an aristocrat. Notice the date and handle with care if you cannot read Japanese, since this is the only biography written in English.

HAMEROW, THEODORE S., ed. *Otto von Bismarck: A Historical Assessment*. Boston: D.C. Heath, 1961, 1973. Many different opinions of his contribution to German and European history. A good place to start.

CHAPTER 9

Chimwere and York: Heroes in Two Worlds

Why do historians regard World War I as the beginning of "contemporary history"? How did this first great twentieth-century conflict change the lives of so many people who lived far from the battlefields of Europe? Are the worlds referred to in this title only geographic ones?

Odd as it may seem, it is no accident that historians date the start of what they call "contemporary history" from the beginning of a war that began nearly a century ago, in 1914. By weakening the major European colonial powers, World War I marked the beginning of the end of a time when Europeans dominated the world politically and economically. The "Great War," as it was called until a greater one broke out in 1939, laid the foundation for a century in which non-Europeans would play a more important role than they had earlier. The United States would be one of the new "world powers" of the twentieth century. And, after World War II, many former colonial peoples would emerge as new nations seeking a voice in the international arena.

The First World War was also a turning point in world history because it was the first modern global conflict. Nations and individuals on every continent joined with one side or the other (the Central Powers: Germany, Austria-Hungary, and Turkey, or the Allies: Britain, France, Russia, Italy, and the United States). Many troops from across the globe fought in the war, including some who were subject to the colonial rule of one of the principal combatant states. By bringing so many previously isolated peoples into a major war, World War I began the process of "shrinking the globe" that we are familiar with today. In that sense, at least, it did begin "contemporary history."

Two of the places far removed from the trenches of Europe—but linked in this shrinking world by the war—were the hills and valleys of Malawi in East Africa and those of the Cumberland plateau in eastern Tennessee, U.S.A. This is the story of how the Great War changed the lives of two war heroes, Juma Chimwere and Alvin York. Each was forced to recognize a wider world than the one in which he had been born; each had to deal with changes that came to the lives of his people both during and after the war.

Although he proved to have an extraordinary career, Juma Chimwere had very humble beginnings. Born about 1879—the exact year is unknown—he came from an area of southeastern Malawi that was undergoing significant transitions. A variety of related Bantu-speaking peoples, continuing the movement east and south that they had begun centuries earlier, were establishing claims on the land between Zomba and Mulanje mountains. We know nothing certain about his childhood, except that he was raised in a traditional African extended family that belonged to the Yao tribe or ethnic group; his family was probably allied with a nearby British-appointed leader of the Nyanja ethnic group. In traditional African societies, power and personal identity were tied to family lineages, not to territorial states as we know them in Europe. Chimwere was clearly a child of a traditional African society. His family, unlike many others in East Africa, had not become part of the growing number of Christian or the smaller number of Muslim communities that were found throughout this area.[1]

As European influence expanded in southern Malawi during the first years of his life, Chimwere was attracted to the opportunities it offered. As a young adult, one of his best options was service with the British who controlled Malawi, then called Nyasaland. In December of 1896, he presented himself to the adjutant general of the King's African Rifles (KAR) at Zomba, seeking to enlist in that branch of the British army.[2]

His enlistment papers indicate that he was then just eighteen and a resident of Chikowi village, located within ten miles of the growing British administrative center on the eastern slope of Zomba Mountain. While many young Africans at this time sought the prestige of serving the Europeans and even falsified information on their applications in an effort to be accepted, Chimwere's record seems accurate. At least we know that he returned to the village of Chikowi when he retired after a distinguished twenty-five-year career in the British army.

Chimwere served throughout British Africa during his many years in the KAR. He was sent to posts as far north as Somalia and as far west as Ashanti, on the Gold Coast in West Africa. Generally, the British did not allow African soldiers to serve in their home areas, in case they would be required to put down a native rebellion or other challenge to imperial authority. In the course of his service, Chimwere was, by some accounts, one of the first Malawians to visit London. He was among a distinguished King's African Rifles honor contingent awarded medals by King Edward VII in 1901 for service in the Ashanti expedition, one of several British attempts to place the peoples of the Gold Coast under colonial authority. Having risen rapidly through the ranks, Juma Chimwere was by this time a sergeant in the KAR, one of its senior African noncommissioned officers. After only fifteen years of service, he was the second longest serving askari [black African soldier] in the first battalion of the KAR.

The years just prior to the First World War were quiet ones for the soldiers of the KAR. Colonial rule was well-established throughout most of Africa, and disputes between European powers there were minimal. Colonial military forces were cut back to peacetime levels, and many askari were discharged. Juma, however, was allowed to reenlist twice during this period (in 1908 and 1910), a sign of the respect which his commanding officers had for his abilities.

Chimwere was also respected among the people of his local area. He had three wives and many children. Since his home was not far from the KAR barracks in Zomba, most of his family lived in and around Chikowi village. The extended family included his brother, who lived nearby on the slopes of Zomba Mountain and who looked after family matters while Juma was on duty at the barracks or in the field. This included caring for the many cattle which Juma had accumulated, for he was considered very prosperous by his peers. His intelligence was also respected by his people; had it not been for his military duties, he would have been expected to be an advisor to the local headman [the traditional authority designated by the British to manage local affairs as part of the system of indirect rule in the African colonies].

World War I interrupted Chimwere's life as a joint member, we might say, of both British and African societies, yet it also gave him the opportunity to become a hero in the eyes of both his British rulers and his African peers. His regiment was deployed to British

East Africa (Kenya) to defend the colony against German raids. Early in 1915, German attacks were being launched from bases just south of the frontier between British and German East Africa. Chimwere's regiment was sent into action to attack one such German base, at Mbuyuni.

The small expedition included English, Rhodesian, and Indian soldiers, in addition to KAR units from Uganda and Nyasaland. The main frontal assault on July 14, 1915, was assigned primarily to the First Battalion KAR, including the company Juma served as Colour Sergeant [leader of a platoon-sized unit], with other units attacking on the German flank. The operation was nearly a disaster. Some of the support units bolted and the main attack stalled. Without good communication with the flanking forces, the commanders ordered a retreat.

During this retreat, Chimwere distinguished himself. With all of the European [white] officers in the two attacking companies of his battalion killed in action, Sergeant Chimwere rallied the remaining askari and led them in a short attack, covering the retreat of other forces. Then, although wounded, Chimwere directed his men in gathering all his unit's guns and equipment, as well as the dead and wounded, and, under heavy fire, led them in retreat. For his bravery, Chimwere was recommended for the Victoria Cross, the highest award for gallantry in the British army. However, probably because he was a black colonial soldier, he was awarded the Distinguished Conduct Medal (the next highest award) instead.[3]

During his recovery from his wounds, Juma learned that one of his wives had been unfaithful during his absence. It was to this event, as much as to enemy fire, that Juma attributed his injury; such connections were commonly assumed in many traditional African societies in recognition that individual actions have both social and personal consequences. Thus, when he was well enough to return home on leave, Chimwere divorced this wife. He believed that this would protect him from other misfortunes once he returned to duty. During this leave, he was also the featured askari at a grand military parade in Zomba, where Nyasaland Governor George Smith presented his Distinguished Conduct Medal, an event that impressed many European military observers.[4]

Having been promoted to Regimental Sergeant Major, having been rewarded for his bravery, and having put his personal affairs in order, Chimwere volunteered to return to the East African front for what turned out to be the rest of the war. Even after the armistice, he returned for yet another tour with the KAR. It was during this postwar period that he began to emerge as a respected and assertive leader among his people, although within the constraints of the colonial system.

As he returned to active duty following the armistice, Chimwere asked for and was given permission to wear a special uniform, one which distinguished him from the other askari. But his quest for what the commanding officer of the Second Battalion KAR described as a "certain distinction" was an attempt to gain respect among his fellow Africans for his special service to the British rulers. As for the special uniform, the commanding officer noted that he should "be allowed a little latitude as he certainly has done good work for 2nd regiment and is about the only real Regimental Sergeant Major that we possess."[5] For years, fellow askari recognized Chimwere's leadership ability, his example, and his instruction to younger troops, yet there was a limit to his effective service, and in 1921 he retired from active duty, remaining a member of the KAR reserve for another decade.

During his retirement, he returned to Chikowi village, where he served as the principal counselor to the local chief. Although he never became either a Christian or a Muslim, as did many African leaders, Chimwere was described by his son Titus as "one of the savers, [one who could speak up for his people] because he could speak English [and] could read and write." These skills, which he gained during his military service, remained important in his role as a counselor to his chief.[6] Chimwere served as what we would call a justice of the peace, settling minor local disputes, and as an advisor to both European and African authorities on matters relating to his village and the surrounding area. In the colonial order, he was an important man. Juma accumulated much wealth, most of it in the form of cattle, which he kept on land given to him because of the respect he had earned through his military service.

His standing in European and African society is shown by the fact that he was given special permission to carry a carbine. In colonial Nyasaland, this was a great honor for an African, since laws prohibited African civilians from carrying rifles. Chimwere was allowed this privilege to protect his herds of cattle, as well as the cattle belonging to the local KAR officers' mess [kitchen]. In return for this service to KAR officers, he was frequently invited to visit his former superiors. As a sign of their respect for him, the British KAR officers commissioned a local artist to paint his portrait, and for years it hung in the officers' mess.

While all this may not seem like much honor for a military hero, it is significant because he was an African in a British colonial protectorate at a time when most natives were not highly regarded by their British rulers. In that setting, Chimwere earned the respect of both his own people and of the British, no small achievement. Testimony to how he was viewed by his white superiors can be found in a rare and touching passage from the memoirs of Major General Sir Francis de Guingand, who was commander of Juma's old battalion in 1930, when the World War I hero died of tuberculosis. After seeing that Juma was cared for while the battalion went on maneuvers, he returned to find Chimwere near death and unable to speak. "I felt tears stinging my eyes at the sight of our old comrade so near his last discharge. I touched his hand and left the hut. We attended his funeral in the cool of the next evening, with our band playing those tunes that he loved so well."[7]

Juma Chimwere was able to adapt successfully to the colonial environment and to fit into the European world without abandoning his native traditions. Being a war hero gave him privileges not accorded to other black Africans, but he did not become a full member of the European world. He never became a Christian, for example, and had virtually no formal education. His two sons and his two nephews, for whom he served as a father figure, served in the KAR during World War II, taking the path that he followed to success. Chimwere continued to live in the traditional African fashion, while meeting the challenges of European domination on its own terms. He remained a hero in both worlds. Few Africans could claim that until much later in the twentieth century.

World War I changed Alvin York's life much more decisively than it did Chimwere's. Born in 1887 in Fentress County in northeastern Tennessee, fifty miles from the nearest railroad, York grew up in a world perhaps more isolated from world events than Chimwere's. York, unlike Chimwere, was not a career soldier but a farmer and hunter in the Valley of the Three Forks of the Wolf River. His family worked land settled by his great-grandfather, an acquaintance of Davy Crockett and John Clemens, father of Mark Twain.[8]

York's family, like that of Chimwere, was poor. One of eleven children on a family farm of seventy-five acres, Alvin was taught by his father how to use a muzzle-loading rifle to shoot the heads off turkeys to avoid damaging the meat. Because of the demands of farming, school only lasted for several months in the winter, and young York reached adulthood with about a third-grade education. Hunting was a favorite activity of the men of Fentress County, and Alvin became an excellent marksman who often took home prizes at the frequent shooting contests. One of these involved killing turkeys tethered behind logs so only their heads were visible. He was an excellent shot even when drunk; riding home one night, he shot six of his neighbor's turkeys with six shots—and was hauled into court.[9] As a young man, York also worked as a day laborer on railroad gangs and on road construction crews.

In his late twenties, he developed an interest in a neighbor girl, Gracie Williams. Inspired by her decision not to see him until he stopped his excessive drinking and shooting, and by his mother, he was "saved" at a revival in 1915. He stopped drinking, gambling, and other forms of "hell-raising" (including drunken target practice) and even became an elder in the local Church of Christ in Christian Union. He was committed enough to the church that he led the singing regularly and even conducted services when the pastor was away.[10]

When the United States entered World War I in 1917, York was drafted and struggled with the contradiction between his desire to serve his country and the biblical injunction not to kill. During training, he appealed for Conscientious Objector status on four occasions but was turned down because his particular church had no distinctive pacifist traditions but only followed the Bible, which has mixed views on killing. After joining the 82nd Division, he spent a long night discussing pacifism with a sympathetic battalion commander before deciding, just before he was shipped to France, that God did indeed want him to fight.[11]

The resolution of York's religious struggle was important because it was precisely his ability to kill that made him a hero and changed his life. In the Argonne Forest in France on October 8, 1918, York, armed with only a rifle and pistol, and aided by only seven other men, succeeded in putting thirty-five German machine gun nests out of action. He did this in part by killing twenty-five German machine gunners the way he had killed turkeys tethered behind logs in Tennessee. Each time a German gunner raised his head high enough to fire his gun, York killed him with a single shot to the head. Moving from one nest to another, and using a German prisoner to ask the gunners to surrender, York took 132 prisoners, which he and his small band marched back to Allied lines. For this feat of individual heroism, York was promoted from corporal to sergeant, and he received the Distinguished Service Cross and the Medal of Honor.[12]

A biographer tells us that Alvin York "marched out of the Argonne Forest and into the annals of American legend."[13] An article in the *Saturday Evening Post* portrayed him as the perfect American hero, a simple mountaineer and frontiersman who demonstrated that the old values of shooting straight and loving God could bring victory even in the modern industrial age symbolized by the machine gun.[14] He was greeted by huge crowds when he returned home, much like those that greeted Charles Lindbergh nine years later after he had flown the Atlantic solo. York was further praised when he turned down over $100,000 (an immense fortune for a man who had worked for $1.60 a day two years earlier) in book and movie contracts and other offers after he returned to the United States. He was the first American war hero since Robert E. Lee to refuse to commercialize his success. York's personal manner, like that of Lindbergh later, was "modest and unassuming." A conscientious objector who nevertheless became a war hero, a simple man who traveled thousands of miles to defend his country but who refused money and returned to his humble home to farm and marry his sweetheart: all this seemed to many Americans to be the best of both worlds—the modern and the traditional.[15]

Once the excitement died down, however, the permanent changes in York's life proved to be much greater than those facing Juma Chimwere. Although well-wishers raised money to buy Sergeant York a farm, he lacked the education or business skill to manage it well. A national fund-raising campaign was necessary to retire his mortgage and keep him from going bankrupt. York also wanted to use his fame to improve conditions in his mountains by building schools. He spent years raising funds and fighting political battles to build the York Agricultural Institute, which was opened in 1930. When the Great Depression threatened the continuation of the school, York supported it with his own money, taking out a mortgage on his farm to do so. He did not manage well as president and business manager of the institute and he was replaced in these positions in 1935. One member of the board of directors told him that it was "not good diplomacy to let a man be head of a school who hasn't a college degree."[16] Formal education was becoming more important in York's world than it was in Chimwere's East Africa.

In the midst of all this, Alvin York remained, despite his fame and the problems it brought him, a generous person whose kindness to family and friends left him nearly broke by the end of the 1930s. In addition, because of a dispute with the Internal Revenue Service over taxes it said he owed on royalties paid him from the movie *Sergeant York*, he entered his final years impossibly in debt. House of Representatives Speaker Sam Rayburn arranged a "compromise" with the tax service in 1961 that left him owing "only" $25,000, a sum eventually paid by donations from the public.[17] By this time, York had suffered several strokes; these and severe arthritis left him an invalid by the late 1950s. He died in 1964.

Alvin York certainly received more recognition for his act of heroism during World War I than Juma Chimwere did for his. Highway 127 through eastern Tennessee was named the "Alvin York Highway." No one named a road after Chimwere, nor were any movies made or books written about his life. Alvin York became a living legend; the true story of York became less important to people than the image of sturdy, simple virtue that he represented at a time in American history when many rural Americans were having trouble adjusting to the changes brought by rapid industrialization and urbanization. York became a symbol of a person who had been successful—at least until the end of 1918—without adjusting to modern life. The American people "created a hero in response to a felt need in society, and Alvin York answered that need. His significance lies not in what he was but in what others wanted him to be," wrote York's biographer.[18] Of course, many of his post-World War I difficulties were due to the fact that he was too poorly educated to handle his finances successfully and to manage the educational institution he established. York found it hard to live in two worlds, the simpler one that existed for him before 1918 and the one he was forced into after the war. Perhaps, unlike Chimwere, York tried to do too much after the war.

By contrast, Juma Chimwere's worlds before and after his act of wartime heroism were not that different. He was already a member of two worlds—African and European—before the war and he remained so after the war. As a native in a society dominated by outsiders of a different race, Chimwere was not subjected to the kind of hero-worship that ended up making Alvin York's life so complicated at times after 1918. Chimwere's British superiors were never tempted to use him as a symbol of the outstanding military skills of the Yao tribe. If he was a symbol of anything, it was that of a man who appreciated the British army and remained loyal to it throughout his life.

The changes brought by World War I to Nyasaland were less immediately dramatic than those brought to the United States by its involvement in the war, yet the social and military skills acquired by Chimwere and others would later allow men like him to govern their country after Malawi became independent of British rule in 1964. The changes that confronted the United States after World War I were more dramatic—we think of the Roaring Twenties, the Great Depression, and the New Deal among others. In this environment, Alvin York's heroism made him the symbol of an earlier, simpler time. He was valued because he was a reminder of an earlier world that was (or seemed) less complicated. Chimwere was respected because he had found a way to be part of both an older, traditional world and the newer, more complicated one brought by the British. Such are the issues that the Great War raised for people as different as these two men and their two countries.

Notes

1. I am grateful to Professor Melvin E. Page of East Tennessee State University, whose fieldwork in Malawi and London in the 1970s rescued the story of Juma Chimwere from the oblivion to which it otherwise might have been consigned. Professor Page's notes on Chimwere's service record, held by the Malawi Army Pay and Records Office, as well as interviews with King's African Rifles veterans—including Juma's son Titus Chimwere—were instrumental in reconstructing details of his life and career.

2. Page notes, Chimwere service record.

3. H. Moyse-Bartlett, *The King's African Rifles: A Study in the Military History of East and Central Africa, 1890–1945* (Aldershot, England: Gale & Polden, Ltd., 1956), 291–292; Sir Francis de Guingand, *African Assignment* (London: Hodder & Stoughton, 1953), 40. It is interesting that the discussion of this battle in the best popular history of the East African campaign, Charles Miller's *Battle for the Bundu* (New York: Macmillan, 1974), 132, completely omits Sergeant Chimwere's actions. Miller considers only the actions of European officers.

4. "Rhodesia Native Regiment," [report from Zomba, Nyasaland], *Rhodesia Defence Force Journal* 2, 11 (September 1916): 10.
5. Quoted in personnel file of RSM Juma Chimwere, Malawi Army Pay and Records Office.
6. Page interview I–27, Titus Chimwere, Zomba, September 13, 1972; a detailed description of this and other interviews can be found in Melvin E. Page, "Malawians in the Great War and After, 1914–1925," Ph.D. diss., Michigan State University, 1977, pp. 261–267.
7. Guingand, *African Assignment*, 41.
8. David Lee, *Sergeant York: An American Hero* (Lexington: University Press of Kentucky, 1985), 1–2.
9. Lee, *Sergeant York*, 4–7; Sam K. Cowan, *Sergeant York and His People* (New York: Grosset and Dunlap, 1922), 30, 169, 231, 242.
10. Lee, *Sergeant York,* 8–10, 15.
11. Lee, *Sergeant York,* 17–20; Cowan, *York and His People,* 240–242.
12. Cowan, *York and His People,* 15–44; Lee, *Sergeant York,* 27–48.
13. Lee, *Sergeant York,* 39.
14. Ibid., 54–57.
15. Ibid., 49–68.
16. Ibid., 86, 90.
17. Ibid., 86–87, 128–130.
18. Ibid., 115.

Further Reading

Cowan, Sam K. *Sergeant York and His People.* New York: Grosset and Dunlap, 1922. A popular, entirely positive account of Sergeant York written just after the war. A good example of colorful hero worship.
Lee, David. *Sergeant York: An American Hero.* Lexington: University Press of Kentucky, 1985. Brief, well-written, and with a good analysis of York's image in *America during the years after World War I.*
Pachai, B. Malawi: *The History of the Nation.* London: Longman's, 1973. A general history of Juma Chimwere's homeland from pre-history through independence. It provides a context for his life story.
Page, Melvin E., ed. *Africa and the First World War.* New York: St. Martin's, 1987. Shows the extent to which black Africans were affected by the European war.

CHAPTER 10

Hitler and Stalin:
Ideas and Personality?

How do rulers of spectacular brutality get and keep power in a twentieth-century state? To what extent did their ideas, their personalities, and the mistakes of their opponents contribute to their success?

We choke on the numbers. Adolf Hitler (1889–1945), who ruled Germany from 1933 to his death, began a war in 1939 that resulted in the deaths of at least 40 million people. Over 6 million of these were European Jews and others systematically exterminated in what we call the Holocaust.[1]

Joseph Stalin (1879–1953), sole ruler of the Soviet Union from 1929 to his death, forced millions of peasants off their private land and into large, inefficient, state-run farms in order to rapidly industrialize the giant Russian state. This "Great Leap Forward" in the early 1930s resulted in famine that took 5 million lives in the Ukraine alone between 1932 and 1934. Over a twenty-five year period, millions more were "liquidated" [executed] or sent to slave labor camps for real or imagined—mostly imagined—opposition to Stalin's policies.

All told, a *minimum* of 50 million people died between 1930 and 1950 as a result of the beliefs and actions of these two men. To the extent that numbers matter, it can be argued that Adolf Hitler and Joseph Stalin had greater impact on the history of the twentieth century than any other two people.

Our textbooks tell us that Hitler ruled using a set of political and social beliefs known as Nazism; the term was taken from the name of Hitler's political party, the National Socialist German Worker's Party [Nationalsozialistische Deutsche Arbeiter Partei, or NSDAP in German]. Texts also tell us that Stalin was the successor to Vladimir I. Lenin, the Bolshevik revolutionary whose party seized power in Russia in November 1917, with plans to create a socialist state and spark a worldwide socialist revolution.

What is not always clear in our discussion of the great political ideas of the twentieth century—nationalist, fascist, Nazi, communist, or totalitarian—is the crucial role of individuals such as Hitler and Stalin in shaping and defining them. Each took existing political sentiments (or resentments) in his country and turned them in incredibly brutal directions. They were able to do this because of their unscrupulous determination and because of the disunity, indecision, and scruples of their opponents. The lives of Adolf Hitler and Joseph Stalin show us that the personalities of these leaders were more important than either the historical conditions in which they found themselves or the ideologies they represented, though these two were important as well. Both men had a pronounced sense of mission, or destiny, and emphasized the power of the will. Both were also extremely calculating, devious, and flexible, able to outwait and outwit their opponents.

Adolf Hitler's strong will was evident in his youth. Born in Austria, he was the son of Alois Hitler, a customs official, and his third (and much younger) wife, Klara. Klara's indulgence of her son contributed to his later sense of self-importance. Young Hitler was a bright but moody and erratic student who barely finished secondary school and spent much time as a teenager dreaming of being a great artist, sharing fantasies of greatness with his best friend, and drawing sketches showing how he would rebuild their town of Linz. Hitler's father died in 1903 and Klara was stricken with breast cancer in early 1907. Hitler tenderly nursed his mother in the weeks before her death in December and then used a small orphan's pension to support himself in Vienna, where he twice failed to pass the examination for admission to the Vienna Academy of Art. He spent the next six years, before moving to Munich in 1913, living from hand to mouth, sometimes earning money by drawing watercolor scenes and advertising posters, and arguing politics and dreaming up get-rich-quick schemes while living in shelters for homeless men.[2]

When World War I broke out in 1914, Hitler eagerly volunteered for service in the German army and spent four years on the Western Front, earning an Iron Cross First Class in 1918 as a result of his heroism in battle, an unusually high honor for a corporal. In the army, Hitler found a sense of belonging he had missed since his mother's death. He was, therefore, particularly shocked when, in a hospital recovering from a mustard gas attack, he was told of Germany's defeat. Hitler returned to Munich, where conservative army officers gave him a job investigating "radical" groups. He was asked to speak to returning troops about the evils of socialism in a Germany that had suddenly (with the abdication of the kaiser on November 9, 1918) become a democratic republic. Munich and the rest of Bavaria soon became a center of right-wing opposition to the new national government; it was here that Hitler formulated his new ideology and discovered his power as a speechmaker. His beliefs, expressed in speeches after he joined the small German Workers Party and changed it into the NSDAP, included opposition to democracy and socialism. Popular fears of these ideas were made real by the fact that the largest party in the new German legislature was the Social Democratic Party. Although it was then a middle-class party committed to democracy, the Social Democrats (SPD) had historically promoted Marxist ideas of equality and revolution. They and other mainstream liberal parties were also responsible for the armistice of 1918 and the hated Versailles Treaty of 1919. The armistice was considered a "stab in the back" by right-wing nationalists, since German troops were still on French soil when it was signed. The treaty took territory from Germany, disarmed the country, and imposed oppressively high reparation payments. Hitler railed against all this, but the heart of his ideology and program—from its beginnings in 1919 to his final "testament" in 1945—was his hatred of the Jews.

In later years, Hitler claimed that he formed his antisemitic [anti-Jewish] views while living in Vienna. In his famous political autobiography, *Mein Kampf* [*My Struggle*], written from 1924 to 1926, he describes seeing "filthy" Jews and reading that Jews were not a religious group but an accursed race responsible for all moral and political evil. Some have argued that Hitler's antisemitism could be traced to his fear that one of his grandparents was Jewish, or to the fact that a Jewish physician had failed to cure his beloved mother of cancer. While we may never know the exact source of his deep hostility toward Jews, we do know that by the mid-1920s he had adopted and had begun to popularize a nineteenth-century antisemitic view of history as a struggle between superior and inferior races. The Aryans [his term for Germanic peoples] were locked in constant struggle with lesser races, such as the Slavs. However, the lowest life-form for him was the Jews. The Aryans were the source of all real culture; the Jews were eternal "culture-destroyers." They threatened Germany both as capitalists who had sabotaged the German army in World War I and as the leaders of "Jewish Bolshevism," who wanted to destroy the country through socialist revolution. As early as August 1919, Hitler wrote that the "ultimate goal" of a strong Germany should be "the removal of the Jews altogether."[3]

Given the irrational nature of Hitler's ideology, we can understand his appeal only if we appreciate two additional things: the mood in Germany after World War I and Hitler's gifts as an orator. The defeat left many Germans disoriented and angry. The new republican government—with no troops of its own—had to rely upon the old army's conservative officers to put down several attempts at a communist revolution. Meanwhile, those same officers and their nationalist supporters, the people most responsible for war in 1914, had escaped responsibility for the defeat. Representatives of the new democratic parties were forced to sign the armistice and the hated Versailles Treaty because President Wilson of the United States refused to deal with the "militarists" who had caused the war. The new democratic Weimar Republic, called after the city where the constitution was written, appeared to be imposed on the people as a consequence of defeat. The new government was, therefore, unfairly associated in people's minds with defeat. Right-wing orators such as Hitler loudly blamed the "November criminals" for selling out the nation when, in fact, it was the leaders of the army in 1918 who had desperately requested an armistice so that the retreating army would not be destroyed. By 1923, German inability to pay reparations had led to French occupation of the industrial Ruhr valley. When the Weimar government printed money to pay the workers to go on strike rather than supply the French with iron and steel, it caused a serious inflation, which wiped out the savings of many middle-class Germans. Although the government survived this crisis, the fear it inspired caused many Germans to vote for extremist parties in the early 1930s, when the Great Depression began.

Hitler's oratorical skills allowed him to take advantage of the crisis in 1923. Although his November "Beer Hall Putsch" [an attempt to seize power] failed miserably, he earned much public sympathy when he skillfully turned his trial into an attack on his enemies, proclaiming himself the real patriot and his government prosecutors the true traitors to Germany. A lenient court gave him the minimum five-year term and released him in eight months. It was while he lived comfortably in a Bavarian prison that he wrote *Mein Kampf*.[4] As his court performance showed, Hitler was able to sense the mood of a crowd and respond to it, saying both what he intuitively sensed people wanted to hear and drawing emotional strength from their response. Some called this ability *Fingerspitzengefühl*, or "finger-tip feeling." He was also a great actor who could convince himself that he really believed what he was saying; this skill also helped him captivate and persuade an audience of thousands as easily as a single person.

His program and ability to appeal to the masses made Hitler a leader to be reckoned with when the depression hit Germany in 1930. With a party loyal to its Führer (leader) behind him, Hitler could exploit voters' fears of economic disaster at a time when the Weimar government seemed unable to end unemployment. In a September general election to the Reichstag [legislature], the Nazis increased their number of seats from twelve to 107; Communist representatives also increased from fifty-four to seventy-seven, giving Hitler more reason to warn against "Jewish Bolshevism." The next eighteen months saw more electoral successes for the Nazis. Because the Nazis and Communists refused to cooperate with the Social Democrats and other mainstream parties, the chancellor [head of government, appointed by the president, the formal head of state] had to rule by emergency decree instead of by securing majority votes in the Reichstag. The constitution allowed this, providing the president—at that time the aged World War I hero, Field Marshall Paul von Hindenburg—countersigned the decrees. Even when Hitler's party became the largest in the Reichstag in July 1932, Hindenburg refused to appoint him chancellor, the normal course of action in a parliamentary system of government. Hindenburg disliked "the Bohemian corporal" and was aware of Hitler's announced goal of coming to power legally so that he could then replace the republic with a Nazi dictatorship. A series of conservative chancellors were unable to get Hitler to accept a lesser post than chancellor. Several, therefore, began to intrigue and conspire against each other over how best to "use" Hitler as the "front man" in a government that would really be run by traditional conservatives. They were sure they could control Hitler when they finally convinced Hindenburg to appoint him chancellor on January 30, 1933.

Hitler's political opponents fatally misjudged both their abilities and his. Within six months, all political parties except the National Socialists had disappeared. The Communists and many members of the Social Democratic Party were jailed; soon the other parties "voluntarily" dissolved themselves. Hitler moved quickly to consolidate his power, putting Nazis in charge at all levels of government and in education, the courts, and other professions. To allay fears, he moved more slowly in implementing other key domestic and foreign policy ideas. It was not until the 1935 Nuremberg Laws that Jews were denied citizenship and subjected to other forms of discrimination. All of these measures were enforced by a vigilant secret police (the Gestapo). In foreign policy, he spoke often of his peaceful intentions, even signing a non-aggression treaty with the Poles in 1934, in which he accepted Germany's loss of territory in the east after World War I. He had no intention of honoring this treaty any longer than necessary, and he had every intention of seeking to expand German territory at the expense of the Poles and others in Eastern Europe, including the Russians, as he had said very plainly in *Mein Kampf.*

He had also made his intention to solve the "Jewish problem" by driving them into exile, putting them in jails and concentration camps, and using other, more "thorough," ways clear from the beginning of his political career.[6] Hitler's goals were clear and consistent. His timing was flexible, and this weakened possible opponents in Germany and abroad, who were pleased with full employment and the new sense of order that the Nazi regime brought. His ability to pursue his goals indirectly also eased the conscience of those who wanted to believe that Hitler's speeches were only designed to play to the prejudices of his uneducated followers. He didn't really mean what he said. He couldn't possibly be as dangerous as he sounded, they told themselves. But he did and he was. In 1938, British Prime Minister Neville Chamberlain believed Hitler's statement that he only wanted to annex the German portion of Czechoslovakia (the Sudetenland) because the Germans there were being mistreated. He added that this was his last territorial claim in Europe and that he was only trying to rectify the wrongs of the Versailles Treaty. Western leaders believed him, even though he was lying about all of this. Conscience, Hitler once said, was "a Jewish invention, a blemish like circumcision."[7]

Germans and others finally found out what they were dealing with when Hitler, after peacefully annexing Austria in 1938 and the rest of Czechoslovakia in 1939, attacked Poland on September 1, 1939, beginning World War II when the French and British declared war on him in response. At first, things went well for Hitler. Poland was conquered in two weeks. The following spring, Hitler's armies moved west, conquering Holland in four days, Belgium in eight, and—to everyone's surprise—France in only six weeks. Hitler was unable to conquer Britain in 1940, however, and despite victories in the Mediterranean and North Africa, the Nazi juggernaut slowed by the end of 1941. Hitler attacked the Soviet Union in June 1941 but was unable to win a quick victory before winter set in. Undaunted, he declared war on the United States after Japan attacked Pearl Harbor in December. From that point on, Hitler's defeat was only a matter of time. His enemies could simply outproduce him. In 1943, for example, when German wartime production was beginning to reach its peak, Germany produced forty-three thousand war machines (from tanks and planes to artillery and battleships), compared with twenty-six thousand the previous year, in spite of constant British and American bombing of German cities. However, Allied (British, United States, Russian) production figures rose from one hundred thousand to one hundred fifty thousand during the same period.[8]

While the war was going on, however, Hitler did not forget his plan to eliminate the Jews. His war in the east coincided with the establishment of death camps, the largest in Poland, where millions of Jews from Germany and the conquered territories were shot, gassed, or worked to death. Hitler's willingness to use valuable manpower and railroad cars for the deportations and executions, which lasted up to the final weeks of the war, shows how seriously he took this ideological goal. The fact that millions of ordinary (non-Nazi) Germans were willing, even eager, to help him says something about Hitler's power over his nation and about the deeply rooted nature of antisemitism in German society at that time.[9]

Until Hitler committed suicide in his Berlin bunker on April 30, 1945, he retained his power over Germany. German soldiers fought hopelessly on, until word of his death was announced, because he had forbidden them to surrender. His faithful architect and munitions minister, Albert Speer, said that only after Hitler's death "was the spell broken, the magic extinguished."[10] However, Nazism as a unique set of ideas did not survive Adolf Hitler. That is one important difference between the ideas of Hitler and Stalin, for the socialist idea and the Soviet Union did survive the death of Joseph Stalin, by almost fifty years. But then, Stalin did not create the idea of socialism the way Hitler created Nazism. Stalin learned his ideas and practices from his great teacher, Lenin; a review of Stalin's life can help us better understand the sort of student he was.

Joseph Stalin was not even Russian. The man who built a strong Russian state was born in Georgia, one of the small states in the Caucasus Mountains which became part of the Imperial Russian Empire in the nineteenth century. Born Iosif Dzhugashvili (he took the revolutionary name Stalin, "Man of Steel," years later), the future ruler was the son of a drunken, illiterate shoemaker, Vissarion, and his pious and independent wife, Ekaterina. Young Joseph was beaten by his father and, like Hitler, was raised by his mother, who had high hopes for him. She was determined that he become a priest. Ekaterina enrolled her son in a church-run elementary school, where the great self-confidence instilled by his mother helped him graduate at the head of his class in 1894. When he entered the theological seminary in nearby Tiflis (today Tbilisi), his ambitions changed. He resented the strict authority and the attempt to "Russify" the Georgian students at the seminary and, with others, turned to reading forbidden Western books, many about socialism. His grades dropped and, at the end of his third year, he was expelled for failing to show up for final examinations. It didn't matter; by this time, he had decided on a new career—that of professional revolutionary.[11]

Since class differences and hatreds were very strong in Russia, many idealistic young people were attracted to the ideas of nineteenth-century German thinker Karl Marx. After observing the development of new classes during the Industrial Revolution, and the conditions of the factory workers, Marx predicted that these workers (proletarians) would overthrow the capitalist classes (bourgeoisie) when the time was right. Then the process of creating a truly classless society could begin. By 1899, when Stalin became a full-time revolutionary in the ranks of the Social Democrats, as the Marxists were known, a split was beginning to develop. A more traditional group felt that a workers' revolution had to wait until the development of industrial capitalism was more advanced. Russia's process of industrialization began only in the late nineteenth century. Another group wanted to speed up the process through the use of a dedicated corps of elite revolutionary leaders who would become the "dictatorship of the proletariat" and would organize the workers to immediately destroy the capitalist classes, not through legal means such as used by the Social Democrats in Germany, but through violent revolution. The leader of this second group was Vladimir I. Lenin, a determined and calculating person who challenged the older view at a party congress in 1903. When he won on several issues, he began to call his group the Bolsheviks (meaning "majority" in Russian) and his opponents Mensheviks ("minority"). The names stuck and young Stalin, unlike many of his fellow Georgian revolutionaries, was immediately attracted to the ideas and radical program of Lenin, who became a father-figure to the man whose father had disappeared when Stalin was eleven.

Between 1900 and 1917, Stalin organized frequently bloody demonstrations of workers in his native Caucasus, hid from the Tsarist police, and was connected with a dramatic bank robbery (called by the party an "expropriation") to secure funds for the party. During these years, he was arrested eight times, sent into exile in northern Russia seven times, and escaped six times. His last exile was in Siberia from 1913 to 1917; he was freed from this only by the March Revolution of 1917 that overthrew the Tsarist government.

Stalin met his hero, Lenin, at a Social Democratic Party congress in Finland in 1905. During these years in exile, Lenin came to appreciate the younger man's hard work and ruthlessness.[12] Stalin was attracted to Lenin during these years because both of them, like Hitler, had dualistic views of the world. "Either the bourgeoisie with its capitalism, or the proletariat with its socialism," Stalin wrote later: there could be no middle ground. This "either-or" view led Lenin to reject compromise and insist on a further revolution when he returned to Russia from abroad in April 1917. The liberals who had taken over after the tsar was overthrown were not ready to eliminate capitalism—or end the disastrous Russian participation in World War I which had caused the tsar's downfall. Lenin was willing to do both, even if it took a bloody civil war. Stalin admired this "hardness" in Lenin and would later identify everything he did as Leninism. He identified himself and his policies with Lenin's brand of socialism in the same way that Hitler identified himself and his policies with Germany. One could not differ with either man without being seen as a traitor.[13]

Lenin and his fellow Bolsheviks were successful in November 1917 in overthrowing the liberal Provisional Government and, in the next five years, gave Stalin further examples of his hardness. Lenin's first action was to suspend an assembly that had been elected earlier to write a constitution. Since he had secured power by promising the people "peace, land, and bread," his next hard decision was to sign a peace treaty with the Germans in March 1918. This Treaty of Brest-Litovsk, which surrendered a third of Russia's people and farmland and over half of its industry,[14] was opposed by most of the other Bolsheviks, who had to be persuaded by Lenin that the Russian people would overthrow them if they didn't end the war. Since many in the Russian upper and middle classes opposed Bolshevik plans to give *their* land to the peasants, the Bolshevik leaders had to fight a bitter civil war for three years against the conservative White armies in order to survive.

During this time, Stalin, who had become almost Lenin's second in command during 1917, was eclipsed in the leadership by Lev Trotsky, the "organizer of victory," a brilliant military leader. Stalin, a quiet, behind-the-scenes organizer, disliked Trotsky, who was a popular, colorful orator. Stalin also distrusted Trotsky's idea that the revolution had to spread and become a world revolution (he especially hoped for a socialist government in Germany) before it could really succeed in Russia. Stalin was becoming a believer in what he would later call "socialism in one country"—Russia. Lenin respected the different skills of each of these men and tried to end their feuding. Their fighting was particularly nasty during the civil war, when Stalin insisted on military command and in the battle against the Poles in 1920 made some decisions which resulted in a Red Army defeat. In 1922, Lenin recognized Stalin's organizational skills and devotion to work by making him the General Secretary of the Communist Party, responsible for supervising and recommending appointment of party officials throughout the country. At the same time, he offered Trotsky a position as vice-chair of a state body, the Council of People's Commissars (the cabinet), which would have put him in line to succeed Lenin, who was the chairman. Trotsky refused "for obscure reasons."[15] It was a mistake.

Lenin suffered his first stroke in May 1922 and died in January 1924. Although he could not appoint a successor, mainly because his position as leader was based more upon his charisma [ability to inspire allegiance and devotion in his followers] than on any office he held, he did leave a final "testament" which recommended, among other things, that Stalin be removed as general secretary of the party because of his "rudeness" and difficulty in getting along with others. Since Stalin was obviously not charismatic, his career might have ended there if he had not been able to use his position as general secretary to pack party meetings with his supporters. He was also able to use his political skills to manipulate and play on the fears of other party leaders, Trotsky, Grigori Zinoviev, Lev Kamenev, and Nikolai Bukharin. In 1924, Zinoviev and Kamenev supported Stalin's continuation as general secretary because they feared Trotsky's power. A year later, they attacked Stalin at the party congress, accusing him of trying to take Lenin's place as *vozhd'* [a term for unquestioned leader, similar to Hitler's title of *Führer* in Germany], but were defeated, with Trotsky remaining aloof. By 1926, Trotsky had joined the other two, but Stalin's hand-picked congress delegates expelled all three from the party in 1927.

During all this, Stalin remained allied with Bukharin, then editor of the party newspaper, *Pravda,* and a person who also opposed Trotsky's emphasis on world revolution. However, Stalin and Bukharin disagreed on policy toward the peasants, though they covered this up until 1928. Bukharin supported the New Economic Policy (NEP) that Lenin had established in 1921. Instead of seizing grain from the peasants to feed the cities, as was done during the civil war, the NEP restored a money economy and allowed peasants to sell any surplus beyond what the government needed. Using a grain shortage in 1928 as an excuse, Stalin moved to eliminate NEP as a concession to capitalism; Bukharin's opposition allowed Stalin to expel him from the Politburo (the decision-making body in the party) in 1929. Throughout this process of consolidating his power, Stalin consistently reminded party members of Lenin's calls for unity and moderation, even as he was preparing to undertake more radical measures against the peasants. In 1927, knowing his men now controlled the party congress, he offered to resign as general secretary to honor's Lenin's wish. The congress unanimously asked him to stay.[16]

With virtually unlimited power by 1929, Stalin could begin his "second revolution," one that would make him as great as Lenin, whose embalmed body was on display near the Kremlin. Between 1929 and 1935, Stalin undertook a massive program to collectivize agriculture and an equally massive program of industrialization through a series of Five Year Plans. His goal was to catch up with the "enemies" of socialism in the West. It worked, up to a point. Steel production, for example, went from 4.4 million tons in 1928 to 6 million tons in 1933 and, by the end of 1934, 90 percent of the farmland in the USSR was in the collective farms. But the costs were great. The kulaks (wealthier peasants) were eliminated as a class; those who resisted having their property collectivized were sent to labor camps or shot. Two hundred forty thousand kulak families were exiled by 1933; many of those died. Famines resulted, but the resulting deaths were denied by the government. Up to 4 million slaves, 10 percent of the total labor force, worked at any one time in the labor camps. Many millions of them died as well during the Stalin years.[17]

Just as many Germans supported Hitler's large-scale murders (which were different from Stalin's because you can change your class easier than you can your "race"), so, too, many Russians supported Stalin's policies to build a strong socialist state in Russia, even with the deaths involved. Both inside and outside the Communist Party, many took the idea of class struggle very seriously and had been troubled by the NEP compromise with capitalism. One story told how two young boys, sons of a champion metalworker, threw a classmate under the wheels of a streetcar because he was the son of a doctor and, thus, their class enemy. In addition, many of the newer party members recruited by Stalin liked his emphasis on building a strong, industrialized Russia able to compete with foreign capitalist states. And Stalin was always able to explain to his people exactly why Lenin would have wanted him to do what he was doing.[18] His actions were—or were made to seem—ideologically correct.

Less easy to explain in ideological terms was Stalin's decision to "purge," or "liquidate," nearly all of the Old Bolsheviks (those who had worked with Lenin) in a series of "show trials." Until the 1930s, those who fell from favor were expelled from the party and, in serious cases, exiled from the country. But, beginning in 1934 and continuing until 1938, Stalin accused former political enemies as well as military leaders of treason, made them confess to things they had not done in carefully scripted trials, then had them jailed and/or shot. Scholars explain this by pointing out that Stalin was both paranoid, fearing numerous secret enemies, and vengeful. One writes that "Stalin was unhappy at not being able to convince everyone, 'himself included,' that he was greater than everyone"; therefore, anyone who questioned—or even seemed to question—his perfection was seen as a class enemy. After all, since Stalin perfectly embodied the Bolshevik cause, anyone who was not slavishly loyal had to be eliminated.[19] Whatever the cause, this aspect of Stalin's personality created an atmosphere of terror that had people shooting themselves or jumping out of windows when they heard the NKVD (secret police) knock on their door in the middle of the night.

Stalin's purges of military leaders help explain why Hitler's armies were able to march hundreds of miles into Soviet territory and take 3.5 million prisoners in the first six months after they attacked in June 1941. Stalin's people did recover; they had population, geography, and climate (a vast country and the Russian winter that had defeated Napoleon in 1812) on their side, not to mention help from Britain and the United States. During the war, Stalin downplayed his socialist goals and appealed to Russians to remember how they had defeated Western armies in the past. World War II became the "Great Patriotic War." These were years of triumph for the grandson of Georgian serfs. He was accepted as an equal by President Roosevelt of the United States and Winston Churchill of Great Britain and, at the end of the war, his troops remained in Eastern Europe, creating, in effect, the largest empire in Russian history. When the Western leaders came to him, at Yalta in February 1945, to divide up the spoils of Hitler's empire, it was, in the words of one historian, "that moment in Stalin's career when reality came closest to confirming his image of himself."[20]

The postwar years, however, saw Stalin return to the policies of repression, terror, and paranoia that marked his rule in the 1930s. Returning prisoners of war were told they were traitors for allowing themselves to be captured. For that, and for being tainted with exposure to foreign ideas, they were jailed. Cooperation with his former allies ended, the "iron curtain" went up, and the Cold War began. In 1953, he was—many believe—on the verge of launching a new set of purges. Some Jewish physicians had already been accused of poisoning Soviet leaders and were to be tried when Stalin's death, from a stroke on March 5, intervened. Three years after his death, the new Russian leader, Nikita Khrushchev, made a "secret speech" at the party congress, condemning Stalin's purges of the 1930s and his "cult of personality"—but not the destruction of the peasants or the deadly labor camps. It was not until the Soviet Union itself was near collapse in the late 1980s that other criticisms were heard. What may surprise us is that, even today in the former Soviet Union, there are people willing to display Stalin's picture in parades and lament the "good old days" of his dictatorship. At least Russia was strong—and orderly—in those days.[21]

All told, Adolf Hitler and Joseph Stalin seem to qualify for a high position on any list of the ten individuals who really made the greatest difference in history. Historians and political scientists often join these two men and their governments together under the label "totalitarian." By this, they mean that both states were ruled by a single political party, tried to control the social and intellectual as well as the political lives of their citizens, and used systematic terror to do this. While this term helps us see how these two dictatorships were similar, it also obscures the real differences. No other totalitarian state was as systematically racist and antisemitic as Hitler's Germany. No other totalitarian state engaged in the bizarre purge trials which Stalin established in the 1930s. It is one thing to think about getting rid of all the Jews in Europe or to think about how nice it would be to destroy all your class enemies. To be ruthless enough to actually do these things is another matter. When we look at what they did and try to understand what motivated them—consciously or unconsciously—to do it, it is, in the words of historian Alan Bullock, "hard to imagine" anyone but Hitler doing what he did and "equally difficult to imagine any other Soviet leader than Stalin" doing the things he did.[22] Others thought about doing such things, but Hitler and Stalin acted. Even harder to explain than what they did is why so many sane, sensible people let them do it.

Notes

1. Estimates of the number of Jews destroyed in the Holocaust range from 5.6 to 6.9 million, out of a total European Jewish population in 1939 of 11 million. Millions of others, including Gypsies and various disabled peoples, were also killed in this attempt to rid Europe of inferior or "subhuman" peoples. See Alan Bullock, *Hitler and Stalin: Parallel Lives* (New York: Alfred A. Knopf, 1992), Appendix III, 989; for the full scope and context, see also *Century of Genocide: Eyewitness Accounts*

and Critical Views, ed. Samuel Totten, William S. Parsons, Israel W. Charny (New York: Garland Publishing Company, 1997).

2. Alan Bullock, *Hitler: A Study in Tyranny,* rev. ed. (London: Odhams Books Ltd, 1964), 33–36.

3. Adolf Hitler, *Mein Kampf* (New York: Reynal and Hitchcock, 1939), 73–78; see also the chapter on "Nation and Race," 389–455; Ian Kershaw, *Hitler* (London: Longmans, 1991), 19–28; Bullock, *Parallel Lives,* 71.

4. Joachim Fest, *Hitler,* trans. Richard and Clara Winston (New York: Random House, 1974), 182–196.

5. Bullock, *A Study in Tyranny,* 377–378.

6. See Eberhard Jäckel, *Hitler's Weltanschauung [Worldview],* trans. Herbert Arnold (Middletown, CT: Wesleyan University Press, 1972), 27–66.

7. Bullock, *Parallel Lives,* 386.

8. Bullock, *Parallel Lives,* 802.

9. While there has long been agreement on the importance of antisemitism in Hitler's ideology, only relatively recently did Daniel Goldhagen argue for an "eliminationist antisemitism" among the German people as a whole. See his controversial book, *Hitler's Willing Executioners, Ordinary Germans and the Holocaust* (New York: Alfred A. Knopf, 1996).

10. Albert Speer, *Inside the Third Reich,* trans. Richard and Clara Winston (New York: Macmillan, 1970), 488–89.

11. See Robert Tucker, *Stalin as Revolutionary, 1879–1929: A Study in History and Personality* (New York: W. W. Norton, 1973), 64–91.

12. Tucker, *Stalin as Revolutionary,* 91–108; see also the excellent brief "Chronology of Stalin's Life" in Robert H. McNeal, *Stalin, Man and Ruler* (New York: New York University Press, 1988), 317–323.

13. Tucker, *Stalin as Revolutionary,* 119, 130–143; McNeal, *Stalin,* 314.

14. See Bullock, *Parallel Lives,* 62; the Russians retrieved this territory when the Germans were defeated less than a year later in the West.

15. Tucker, *Stalin as Revolutionary,* 336.

16. Bullock, *Parallel Lives,* 175–176, 205.

17. Bullock, *Parallel Lives,* 256–395; Edvard Radzinsky, *Stalin,* trans. H. T. Willetts (New York: Doubleday, 1996), 249.

18. McNeal, *Stalin,* 312; Radzinsky, *Stalin,* 232; Tucker, *Stalin as Revolutionary,* 321–324; Bullock, *Parallel Lives,* 202.

19. Tucker, *Stalin as Revolutionary,* 439, 450–451.

20. Bullock, *Parallel Lives,* 875.

21. Radzinsky, *Stalin,* 583–584.

22. Bullock, *Parallel Lives,* 977.

Further Reading

BULLOCK, ALAN. *Hitler: A Study in Tyranny.* rev. ed. London: Odhams Books, 1964. See especially Chapter 7, "The Dictator," for an excellent look at Hitler's personality; see also Bullock's later comparative biography, *Hitler and Stalin: Parallel Lives.* New York: Knopf, 1992.

KOESTLER, ARTHUR. *Darkness at Noon.* New York: Macmillan, 1941; also later printings. Though a fictional account, this work dramatically portrays the state of mind of those who participated in the show trials and tries to explain why many willingly signed false confessions.

RADZINSKY, EDVARD. *Stalin.* Trans. H. T. Willetts. New York: Doubleday, 1996. Written by a playwright rather than a historian, this contains many anecdotes and a few interesting insights—among them a new date of birth for Stalin.

TUCKER, ROBERT C. *Stalin as Revolutionary, 1879–1929: A Study in History and Personality.* New York: W. W. Norton, 1973. See especially Chapter 12, "The Decisive Trifle," on Stalin's personality.

CHAPTER 11

Eva Perón and Golda Meir: Helping the Dispossessed— Two Models

How did the personalities of two leaders affect the way they chose to help the dispossessed in their two very different cultural communities? Is power best exercised in formal or informal ways?

An old Russian proverb calls poverty "the sin the rich cannot forgive." Whether or not this is true, it is clear that, during the past century, large numbers of people have been forced into poverty or homelessness by wars, revolutions, and economic inequalities. Since we no longer regard poverty as inevitable, as many did before the Industrial Revolution, private and government efforts to help such people have increased.

The lives of two twentieth-century women, Eva Perón of Argentina (1919–1952) and Golda Meir of Israel (1898–1978) illustrate two vastly different ways of aiding the dispossessed. Eva Perón was the wife of the president of Argentina, Juan Perón, and was his "ambassador" to the poor, or *descamisados* ("shirtless ones"), from 1946 to her death in 1952. Golda Meir spent much of her life working for the Zionist [Jewish nationalist] movement in Palestine before serving as minister of labor, foreign minister, and, finally, prime minister of the state of Israel from 1969 to 1974.

Both of these powerful, determined women helped the dispossessed. Eva Perón, still a legendary figure in Argentina, did it by creating what *Time* magazine called "the splashiest giveaway machine the world ever saw."[1] Meir, who seemed to some to be the archetypal Jewish grandmother, helped her people by working to establish an independent state characterized by strong social welfare institutions. Their quite different approaches to social justice grew out of the different histories and cultures of the Jewish and Argentine peoples, as well as from the very different personalities of these two women.

Any comparison of them is made more difficult by the controversial nature of Eva Perón's career, as well as by a general North American ignorance of Latin American political traditions. North Americans tend to be more sympathetic to a leader like Golda Meir because she adopted a policy of national self-determination and a social welfare ideology more familiar in the United States. Eva Perón's behavior, by contrast, is not only unfamiliar, but it also seems irrational. Golda Meir strikes us as better organized, employing public institutions in the pursuit of her cause; Eva Perón, on the other hand, was charismatic [having personal magnetism or charm] and spontaneous, depending on personal power rather than on institutions, to reach her goals. Of the two, Eva was the more fascinating.

Born the illegitimate daughter of Juana Ibarguren and Juan Duarte in the small village of Los Toldos, Eva watched her mother struggle to feed five children after the death of her father, when Eva was six. She grew up aware of the pain of being poor. When she and her four illegitimate siblings walked twenty miles to attend her father's funeral, they were initially turned away by the wealthier "legal" family and were allowed to attend only when the mayor intervened. Years later, she wrote in her autobiography that she "was sad for many days when I first realized that there were poor and rich in the world; . . . the fact of the existence of the poor did not hurt me so much as the knowledge that, at the same time, the rich existed."[2]

At age fifteen, Eva went to Buenos Aires, then the third-largest city in the western hemisphere, to become an actress. Exactly how she got there and what she did after she arrived is uncertain; Evita ("little Eva," the nickname by which she later became famous) spoke little about her early life. She had her birth certificate changed so she would appear legitimate, and she distorted much of what she did reveal. Her enemies accused her of being a prostitute during her early years in the capital, and she did have a number of lovers. But it is more likely that she earned a meager living through a series of temporary acting jobs with traveling companies until she was able to achieve moderate success as a radio actress in the early 1940s.[3]

Eva Duarte's life changed dramatically in January of 1944, when she became the mistress of Colonel Juan Perón, minister of labor and soon-to-be minister of war in the military government that had come to power eighteen months earlier. In the former position, he appealed to Argentine workers (and undercut the Communist and Socialist union leaders) by organizing government-sponsored unions that raised salaries and increased benefits for the workers, whose interests had been ignored by previous liberal governments. As minister of war, he maintained the support of conservatives in the army by assuring them that the privileges he was granting workers were "strictly limited by the powers of the State."[4]

Despite these assurances, it was plain that, true to the Latin American political tradition, Perón was supporting the workers in order to build a personal power base, independent of the military. When new laws guaranteeing higher wages or shorter hours were proposed or signed, the minister of labor himself announced the proposal or signed the bill. During strikes, Perón personally visited the strikers and was photographed listening to their complaints, and he often took to the radio to announce such things as new health insurance or retirement benefits. Argentina was still a country of huge cattle ranches, and towns were often hundreds of miles apart. The rural poor who migrated to Buenos Aires in large numbers during the first half of the twentieth century were accustomed, not to democracy, but to rule by local strongmen *(caudillos)* who governed—often extra-legally—by establishing a personal bond with their people. By courting the previously neglected urban workers, Juan Perón successfully appealed to this populist, personalist tradition.[5] His mistress, Evita, would later, as his wife, use this tradition in a particularly dramatic and feminine way to make her mark on history.

Before this could happen, Juan Perón had to become the sole ruler of Argentina. By 1945, Perón, who had added the title of vice-president in late 1944, had clearly become the most powerful of the military leaders. Fear of his growing power led the other generals to demand Perón's resignation on October 9, 1945, citing as a reason that he lived openly with his mistress, Evita. After his resignation and a farewell speech to employees at the Ministry of Labor (which he cleverly had broadcast on the radio), Perón was imprisoned.

Later Peronist propaganda claims that, during the next week, Evita went to the working-class neighborhoods in Buenos Aires and rallied union leaders, who encouraged three hundred thousand workers, derisively called "shirtless ones" by the conservative press, to descend on the central square in the capital to demand the release of Perón.[6] [*Descamisados,* shirtless ones, did not wear jackets; they were not literally shirtless.] Eva encouraged Perón not to give up while throngs of workers, fearing the loss of Perón would mean the loss of their recent gains, took over the city and gathered in the Plaza de Mayo on October 17. Overwhelmed by the size of the crowd organized by Perón's supporters in the unions and at the Ministry of Labor, the military leaders released Perón from prison that night. He gave an impromptu speech from the balcony of the presidential palace, announcing that he would run for president in the next general election. Perón married Evita five days later and won the election of February 1946 with fifty-two percent of the vote. He won a second term as president in 1951 by an even larger margin and retained power until 1955 by implementing a policy of economic nationalism (buying back utilities and industries from foreigners, especially the British) which appealed to both the army and the organized working class. Within a year of her husband's first election, Evita was playing a key role—some say she overshadowed him—in keeping working-class support.

She did this primarily through her creation (almost by accident) of what became known as the "Eva Perón Foundation." It was customary for the President's wife to be asked to lead Argentina's largest private charity. However, the wealthy upper-class women of Buenos Aires who ran this organization snubbed Eva Perón because of her lower-class background. Evita then began her own social aid, or welfare, foundation, which later took her name. Within four years, it became a massive welfare organization. By 1951, the foundation had built one thousand schools, 600 new homes, and 60 hospitals, and it was training thirteen hundred nursing students a year and would open 35 clinics that year alone. By this time, it had assets of over $200 million and fourteen thousand permanent employees, including thousands of construction workers, and even a staff of priests.[7]

What made Eva's foundation unique was that although it was one woman's personal patronage system, it was a semi-official one, supported with both voluntary and semi-coerced private funds and outright government grants. Businesspeople were "expected" to contribute; one who did not had his factory closed for several years for violations of health regulations. When new collective bargaining agreements were signed, union members "donated" the first month's salary increase to the foundation. It also received 20 percent of the proceeds from the national lottery and other state revenues.[8]

Evita ran the semi-official foundation in an extremely personal fashion and encouraged people to write her directly about their problems. She claimed to receive thousands of letters each day. Several times a week, in the fashion of the monarchs of old Spain, she granted audiences to the poor of her "kingdom." She talked to the destitute for hours at a time in her office, giving them everything from homes and shoes to cooking pots and cash. Although this was stage-managed, with floodlights over her desk and photographers present, witnesses reported that she was genuinely kind to all she met and interested in their problems. Father Hernán Benítez, her confessor, present at many of these sessions, said later, "I saw her kiss the leprous. I saw her kiss those who were suffering from tuberculosis or cancer. I saw her distribute . . . a love that rescues charity, removing that burden of injury to the poor that charity implies."[9] Indeed, Evita despised the idea of charity, which she believed placed an obligation on the recipients and gave the upper-class "oligarchs," as they were called in Argentina, a sense of superiority. She regarded her gifts as social justice, as "reparations" for past wrongs inflicted on the lower classes. For that reason, she insisted on attractive interior decorations in her hospitals and children's homes and often used expensive materials such as marble in their construction. She believed the poor deserved it. In a published series of lectures and in her autobiography, largely written by others but reflecting her views, she wrote that many of the social welfare buildings she saw in Europe "are cold and poor. Many have been built according to the standards of the rich . . . and when the rich think of the poor, they think poorly. Others have been erected by State standards; and the State can only build bureaucratically, that is . . . with coldness, from which love is lacking."[10] We could have no clearer expression of the personalist Latin American political culture which produced both Evita and her "reform."

Given this genuine sympathy for the poor, especially when combined with her beauty, dedication to working long hours, and skillful self-promotion, it is not surprising that many poor Argentines began to see Evita as a holy person, "the Lady of Hope" (a title created by a newspaper she owned) who was giving her life for the poor. She was literally working herself to death. Months before her early death from uterine cancer on July 26, 1952, something she could have avoided by agreeing to surgery thirty months earlier, she was being referred to as a "saint" by many Argentines. Shortly before her death, the Peronist-dominated legislature voted her the title of "Spiritual Chief of the Nation." While much of this myth of "Saint Evita" was consciously contrived to gain support for the government, there is some evidence that Eva herself was changed by her contact with the poor and that she came to believe or even transcend the Peronist propaganda. The president's wife who, on a "goodwill" trip to Europe in 1947, had worn so much expensive fur and jewelry that she alienated many Europeans, in her last years wore less jewelry and more sober business suits while working nearly full-time at the foundation. "Her work acquired the importance and sanctity of a 'mission'. . . . Even when she was exhausted and obviously ill, she continued to work. Of all the many distortions surrounding her life the least outrageous and closest to the truth is the suggestion that she elected to die for Perón and Peronism." During her final two years of life, she appears to have accepted her own "martyrdom" by "increasing her activity to levels that would have been sustained with difficulty even by a healthy person."[11]

This view of Eva Perón is controversial because many see it as based on propaganda by a dictatorial regime that jailed its political opponents, ended press freedoms, and reshaped the political system to eliminate opposition parties. Evita's speeches and written works are propaganda works full of sentimental exaggeration of Juan Perón's virtues. He was a "genius," a "meteor that burns to illuminate our age," a man with "no defects," yet "humble even to the smallest detail." Perón is compared to Christ and Napoleon, and Evita claims to be "the shadow of the Leader," a person willing "to give her life [for him] at any time" and "a link stretched between the hopes of the people and the fulfilling hands of Perón."[12] Only by appreciating the importance of the personal bond between a leader and his or her followers in the Latin American *caudillo* tradition can we begin to understand the success of the Peróns—and the enduring quality of the myth of Evita.

Although Eva Perón could be vindictive toward enemies and to those who failed to flatter her sufficiently—it was said that one young man was jailed for not donating his radio quiz show winnings to the foundation—historians disagree on whether she sought power for herself or was only "the shadow of the Leader." Perón made her the *de facto* head [leader "in fact," though not "in law"—*de jure*] of the Ministry of Labor (the official minister was José Freire), where she purged all labor leaders not completely subservient to Perón. Evita also supported women's suffrage, a reality by 1948, and organized the Peronist Women's Party in 1949 to mobilize women's votes for Perón. Two million women voted in the 1951 presidential election, contributing to Perón's victory margin. Evita was not a feminist, however. She claimed that most feminists wanted to make women too much like men, and she wrote that women "suffer from love more than men."[13] In her work with both the labor unions and women's groups, Eva was careful not to upstage her husband. Only in 1951, when she tolerated a popular campaign by the workers' organizations to put her on the ballot as a vice-presidential candidate, did the question of whether she was seeking power for herself arise. After she was pressured by a crowd on August 22 to accept the nomination, she appeared to do so by saying, "I will do what the people say." Perón, aware that the army would not accept a female commander-in-chief, told her to refuse, which she did ten days later. By this time, she was already so ill that she was forced to spend most of her remaining months of life in bed. In sum, there is little evidence that Evita sought power for herself; most of her activities suggest that she did, in fact, see herself as Perón's "shadow."

However, Evita remains a legend. Whether people loved her or hated her, whether she was the "lady of hope" or "the great whore" *(la gran puta)*, the charismatic nature of Evita's power stirred emotions outside the boundaries of formal legal bureaucratic authority. Her supporters saw her bond with them as one of love; her middle- and upper-class enemies saw her power as "mystical, irrational, impulsive, [and] disordered."[14]

One way to gauge public perceptions of Eva Perón and Golda Meir (in the United States, at least) is to review obituary notices. *Time* magazine's obituary for Evita was entitled "Cinderella from the Pampas"; *Newsweek* called her a "tough, indefatigable" woman who "tied thousands around her much beringed finger." *Life* admitted she had become "the most powerful woman in the western hemisphere" but also belittled her as "the most spectacular Cinderella girl of her time." Only *The New York Times* avoided flippancy and referred to her as Perón's "most faithful and trusted collaborator" who exerted "tremendous power," even from her sickbed. In contrast, when Golda Meir died in 1978, *The New York Times* honored the former prime minister of Israel with two full pages, which included many references to her toughness, sense of humor, and use of plain language. *Time* called her "a tough maternal legend," and American conservative commentator William F. Buckley asked that "God be with her. She will look after Him."[15]

It is not surprising that Golda Meir is treated with greater seriousness by journalists and historians. The two women were a world apart geographically, philosophically, and temperamentally. If Eva's brief career demonstrates the impact of charismatic leadership on the long-term *memory* of a Latin American people, Golda Meir's much longer career demonstrates how a life of commitment to institutionalizing an idea can contribute to long-term *change* for a people. Like Eva Perón, she was not willing to accept the lot of the dispossessed—Jews without a state, in this case—but, unlike her, Meir wanted to create an environment and state in Palestine that would guarantee the Jewish dispossessed long-term security.

Golda Mabrovitch was born in Russia and could remember her father boarding up the family home in Kiev after he had been warned of a pogrom [attack on Jews, often government-sponsored]. She recalled thinking that maybe Jews should move to a place where the government would not let this happen. The Mabrovitch family moved to the United States in 1906, and she finished high school in Milwaukee after spending some time with her sister and brother-in-law in Denver. Her energy and organizational skills were shown as early as age eleven, when she organized a group of classmates who secured the donation of a hall, knocked on doors, and painted posters, asking parents to attend a meeting, where she gave a speech pleading for money to buy school books (public school in Milwaukee was free; books were not).

While in high school, Meir decided to join the movement to establish a Jewish state in Palestine [Zionism], a cause to which she devoted her life. "The Jews must have a land of their own again— and I must help build it, not by making speeches or raising funds, but by living and working there [in Palestine]."[16] But first she had to convince her boyfriend, Morris Meyerson, to go with her. She would not marry him until he did. They were married in 1917, but it was not until May 1921 that the Meyersons and a small group of fellow adventurers boarded the barely seaworthy *SS Pocahontas* for the long journey to Palestine. When they finally arrived at the barren, windswept railroad station on the edge of the frontier city of Tel Aviv, one member of the party said jokingly, "Well, Goldie, you wanted to come to Eretz Yisroel [the land of Israel]. Here we are. Now we can all go back—it's enough." She was not amused.[17]

She and Morris plunged into the life of agricultural workers at the Merhavia kibbutz in the valley of Jezreel. The kibbutzim were farming communes established on usually poor or swampy land not previously cultivated. By living on the land and sharing hard work and their few possessions, these Jewish pioneers hoped to build a Jewish community in Palestine; they wished to "redeem" themselves and the land at the same time. By 1951, kibbutzim in the state of Israel supported over a million immigrants.

Although Golda loved Merhavia, Morris disliked communal living and did not want to have children there, since kibbutz children were raised in nurseries and not exclusively by their parents. When he took ill in 1923, the couple moved to Tel Aviv and then Jerusalem. Two children, Menachem and Sarah, were born in the 1920s; during these years, Mrs. Meyerson lived as an impoverished homemaker, taking in laundry to pay Sarah's nursery school fees. The poverty bothered her less than being isolated from the important political and social work being done around her: "Instead of actively helping build the Jewish national home . . . I found myself cooped up in a tiny apartment in Jerusalem, all my thoughts and energy concentrated on making do with Morris' wages." Frustrated, she finally accepted a position working for the General Federation of Jewish Labor (Histadrut), and this led to her separation from her husband. Despite "bitter regret" at the failure of her marriage and the "inner struggles and despairs" of a working mother, Meir [the Hebrew form of Meyerson] remained an active, full-time worker in Histadrut and Mapai [the Labor Party] the rest of her life.[18]

One of the clearest differences between Eva Perón and Golda Meir is that Evita's career was possible because of her marriage and intense support for her husband, while Meir's career was made possible by the failure of her marriage. Morris, more poet than politician, had not wanted her to join the Zionist movement in the first place.[19] Another clear difference, of course, is that Eva started at the top in her attempt to help the less fortunate in her society; Meir spent many years working in many Zionist organizations before becoming the leader of her people.

From 1932 to 1934, Meir was back in the United States, giving speeches and raising money for rebuilding in Palestine. In 1934, she joined the executive committee of Histadrut and, within a few years, was in charge of mutual aid funds for all Jewish workers in Palestine. In 1937, it was back to the United States to raise money to build a Jewish harbor in Tel Aviv when the British, who controlled Palestine as a "mandate" from the League of Nations, closed the harbor at Jaffa after Arab riots in 1936.

By the late 1930s, the outline of future Arab-Jewish conflict was emerging. Arabs feared and resented Jewish immigration to Palestine. On the other hand, Hitler's persecution of German Jews made it clear to the *yishuv* [Jewish community in Palestine] that many more Jews from Europe needed a place of refuge. The British, in charge of Palestine, tried to slow Jewish immigration to Palestine in order to please the Arabs. Jews felt betrayed because the British in 1917, during World War I, had promised the Zionists "a Jewish homeland" in Palestine. But the language of this promise, in the form of the Balfour Declaration, did not promise a national state; it was deliberately and diplomatically vague.

Continued British refusal to allow free Jewish entry into Palestine during World War II, and even after 1945, when the extent of the Holocaust [destruction of 6 million Jews in Europe by the Nazis] became known, made it inevitable that Jews would fight the British, if necessary, to create their own state. In 1946, testifying before an Anglo-American Committee of Inquiry examining the question of Jewish immigration to Palestine, Meir described the two goals that motivated her and most other Jewish workers in Palestine: to create "an independent Jewish life in the Jewish homeland" and "to create a new society . . . of equality, justice, and cooperation." Socialist economic organization, such as that found in the kibbutzim, and national political independence were goals of these soon-to-be Israelis. Both, as well as humanitarian concern for the survivors of Hitler's death camps, required unrestricted Jewish immigration.[20]

No one was surprised that Meir, by then a leading member of the Labor Party, was one of the signers of the Israeli declaration of independence in May 1948, written after the Arab nations rejected the United Nations' plan to partition Palestine into separate Jewish and Arab states. During the previous months, to prepare for the expected Arab attempts to destroy the new state, Meir raised $50 million among American Jews for military supplies. When she returned home, David Ben-Gurion, Israel's first prime minister, said that "someday when history will be written, it will be said that there was a Jewish woman who got the money which made the state possible."[21]

In 1948, when Eva Perón was expanding the work of her foundation, Golda Meir was serving her new state as its first ambassador to Moscow. A year later, she became minister of labor in the Israeli cabinet. While Perón was building hundreds of schools and dozens of hospitals for the Argentine poor, Meir was feeding, housing, and finding jobs for nearly seven hundred thousand new immigrants who had poured into Israel by 1951. In 1949, her ministry began to build thirty thousand housing units; she also organized a large road-building program.[22]

As Israeli foreign minister in 1956, Meir had to defend her country's strike against the Arab armies massing on its borders in October of that year. "If hostile forces gather for our proposed destruction," she explained, "they must not demand that we provide them with ideal conditions for the realization of their plans." This is only one example of Golda Meir's tough language. When asked about the possibility of compromise with the Arabs after a later war, in 1967, she responded, "The Arabs wish us dead. We want to live. That's very hard to compromise."[23]

Up through her period of service as prime minister, which included the Yom Kippur war of 1973, Meir continued to think of herself as a "leader who was a woman rather than a woman leader." When someone asked her how it felt to be a woman minister, she replied, "I don't know. I was never a man minister." On another occasion, when the cabinet was discussing an outbreak of assaults on women at night, one member of a conservative religious group suggested a curfew for women after dark. Meir remarked, "But it's the men who are attacking the women. If there is to be a curfew, let the men stay at home, not the women."[24] Meir's attitude toward women and her language, like her method of helping the poor, were as rational and straightforward as those of her Argentine counterpart were sentimental.

In her autobiography, Golda Meir noted with pride that the Jewish population of Palestine had grown from eighty thousand people in 1921 to over 3 million in 1975. She also expressed her belief that Israel would someday find peace with its neighbors but added that "no one will make peace with a weak Israel. If Israel is not strong, there will be no peace."[25]

Despite continuing hostility in Arab-Israeli relations in the years since Golda Meir's death, it is clear that many Jews have found a measure of security in the Jewish state thanks to the systematic efforts at nation-building by her and her Labor Party colleagues. Although Eva Perón's memory still lives in Argentina and helped inspire a revolutionary movement in the 1970s, it is more difficult to see the lasting effects of her work. Inflation eroded the economic gains made by the poor under the Peróns in the late 1940s. Three years after Evita's death, Juan Perón was overthrown in a military coup and, although the Peronist Party remained active and was even able to bring Juan Perón back as president in 1973 until his death in 1974, Evita's work in helping the dispossessed of her country left few concrete results. But, then, the goals of these two strong women were quite different. Golda Meir wanted the Jews of the world to know there was one place where they would be safe and could feel at home. She succeeded in helping to create such a place. Andrew Lloyd Webber and Tim Rice, in their 1978 musical, "Evita," have the title character say that she was not concerned with the repressive side of her government; she was "in business . . . to give all my *descamisados* a magical moment or two." If this was her goal, she, too, succeeded.

Notes

1. *Time,* Aug. 4, 1952, 33. Eva Perón will be referred to as Eva or Evita throughout this chapter to avoid confusing her with her husband.
2. Eva Perón, *My Mission in Life,* trans. Ethel Cherry (New York: Vantage Press, 1953), 6.
3. The most balanced account of this period in Eva's life is found in Nicholas Fraser and Marysa Navarro, *Eva Perón* (New York: W. W. Norton, 1980), 20–27; see also John Barnes, *Evita: First Lady. A Biography of Eva Perón* (New York: Grove Press, 1978), 20–22.
4. Fraser and Navarro, *Eva Perón,* 40.

5. Robert Crassweller, *Perón and the Enigmas of Argentina* (New York: W. W. Norton, 1987), 120, 223; Robert J. Alexander, *Juan Domingo Perón: A History* (Boulder, CO: Westview Press, 1979), 37–39; Susan and Peter Calvert, *Argentina: Political Culture and Instability* (Pittsburgh: University of Pittsburgh Press, 1989), 80–84; Glen Caudill Dealy, *The Latin Americans: Spirit and Ethos* (Boulder, CO: Westview Press, 1992), 58–61.

6. See Eva Perón, *My Mission,* 27–28, 30.

7. Barnes, *Evita,* 14; Crassweller, *Enigmas,* 209–210; Richard Bourne, "Eva Perón," in *Political Leaders of Latin America* (New York: Alfred A. Knopf, 1970), 270.

8. Fraser and Navarro, *Eva Perón,* 119; Alexander, *Perón,* 83; Crassweller, *Enigmas,* 210.

9. Fraser and Navarro, *Eva Perón,* 122–126; Eva Perón, *My Mission,* 117–119.

10. Eva Perón, *History of Peronism* (Buenos Aires: Servicio Internacional Publicaciones Argentinas, 1952), 188–189; *My Mission,* 125–126, 144, 154–159. Eva's genuine concern for the poor is made clear in Alicia Dujovne Ortiz's biography, *Eva Perón,* trans. Shawn Fields (New York: St. Marti's Press, 1966), 180–222, 235.

11. Fraser and Navarro, *Eva Perón,* 125, 135; J. M. Taylor, *Eva Perón: The Myths of a Woman* (Chicago: University of Chicago Press, 1979), 57.

12. Eva Perón, *History of Peronism,* 12, 28–29, 56, 104, 141; *My Mission,* 61, 80, 176.

13. Barnes, *Evita,* 74–76; Eva Perón, *My Mission,* 51, 185.

14. See Taylor, *Myths of a Woman,* 11–19, 86–87, 104. She suggests that Eva's power was not only personal but also different from the personal power of her husband, because the personal, extra-legal power of a woman stirs different fears in a macho, male-dominated society like that in Latin America than does the same extra-legal power when exercised by a man. See also Marysa Navarro, "Evita's Charismatic Leadership," in *Latin American Populism in Comparative Perspective,* ed. Michael L. Conniff (Albuquerque: University of New Mexico Press, 1982), 47–66, for a summary of how Evita "moved outside of the institutional structure."

15. *Time,* August 4, 1952, 33; Dec. 18, 1978, 42–43; *Newsweek,* August 4, 1952, 47; *Life,* August 4, 1952, 32; *The New York Times,* July 27, 1952, 56; December 9, 1978, 6–7; *The National Review,* January 5, 1979, 18.

16. Marie Syrkin, *Golda Meir: Israel's Leader* (New York: Putnam's Sons, 1969), 14–37; Ralph G. Martin, *Golda: A Biography* (New York: Ballantine Books, 1990), 7–8, 12–13, 33–34, 44–45, 59, 63; Golda Meir, *My Life* (New York: Putnam's Sons, 1975), 22–25, 63. Golda Meir's married name was Meyerson, only changed to the Hebrew Meir in 1956 as a

requirement for serving in the Israeli cabinet. To avoid confusion, she is generally referred to as Meir in this chapter.

17. Meir, *My Life*, 77–78.
18. Syrkin, *Golda Meir*, 69–92; Meir, *My Life*, 112–115, and "Woman's Lib—1930" in Golda Meir, *A Land of Our Own: An Oral Autobiography*, ed. Marie Syrkin (New York: Putnam's Sons, 1973), 43–45.
19. Martin, *Golda*, 62.
20. Meir, "The Goal of Jewish Workers," in *A Land of Our Own*, 52–57.
21. Syrkin, *Golda Meir*, 191.
22. Ibid., 235–243.
23. Meir, *A Land of Our Own*, 94; *Time*, December 8, 1978, 43.
24. Syrkin, *Golda Meir*, 11, 97; Meir, *A Land of Our Own*, 240.
25. Meir, *My Life*, 459–460.

Further Reading

FRASER, NICHOLAS, and MARYSA NAVARRO. *Eva Perón*. New York: W. W. Norton, 1980. The most balanced treatment of her life to date.

MEIR, GOLDA. *My Life*. New York: Putnam's Sons, 1975. Popular autobiography; gives readers a good look at her personality.

PERÓN, EVA DUARTE DE. *My Mission in Life*, Trans. ETHEL CHERRY. New York: Vantage Press, 1953. Although much of this was ghost-written for Evita and changed by her husband, it shows how she wished to be seen and also serves as an excellent example of Peronist propaganda.

SYRKIN, MARIE. *Golda Meir, Israel's Leader*. New York: Putnam's Sons, 1969. Clear, written by a friend a decade before Meir died.

CHAPTER 12

M. K. Gandhi and Ho Chi Minh: Paths to Independence

When you wish to get foreign rulers to leave your country, which approach is best—violent or nonviolent resistance? Could Gandhi's approach have worked elsewhere?

The contrast between these men and their respective challenges is a striking one. Mohandas Karamchand Gandhi (1869–1948) led a large, religiously inspired, non-violent resistance movement against the British government of India in the 1920s and 1930s. The British ended nearly 200 years of political and economic domination of India peacefully in 1947, in part because of the work of Gandhi and in part because economic conditions at that time dictated a reduction of the "burdens" of empire.

At the same time the British were leaving India, the French were making a desperate military attempt to retain control of the colonial possessions they had held in Indochina since 1885. Ho Chi Minh (1890–1969), communist president of the Democratic Republic of Vietnam established in northern Vietnam in 1945, used violent resistance to defeat the French between 1946 and 1954. The struggle continued in the 1960s, when the Americans sent up to half a million troops to Vietnam at one point in support of the anticommunist South Vietnamese government. Ho Chi Minh died before the last American troops left Vietnam in 1973 and before DRV or North Vietnamese troops conquered the regime in the south in 1975.

Ho Chi Minh was honored posthumously when the capital of the former South Vietnam, Saigon, was renamed Ho Chi Minh City in 1975. Gandhi lived long enough to see the British leave India and was disappointed with the results. The Indian subcontinent was split into separate Hindu and Muslim nations. Fifteen million people fled in fear in order to relocate themselves in either Hindu India or Muslim Pakistan. Several million died from riots, civil war, and disease. Gandhi saw this as betrayal of at least three of his cherished beliefs: nonviolent action to bring about change, Hindu-Muslim "unity in diversity" in India, and the basic goodness of humanity. It may be ironic that Ho, who used violence to free his country, died of a heart attack in 1969, while Gandhi, the man of nonviolence, was assassinated by a Hindu fanatic on January 1948.

Mohandas Gandhi (called the Mahatma, or "Great-Souled One" by his followers) saw himself primarily as a moral teacher for whom the political arena was only one of many places where a person should serve Truth.

Ho Chi Minh (born Nguyen Sinh Cung[1]) saw himself primarily as a man struggling for the independence and unification of his country. For him, questions of morality or theory, even those connected with the Marxist philosophy to which he committed himself, were secondary.

Gandhi wanted Indians to achieve political independence and, more important to him, spiritual maturity through the use of *satyagraha*, or "truth-force." He refused aid, especially military aid, from outsiders. Ho, on the other hand, did not hesitate to accept large amounts of military economic aid from both China and Russia in order to battle the French and Americans.

However, despite these personal and political differences, Gandhi and Ho Chi Minh had two things in common, both important in any independence movement. Despite their disclaimers, both were popular, even charismatic[2] leaders. Each became a personal inspiration to those wishing freedom from foreign rule. Second, these men were the first in their respective countries to bring the rural masses into political life through careful, shrewd organization. Gandhi and Ho embodied, respectively, Indian and Vietnamese nationalism. The fact that each did so, while being so different from the other, and living in social and political settings that were quite different, illustrates the adaptability and appeal of nationalism during the twentieth century.

Little in Gandhi's early life, except his mother's religiosity, suggested he would be the leader he later became. Young Mohandas seemed "to have little ability and less talent." He was shy, afraid of being ridiculed by others, and a "mediocre student."[3] Gandhi was impressed by his mother's frequent fasts for self-purification, her daily prayer, and her strict prohibitions against smoking, drinking, and eating meat. Putlibai's moral influence on her son's life was significant. Even as a boy, Gandhi was scrupulous about truth. He refused to cheat on a spelling test, even when his teacher gave him permission by pointing to the correct answer on a neighbor's paper (the teacher wanted to impress a visiting British school inspector with his bright students).[4]

Despite his conscientiousness, Gandhi's academic record improved little. His arranged marriage at age thirteen did not help. He was jealous of his wife, Kasturbai, and for a number of years "their life jerked along through a series of tiffs and sulks." By the time he took an entrance examination for Bombay University, his score was 247.5 out of a possible 625.[5] It was also during this time, at age sixteen, that Gandhi had a traumatic experience in association with his father's death. On the night his father died, Gandhi left his father's bedside temporarily to indulge in "animal passion" with his wife. A messenger soon told him that his father had died. In his autobiography, Gandhi recalled this lapse of duty as "a blot I have never been able to efface or forget." To make his guilt feelings worse, Kasturbai was very pregnant at the time, and the child died soon after birth. All this, psychologists tell us, helps explain Gandhi's later decision to abstain from sex altogether. And that decision influenced Gandhi's politics.[6]

Meanwhile, Gandhi, with family urging, settled upon the career of a lawyer. Since legal training could be more easily obtained in London, Gandhi set sail for England in September 1888 after getting his mother's permission and taking a vow to stay away from wine, women, and meat while abroad. His wife and young son stayed at home. It was during three years in London, and as a direct result of his vegetarian vow, that Gandhi began to come alive, intellectually and spiritually. He discovered that English vegetarians could argue a case for avoiding meat which was far more logical than his mother's simple religious prohibition. He also discovered the classic Indian religious work, the *Bhagavad-Gita*, in English translation, and he encountered a number of Western advocates of Eastern ideas. In short, he began to discover the East through the West and to create a philosophy of life that tempered Eastern ideas with a Western sense of precisely how to apply those ideas.

Upon returning to India in 1891, Gandhi's new inner determination was revealed as a result of two insults he suffered. On one occasion, he went to a British official in Kathiawar (his home province in western India) to plead on behalf of his brother; when he insisted on presenting a case that the Englishman did not wish to hear, he was unceremoniously thrown out of the office. In April 1893, Gandhi was hired by some Muslims in his home city of Porbandar to do some legal work for their firm in South Africa. Shortly after his arrival in this white-ruled colony, Gandhi was thrown out of a first-class train compartment just because he was "coloured."[7] These two incidents crystallized his desire to become a reformer and fight injustice.

That fight would keep Gandhi in South Africa until 1914. At first, he followed traditional political methods such as collecting names on a petition when the government of the province of Natal tried to deny the vote to Indians.[8] After 1904, however, Gandhi's personal and political style began to change. At that time, he took up communal living on a farm he bought near Johannesburg. Several years later, he adopted (without consulting his wife) the Hindu practice of brahmacharya, or complete sexual abstinence. In 1906, Gandhi coined the word *satyagraha*, or "truth-force," to describe a new type of nonviolent resistance to the government that the Indians tried to stop a Registration Act that would make them second-class citizens.

Satyagraha involves selective non-violent law-breaking by large numbers of people. As Gandhi explained this idea, it was not mere pacifism or a clever political tactic. It was, rather, a way of confronting Truth within oneself by deciding to take a stand on a clear moral issue. It was also a way of forcing one's opponent to confront Truth by allowing oneself to be arrested or even beaten after breaking an unjust law. Gandhi believed that such actions could lead to the conversion of one's political opponent and that such conversion was more important than political success or failure. "Satyagraha," he wrote, "postulates the conquest of the adversary by suffering in one's own person."[9]

Although Gandhi's personal philosophy, and especially his belief in satyagraha, was fully formed by the time he returned to India from South Africa in 1914, he was not yet anti-British or even an advocate of Indian independence. He still believed in the British empire and even recruited for the British army in 1918. That would soon change. When the British government refused to restore civil liberties that had been curtailed during the war, Gandhi asked Indians to engage in a kind of economic sit-down strike (hartal) and to combine this with selective civil disobedience. The hartal was a success, but some outbreaks of violence caused Gandhi to call off the satyagraha campaign in April 1919 and a smaller one planned for 1922. More serious than Indian violence, however, was the killing of 379 unarmed civilians by a British general in Amritsar (troops fired 1,650 rounds, and there were 1,516 casualties).[10] The Amritsar massacre in 1919 led Gandhi to proclaim a policy of "non-cooperation" with the British government of India. The keynote of this campaign, which urged people to boycott all British goods, honors, and services, including courts, schools, and jobs, was a seven-month tour of the country by Gandhi. During what seemed to some like revival meetings, he urged peasants and others attending his speeches to spin their own clothes and called spinning a "sacrament." Gandhi would then ask people to place any foreign-made clothing they were wearing in a huge pile. Sometimes there were a few naked people in the crowd; always there was a match to light the bonfire. The fires symbolized both Indian economic dependence on the British and a growing determination to end that dependence.

Gandhi's advocacy of the spinning wheel was most important, however, as a way of communicating with the millions of Indian peasants. Like his adoption of a simple cloth garment instead of European clothes, it was Gandhi's way of identifying with the poor and creating a bridge between the Indian masses and their leaders. While he intended these actions as forms of communal spiritual uplift, there is no doubt that they were also politically astute. Gandhi was the first Indian political leader to cultivate the peasants by living with them and making sure that the political organization he headed (the Indian National Congress) held its annual meetings in rural areas.

By 1929, demands for complete independence from Britain were growing among Indian leaders. Gandhi returned to the headlines by organizing what became known as the Great Salt March. In what history records as his "finest hour," Gandhi walked 241 miles in twenty-four days, collecting praise from the peasants and a crowd of several thousand. "We march in the name of God," Gandhi said, promising to "give a signal to the nation" when he arrived at the sea. On the beach at Dandi, the Mahatma defied the British rulers of India (who had a monopoly on the production and sale of salt) by picking up a handful of salt from the beach while one of his followers cried, "Hail, Deliverer." It was a moment, in the words of Gandhi's biographer, Louis Fischer, that required "imagination, dignity, and the sense of showmanship of a great artist."[11] And it worked. All across India, peasants began defying the British, wading into the ocean, and producing salt. The British, of course, had to arrest them, even though many English people themselves thought the salt monopoly just the sort of silly law that a revolutionary could exploit.

As a result of this protest, Gandhi went to jail, where he stayed, off and on, for several years. During this time, he displayed his seriousness as a religious reformer within his own community by undertaking a fast—which almost killed him—to convince Hindus to change their attitude toward the outcasts, or "untouchables." For centuries, this group of people was considered religiously unclean and fit only for the most degrading chores. Gandhi called them "Harijan," or "Children of God," and wished to see a Hindu change of heart that would see them as equal. His fast resulted in the beginnings of such a change. Long-term changes were less dramatic, but, at the time, no one wanted the death of the Mahatma on his or her conscience.

Gandhi undertook this and other fasts during his life out of love and, like satyagraha, as a way to change the hearts of his opponents. He claimed that he did not fast in order to coerce people to come to terms, yet that is exactly how most ordinary people saw the situation. Before his death, Gandhi had fasted a total of 138 days, thirty-five against untouchability, twenty-nine for Hindu-Muslim unity, twenty-eight as penance for a comrade's moral lapse, and eighteen in repentance for a violent action committed by others.[12] In this area, as in many others, Gandhi was the "practical idealist," the holy man whom the politicians feared.

If we accept the sincerity of Gandhi's search for Truth, a search which led him to advocate strict nonviolence "in thought, word, and deed," we can appreciate his bitter disappointment during the last months of his life, when Hindus and Muslims began to kill one another. Gandhi was not able to hold his people together, but he was still the Mahatma. As he walked through the strife-torn villages, talking and praying from both Hindu and Muslim scriptures, people often did stop fighting—at least temporarily. His last fast in New Delhi brought Hindu and Muslim leaders in India together—again, temporarily—several weeks before his death, which was mourned by members of all faiths in India.

Despite his personal disappointments, Gandhi can be congratulated on his success in freeing his country from foreign rule, whatever the problems that followed. It took the Vietnamese, after all, a full generation longer to get the foreigners out after World War II. Of course, they suffered by having the less "liberal" French as their colonial rulers; they were also hindered by the fact that those most able to free Vietnam were communists. This meant that the fight against Vietnamese independence could be turned into an anti-communist war. That the Vietnamese succeeded in creating an independent nation-state in Southeast Asia is a tribute to Ho Chi Minh, a man who gave himself the following "advice" in a poem written while in a Chinese prison during World War II:

Without the cold and desolation of winter
There could not be the warmth and splendor of spring.
Calamity has tempered and hardened me,
And turned my mind into steel.[13]

If Gandhi was a man whose adult life was guided by a persistent search for Truth and a desire to teach the ways of Truth-seeking to others, the life of Ho Chi Minh was dominated from early childhood by the pride of a revolutionary willing to use whatever means were necessary to free his country from colonial rule. The region where he was born, Nghe Tinh, along the central coast near the Gulf of Tonkin, was famous as a haven for revolutionaries, and Ho's father, Nguyen Sinh Sac, was himself a patriotic dissenter who lost his government job in 1907 for displaying anti-French sympathies. Ho's psychological development, like that of Gandhi, was influenced by his relationship with his father, who gave the boy something to revolt against by leading an irresponsible life while Ho was growing up. In particular, Nguyen Sinh Sac once left ten-year-old Ho at home alone with his mother, who was about to have a child. When Ho's mother died while his father was gone, we can assume the experience might have created both guilt feelings and anger in the young boy.[14] By becoming a nationalist revolutionary, Ho could express his rebellion against his authority-figure father and remain true to his father's dislike of the French.

Modern revolutionaries, especially those in poor colonies, usually have to travel abroad to secure part of their training. After attending high school in the city of Hue, Ho taught for a few months before signing on as part of the kitchen crew of a French passenger liner. He spent two years at sea, visiting ports in North Africa,

Europe, and even the United States, where he later claimed to have been impressed by the rights enjoyed by citizens of New York's Chinatown. During World War I, Ho lived in London, earning money by working as a gardener, washing dishes, and shoveling snow.[15] From 1917 to 1923, he lived in France, getting to know French people who were not as brutal as the colonizers he knew in Indochina, and trying to connect his recent experiences as a proletarian [Marxist term for members of the landless urban working class] with his desire for national independence for his people. Ho became a respected member of the French Socialist Party, founded and edited a newspaper, *La Paria (The Outcast)*, and wrote a bitter pamphlet denouncing the economic and human cost of French colonialism, especially in Indochina. An interesting theme of his early articles is his repeated contention that the French were poisoning the Vietnamese by forcing them to use opium and alcohol in order to enrich French businesspeople.[16]

While in France, Ho was given a copy of Lenin's "Thesis on the National and Colonial Questions." It convinced him, he wrote later, that only the communists were really serious about freeing colonial peoples. He became a founding member of the French Communist Party and, in late 1923, traveled to Moscow. There he studied, wrote articles for *Pravda*, a leading Communist paper, and became an active and respected member of the Comintern, an agency established to promote revolutions outside Russia. For the next fifteen years, Ho travelled through Asia, organizing revolutionary groups, dodging arrest, and serving as official Comintern spokesman at international meetings. It was also during these years that Ho began to develop his relationship with the peasants. He lived simply among them; much like Gandhi, he stressed the importance of hygiene and education and got along very well with children. After World War II, Ho cultivated this image of simplicity, especially in dealings with Westerners. One French journalist who interviewed him in 1946 commented on "the disarming gaze of a Franciscan Gandhi." Another French official, who had to work out an agreement with Ho, referred to his "prestige and popularity in the eyes of the people" and added that he had no doubt Ho "had aspirations . . . of becoming the Gandhi of Indochina."[17]

However, if Ho wished to suggest a similarity with Gandhi based upon their shared concern for the poor, their popularity, and their determination to put up with hardship (all of which was true), it is also certain that Ho did not want to be a Gandhi. As early as 1922, he had written an article contrasting the brutality of French rule in Indochina with the relative mildness of British rule in India and Ireland. "The Gandhis and the De Valeras [Irish leader] would have long since entered heaven had they been born in one of the French colonies," he wrote. Necessity made Ho Chi Minh less of a spiritual leader of his people and more of a dedicated anti-colonialist and nationalist who used communist ideology and skillful organization as the means to his end—a united Vietnam. For Gandhi, both the means (non-violence) and the end (Truth) were different.

Of course, their enemies were also different. While the British were willing to leave India at the end of World War II, the French, who had been replaced by the Japanese as rulers in Indochina during World War II, wanted to retain their colony after the Japanese left. At the end of the war, Ho's guerrilla forces took control in the north and proclaimed Vietnamese independence. Ho apparently believed that he might be able to convince the French to leave, and he tried to make it easier for them by downplaying his communism. The French, however, refused to end colonial rule and gambled on a war to suppress the Viet-minh revolutionaries, as Ho's men were called. They lost. An eight-year struggle ended in 1954, when a major French fortress at Dien Bien Phu was captured by the communists. An agreement that year divided the country, leaving Ho's Democratic Republic of Vietnam in charge in the north and calling for elections in two years to establish a single government for Vietnam. Ho's problems with the French were over; difficulties with the Americans were to follow.

In the final months of World War II, Ho's relations with Americans had been reasonably good. A downed American airman who worked with Ho for several months in 1945 reported that he was "an awfully sweet guy." Ho wrote letters to President Truman in 1945 and 1946, asking for aid against the French, and some Americans believed later that Ho could have developed as an "independent" communist leader, such as Marshall Tito did in Yugoslavia.[18] Truman thought otherwise, opted for a tough line against communists everywhere after 1947, and by 1950 (after the Korean war began) had supplied the French with $4 billion of aid to fight their war in Indochina. By 1954, the United States was paying 78 percent of the French war bill in Vietnam, more than the percentage of external aid Ho was receiving from his Russian and Chinese supporters.[19] Ho Chi Minh's communist-led independence movement became, by the 1950s, the target of American policy makers bent on containing communism in Asia.

This fact, combined with Ho's continued determination to drive out the foreigners and unify the country, perhaps made inevitable the events of the next twenty years. The United States supported a decision to cancel the 1956 elections, which Ho would probably have won, and instead sponsored an anti-communist state, the Republic of Vietnam, in the southern half of the country. Within a few years, Ho's government was supplying communist-led guerrillas operating in the south (the Viet Cong). Although the government of South Vietnam remained weaker than the one in the north, the weight of American military power, applied through bombing of North Vietnam and large-scale American troop deployments in the south after 1965, was sufficient to delay a final victory by Ho's troops until 1975. Faced with widespread domestic protests against the war and a substantial death toll in a guerrilla war against an elusive enemy, the American government withdrew its troops from Vietnam in 1973.

Ho Chi Minh combined nationalism with communist ideology. Whether that made his struggle for independence and unification of his country more difficult or easier after 1945 is difficult to say. Aid from other communist countries helped him sustain his struggle, yet had he not been a communist, he might have avoided a long struggle with the Americans. Of course, had the French been less intransigent, he might not have seen communism as the best response to colonial exploitation.

Mohandas K. Gandhi combined his nationalism with a search for moral Truth for himself and his people. One scholar noted that young Gandhi himself has suffered from the British definition of courage, which defines this virtue in largely military terms. He, therefore, called the attention of Indians to their own tradition of courage, which often defines it in non-aggressive terms, as a moral quality which allows a person to suffer pain without striking back, something we might call an Indian version of "turning the other cheek."[20] Whether that made his struggle against the British longer or shorter, harder or easier, is difficult to know. Gandhi could have called for a full-scale war of independence against the British in 1922 or 1931 after the salt tax protests. Because such a conflict would certainly have been violent, Gandhi refused to approve such a struggle. He withdrew on both occasions, to jail or to his ashram, until such time as the people would be spiritually more mature and able to practice satyagraha wholeheartedly. That day never came. When the British finally left peacefully in 1947, Hindus and Muslims resorted to violence against each other to achieve their respective national goals.

It is intriguing to ask what might have been: had Ho tried nonviolence, had Gandhi accepted violence, had Ho not been communist, had the Americans not been so anti-communist, had ruthlessness against opponents been a sustained instead of an incidental British policy in India.

Regardless of their considerable differences, these two men were genuine national leaders. Despite talk of a "shrinking world" common among twentieth-century journalists and scholars, our planet was culturally varied enough for people to respond to satyagraha in one part of Asia and to sustained guerrilla warfare in another. On one thing people of differing convictions in these countries and elsewhere can agree: however well or badly the Indians or Vietnamese might have been in their respective struggles, their independence movements took the form they did largely because of the actions and beliefs of these charismatic leaders. India and Vietnam are today quite different than either Gandhi or Ho Chi Minh might have expected. But they are fully independent nations, each with some status in its part of Asia, and in the world. That is something of which Gandhi and Ho Chi Minh would have been very proud.

Notes

1. For a list of Ho Chi Minh's twenty aliases, including information on when and where he used each, see James Pinckney Harrison, *The Endless War: Fifty Years of Struggle in Vietnam* (New York: Free Press/ Macmillan, 1982), 38. To simplify matters, he will simply be called Ho Chi Minh (He Who Enlightens) throughout this chapter.
2. While this word has a specific religious meaning, it is used here in its social-political sense, as that "rare personal quality that attributed to leaders who arouse fervent popular devotion and enthusiasm." See *American Heritage Dictionary of the English Language,* 3rd ed. (Boston: Houghton Mifflin, 1992), 322.
3. Louis Fischer, *Gandhi: His Life and Message for the World* (New York: Mentor, 1954), 9–10.
4. Geoffrey Ashe, *Gandhi* (New York: Stein and Day, 1968), 6–7.

5. Ashe, *Gandhi*, 9, 14.
6. Mohandas K. Gandhi, *An Autobiography: The Story of My Experiments with Truth* (Boston: Beacon Press, 1957), 30–31; see E. Victor Wolfenstein, *The Revolutionary Personality: Lenin, Trotsky, Gandhi* (Princeton: Princeton University Press, 1967), 73–88; Erik H. Erikson, *Gandhi's Truth: On the Origins of Militant Nonviolence* (New York: W. W. Norton, 1960).
7. Gandhi, *Autobiography*, 97–99, 111–112; at about the time Gandhi arrived, the South African provinces of the British empire were ruled by six hundred thousand whites outnumbered by 2 million blacks and sixty-five thousand Indians. See Fischer, *Gandhi: Life and Message*, 22–25.
8. Ashe, *Gandhi*, 59.
9. Ibid., 100–103; M. K. Gandhi, *Satyagraha in South Africa*, translated from the Gujarati by V. G. Desai, rev. 2d ed. (Ahmedabad, India: Navajivan Publishing House, 1950), 102–107, 113–114.
10. Fischer, *Gandhi: Life and Message*, 66.
11. Ibid., 98–99.
12. T. K. Mahadevan, *Gandhi My Refrain: Controversial Essays: 1950–1972* (Bombay: Popular Prakashan, 1973), 196.
13. Ho Chi Minh, *The Prison Diary of Ho Chi Minh*, trans. Aileen Palmer, introduction by Harrison E. Salisbury (New York: Bantam, 1971), 28.
14. Jean Lacouture, *Ho Chi Minh: A Political Biography*, translated from French by Peter Wiles (New York: Random House, 1968), 6–15; David G. Marr, *Vietnamese Anticolonialism, 1885–1925* (Berkeley: University of California Press, 1971), 254–255.
15. Lacouture, *Ho Chi Minh*, 17–20; Bernard Fall, *The Two Viet-Nams: A Political and Military Analysis*, 2d rev. ed. (New York: Frederick A. Praeger, 1967), 85; Charles Fenn, *Ho Chi Minh: A Biographical Introduction* (New York: Charles Scribner's Sons, 1973), 26.
16. Ho Chi Minh, *On Revolution: Selected Writings, 1920–1966*, edited with an introduction by Bernard Fall (New York: Frederick A. Praeger, 1967), see 68–123 for his pamphlet on French colonialism and his references to opium and alcohol on 4, 19, 69, 76–79, 144.
17. Lacouture, *Ho Chi Minh*, 124–126; see also 148, 175, 217.
18. Robert Shaplen, "The Enigma of Ho Chi Minh," *The Reporter* (January 1955): 11–13; Harrison, *The Endless War*, 92, 97; Fenn, *Ho Chi Minh*, 84; Bernard Fall, *Viet-Nam Witness, 1953–1966* (New York: Frederick A. Praeger, 1966), 7–8.
19. Harrison, *Endless War*, 117.
20. Susanne Hoeber Rudolph, "The New Courage: An Essay on Gandhi's Psychology," in *Modern India: An Interpretive Anthology*, ed. Thomas R. Metcalf (New Delhi: Sterling Publishers Private Limited, 1990), 323–341.

Further Reading

FISCHER, LOUIS. *Gandhi: His Life and Message for the World.* New York: New American Library, 1954). Short, easy to read. A major film was based on this work.

GANDHI M. K., *Selected Writings.* Selected and edited by Ronald Duncan. New York: Harper and Row, 1972. Best short collection.

HARRISON, JAMES PINCKNEY. *The Endless War: Fifty Years of Struggle in Vietnam.* New York: Macmillan/Free Press, 1982. Good overall picture of this long, complicated conflict.

LACOUTURE, JEAN. *Ho Chi Minh: A Political Biography.* New York: Random House, 1968. An insider's account, interesting and readable.

CHAPTER 13

Teller and Sakharov: Scientists in Politics

What are the political implications of major technological developments? How did the careers of these two "fathers of the H-bomb" differ, and what does this tell us about their respective societies?

It was early on the morning of July 16, 1945. The first atomic bomb had just been detonated in the New Mexico desert. After congratulating themselves on the success of the test, the American scientists boarded the bus which would take them back to their laboratory at Los Alamos. One of them, Edward Teller, turned to take a last look and saw that "the desert winds had shaped the mushroom cloud into a giant question mark."[1]

That question mark, which began our age of nuclear weapons, is an important part of twentieth-century world history. The "small" atomic bombs that destroyed the Japanese cities of Hiroshima and Nagasaki in 1945, bringing World War II to an end, were soon replaced by much larger weapons. Between 1951 and 1954, the Soviet Union and the United States each developed "super" bombs, thermonuclear hydrogen weapons. The first hydrogen bomb, or H-bomb, exploded by the United States on October 31, 1952, was twenty-five times more powerful than the atomic bomb dropped on Hiroshima; it destroyed the entire Pacific island of Elugelab, one mile in diameter. Less than a year later, the Soviets tested their own H-bombs.

These developments accelerated the nuclear arms race that lay at the heart of the "Cold War" between the Soviet Union and the United States from 1945 to the collapse of the USSR in 1991. This nuclear contest formed the backdrop for all actions on the international political stage. During that period, the original 1945 question mark appeared again and again: in novels and movies about nuclear "holocaust," in the many attempts at disarmament by the "superpowers" since the 1950s, and in the frequent protests against nuclear weapons that filled newspapers and television screens from the 1960s through the 1980s.

Given the magnitude of nuclear power, it is not surprising that it is difficult to discuss its possible effects rationally. The problem of nuclear weapons, like all other problems discussed in this book, can be better understood if given a human face. In the case of the H-bomb, the human face is really two faces, those of the American and Russian "fathers of the H-bomb," Edward Teller (1908–2003), the man who first saw the question mark—and his Russian counterpart, Andrei D. Sakharov (1921–1989).

Perhaps it is appropriate that such a crucial development in human history should have two fathers. Both of these men were brilliant physicists. But they were more than that. Following the perfection of an operational, or "deliverable," hydrogen bomb, both Teller and Sakharov increasingly turned their attention to the broader political questions raised by their scientific work. As national heroes for a time, both were in a position to give advice to their governments. Both favored a balance in weapons between the USSR and the United States as a prelude to disarmament, and both pushed for peaceful development of nuclear energy. Otherwise, their paths, like their societies, were different.

Teller pushed for the development of the H-bomb in order to keep up with the Russians; this made him a hero to most Americans and the subject of a *Time* magazine cover story in 1957. A decade later, Andrei Sakharov began his career as a famous Soviet "dissident" when he publicly criticized the closed society and totalitarian government of the Soviet Union. Until late in his life, his many public statements urging greater democracy within the USSR, freedom of thought, free emigration, and arms reduction made him appear a traitor to the government and to many people in the Soviet Union. He lived in "internal exile" in the city of Gorky, guarded by police and kept away from his colleagues and the Western press until freed in December 1986 as part of Premier Mikhail Gorbachev's new policy of "glasnost," or "openness."

Despite their different political careers, Teller and Sakharov's distinct views on the social responsibility of scientists illuminate the fears that beset those who created the nuclear age. Their lives also shed light on "political" scientists in the United States and the Soviet Union, the nations that sustained the nuclear arms race for forty-five years.

Edward Teller was born in Budapest, Hungary, to a lawyer father and a musician mother who was overprotective to the point of tying a string to Edward and his sister when they went swimming. Although his early genius in mathematics irritated his fellow students, his life was more seriously affected by political disorder in Hungary after World War I. An inept Communist government, which lasted a year, was followed by an antisemitic regime which made it necessary for Teller, a Jew, to leave his homeland in order to succeed as a physicist. The political disorder in Hungary during his youth and his family's suffering at the hands of a Communist government in 1919 and again after 1945 helped make him an advocate of "conservative capitalism and a strong military establishment." Years later, he recalled that he "had seen, in Hungary, at least one society that was once healthy go completely to the dogs. I have seen the consequences of a lost war."[3]

During the late 1920s, when Teller was studying physics in Germany, people such as Albert Einstein, Werner Heisenberg, Max Planck, and Niels Bohr were revolutionizing that science by challenging ideas about matter and energy that had been unquestioned since the work of Isaac Newton in the seventeenth century. In 1934, after teaching for several years in Germany, Teller used a Rockefeller Foundation scholarship to study with Niels Bohr in Copenhagen. There he met George Gamow, who invited the newly married Teller to teach with him at George Washington University in Washington, D.C., in 1935. There the Tellers settled down to what they thought would be the quiet life of a professor of theoretical physics.[4]

That hope died in January 1939, when American physicists discovered that German scientists had split the atomic nucleus in December 1938. Within months, physicists around the world understood that the center, or nucleus, of certain atoms could be bombarded with neutrons. This process could lead to a chain reaction, releasing incredible amounts of energy. The trick was to control such a nuclear reaction. Whoever did so first could possess a weapon of immense destructive force. At this time, Germany was ruled by Adolf Hitler, and World War II was only months away.

All of this caused leading American physicists, many of them refugees from Nazi Germany, to push the American government into a serious program of atomic research. After initial disinterest on the part of the military, a famous letter from Albert Einstein to President Franklin Roosevelt stimulated the beginning of an American effort to produce a nuclear chain reaction. After America entered World War II, this effort, known as the Manhattan Project, accelerated and, on December 2, 1942, the first "sustained nuclear chain reaction" was achieved in a laboratory under the football stadium at the University of Chicago.[5] From then on, it was only a matter of time until the first bomb was created in 1945.

The tension between science and politics appeared in Edward Teller's life during these years in the form of two issues. The first was the decision of President Truman to use the new bomb against Japanese cities in order to end the war more quickly and to impress the Soviet Union with U.S. power. In the summer of 1945, some scientists began to circulate a petition asking that the bomb not be used without first warning the Japanese. Teller and some others who favored a demonstration project rather than a drop on a population center refused to circulate the petition at Los Alamos. He had checked with his boss, J. Robert Oppenheimer, who told Teller that he did not think scientists should make "political pronouncements." In a letter to Leo Szilard, the friend who had asked him to circulate the petition, Teller consoled himself by writing that perhaps "actual combat-use" of this terrible new weapon might be the best way to get the facts about nuclear power to the people, who were the ones—in a democracy—who should control its use. In the same letter, Teller suggested scientists were not responsible for political decisions when he wrote, "I feel that I should do the wrong thing if I tried to say how to tie the little toe of the ghost to the bottle from which we just helped it escape."[6] This point he would repeat in the years to come.

A second, more strictly scientific issue which soon involved Teller directly in politics was the possibility of building the "super," or hydrogen, bomb. As early as 1941, he had become fascinated with the idea of capturing the energy of the sun by creating a chain reaction through "fusion" [creating energy by joining several light nuclei to create a heavier nucleus] rather than "fission" [the process of splitting the nucleus used in atomic weapons]. Work on this new super-weapon was opposed by Oppenheimer and most other physicists at the end of World War II. They believed that it would be many years before any other country could develop atomic weapons; Teller alone was realistic about the USSR. He was motivated not by any inside information about the state of Soviet science but by his intense personal distrust of communism. He was proved right when the Soviets exploded their first atomic bomb— called "Joe One" by the Americans—in 1949. Even after that, scientists advising the Atomic Energy Commission (AEC) recommended against work on a hydrogen bomb for moral reasons. Teller pushed the project with the help of Lewis Strauss, member and later chairman of the AEC, and Senator Brien McMahon, chairman of the Joint Congressional Committee on Atomic Energy. It was not until January 31, 1950, that President Truman instructed the AEC to "continue its work on all forms of atomic weapons, including the so-called hydrogen or super bomb."[7] Teller was not only the principal scientific inventor of the hydrogen bomb but also the man whose political activities pushed the American government to develop it. For both of these reasons, he is rightly seen as the "father" of the American H-bomb. After J. Robert Oppenheimer, the man who had chaired the General Advisory Committee that recommended against the H-bomb project, lost his security clearance in 1954 because of past association with communists and errors of judgment that frightened many people during the cold war, Teller became a hero to many Americans. He "hurried the H-bomb," in the words of *Newsweek; Life* magazine embarrassed him by calling the project "Dr. Edward Teller's Magnificent Obsession."[8]

Although he claimed to dislike the publicity that followed his scientific success, Edward Teller thrust himself into the spotlight repeatedly over the next forty years. His public comments have been lonely and controversial ones, ranging from his statement at the 1954 Oppenheimer security hearings that he did not fully trust Oppenheimer, to his 1983 support of President Reagan's plan for a missile defense system for America based on laser and particle-beam technology.[9] Both of these positions, and quite a few he took in between, including his opposition to the 1963 treaty banning nuclear tests in the atmosphere, earned him the enmity of most fellow scientists, who tended to be much more liberal politically than Teller.

However, given Teller's position as a conservative advocate of a strong defense policy, it is interesting that he repeatedly stated that science and politics should be kept quite separate. "The scientist is not responsible for the laws of nature," he wrote in an article addressed to fellow scientists in 1950, urging them to work with him on the hydrogen bomb project. "It is his job to find out how these laws operate . . . to find ways in which these laws can serve the human will." Teller stressed that it was "not the scientist's job to determine whether a hydrogen bomb should be constructed, whether it should be used, or how it should be used. This responsibility rests with the American public and their chosen representatives."[10]

However, in this same article, Teller added that, speaking "as a citizen," he was sure that President Truman had made the correct decision when he ordered the AEC to build an H-bomb. After all, Teller wrote in a remark that was clearly political, we were in a situation "not less dangerous than the one we were facing in 1939 . . . . We must realize that mere plans are not yet bombs, and . . . democracy will not be saved by ideals alone." In other articles written by or about him in the 1950s, Teller returned to his earlier point that scientists have no "special insights into public affairs"; the "person who makes the bombs is not quite the proper person to know what to do with them." Scientists should remain true to the tradition which urged them to "explore the limits of human achievement." Teller was "confident that, whatever the scientists are able to discover or invent, the people will be good enough and wise enough to control for the benefit of everyone."[11]

Over the years, Teller's confidence in the wisdom of the people seemed to diminish, blurring the line—always a thin one—that separated Teller the scientist from Teller the political figure. In 1957 and 1958, he strongly advocated the peaceful uses of "clean" nuclear energy. In one essay, he tried to dispel growing fears of radioactive fallout from nuclear explosions, comparing the danger from such explosions to the "equivalent of smoking one cigarette every two months."

By 1968, Teller and other scientists working on "Project Plowshare" had devised many industrial and scientific uses for nuclear explosives. These included geo-thermal heat production, mining, canal building, and even the construction of highways.[12] Perhaps Teller's opposition to the nuclear test-ban treaty of 1963 indicated most clearly that he was not, in the final analysis, willing to trust "the people" to be "good enough and wise enough" to control nuclear weapons in ways he believed best. "If we renounce nuclear weapons, we open the door to aggression," he stated flatly in 1958. At the congressional hearings on the treaty in the summer of 1963, he went further, calling the test-ban treaty "possibly a step toward war," because it would reduce America's defense against a missile attack—an area in which he was convinced the Russians were ahead.[13]

Teller's sympathetic biographers tell us that while he has been universally respected as a scientist, his performance in the "political theater, where he has been pursuing his scientific goals," finds the audience divided, some cheering and some booing. But Edward Teller pursued not only scientific goals in the political arena, as he did to get the H-bomb built, but also political goals in the political arena. Some of these—for example, particle-beam technology—require scientific work. Teller's apparent difficulty in taking his own advice to make "clear-cut distinctions" between scientific and political questions might account for the fact that he remained, according to his biographers, "a strangely restless and vaguely unhappy man, seemingly traveling about the earth in the quest of some elusive and formless Holy Grail."[14]

Perhaps that lofty but elusive goal Edward Teller sought is a world in which scientists and statesmen from all countries work together to create a peaceful, prosperous planet. Teller's early support for an end to secrecy and for an international control agency for atomic weapons and research suggests this as his goal. If so, his Russian counterpart, Andrei Dmitriyevich Sakharov, was in full agreement. Sakharov's courageous and persistent criticism of the Soviet totalitarian government for more than fifteen years made him a near-martyr in the cause of human freedom. The fact that his political activity pleased liberal intellectuals as much as Teller's dismayed them makes it difficult to see some of the similarities between the views of these two men. At the very least, both were fully aware of how modern science is closely tied to the very unscientific judgments of politicians.

A year before his death, Andrei Sakharov was called "the most admired man of science since Einstein" but also "the conscience of the Soviet people" and "a folk hero for the times."[15] His career began with much less fanfare. A "thin, blond, shy" student, Sakharov graduated from the University of Moscow in 1942 with a record of scientific achievement good enough to exempt him from the army at a time when the USSR was still reeling from Hitler's attack, begun a year earlier. For the rest of the war, Sakharov worked as an engineer at a large arms factory, where his inventions increased arms production. From 1945 to 1947, this son of a physics teacher and a piano player did graduate work in physics at the Lebedev Physical Institute in Moscow, earning a doctorate before being assigned in 1948 to the research group that would develop thermonuclear weapons.

"I found myself," Sakharov recalled twenty-five years later, "in an extraordinary position of material privilege and isolated from the people." For his top secret weapons research in Turkmenia, Sakharov was paid the equivalent of $27,000 annually, high even in the United States in the early 1950s. He was also given special bodyguards and a chauffeur, as well as access to special food and housing. All of this must have been heady wine for a scientist in his twenties who was convinced his work was "essential" to protect his country and to establish a worldwide military equilibrium. Sakharov's work was successful. He was largely responsible for the fact that the Russians caught up with the Americans within three years, exploding their first H-bomb in 1955.

Sakharov's key role in the development of the H-bomb earned him further awards. He was elected a full member of the Soviet Academy of Sciences in 1953, an honor unprecedented for one his age. On three other occasions, he was awarded the title of "Hero of Socialist Labor." Despite these honors, Sakharov became increasingly troubled by some of the moral implications of his work. He noticed that many of the people with whom he worked were talented but cynical, and his uneasiness was increased by an incident in 1955. Following the successful H-bomb test that year, a banquet was held for the officials. Sakharov proposed a toast that "our handiwork would never explode over cities." A general who was director of the test replied that how a weapon is used is no business of the scientists; the same message was delivered to Sakharov in person by Soviet Premier Khrushchev at another banquet in 1961. In 1962, Sakharov tried to stop an atmospheric thermonuclear test that he knew was of no scientific value but that could cause harmful fallout. He failed and said he never got over "the feeling of impotence and fright that seized me on that day." Unlike Teller, Sakharov was very concerned with the danger posed by fallout from tests. He wrote an essay in 1959 expressing concern about the effects of radiation, especially in causing genetic damage, and disputed Teller's claim that radioactive fallout was no worse than an occasional cigarette. Sakharov suggested some of the provisions of the 1963 test-ban treaty, the same one Teller opposed so strongly in the United States.[17]

It took more than ten years for Andrei Sakharov's discontent with the Soviet political system to bloom into full, public dissent. When it did, however, he became a prophet of "perestroika" and "glasnost" nearly twenty years before Mikhail Gorbachev introduced these terms in the late 1980s to describe his policy of "restructuring" and "openness" within the Soviet system. In 1968, Sakharov's essay on "Progress, Co-existence, and Intellectual Freedom" was published in *samizdat* form [illegal manuscripts circulated in typescript] in the Soviet Union. It appeared in the West after a Dutch correspondent in Moscow read the entire essay over the phone in order to smuggle it out.[18] This work made him famous in the West but lost him his right to work on further secret scientific projects in the USSR. In it, Sakharov linked scientific questions such as the "enormous destructive power" of nuclear weapons and "pollution of the environment" to the need for peaceful coexistence and more openness in the Soviet Union. Sakharov initially remained loyal to socialism, calling it the system that has done the most to "glorify the moral significance of labor," yet he also spoke for "convergence" of the capitalist and socialist systems of government and economy as the basis for peace. Such an agreement, or "detente," between the two camps would require greater democracy within the Soviet Union. Sakharov specifically suggested greater intellectual freedom in the USSR, free elections, and even (gradually) a genuine multi-party political system. If this happened, the United States and the USSR could use money saved from the arms race to feed and clothe those in poorer nations.

The leaders of the Soviet Union at that time spurned his advice. In 1970, with two other academicians, Sakharov wrote a letter to state and Communist Party leaders urging a freer flow of information, amnesty for political prisoners, and greater democracy and competition in political and economic life. That year, Sakharov and two other dissidents formed the Moscow Human Rights Committee, a group that appealed to the government on behalf of political prisoners. They especially tried to help those intellectuals forced into psychiatric hospitals for their political statements. Sakharov's "Memorandum" to Communist Party Chairman Leonid Brezhnev in March 1971 asked for "a dialogue with the country's leadership and a frank and public discussion of problems of human rights." In addition to pleas for greater political and economic freedom, this statement also requested prison reform, an end to the death

penalty, improved education and medical care, a fight against alco-
holism in the USSR, and a change in the Soviet legal system to
allow republics within the Union of Soviet Socialist Republics to secede if they wished.[19]

By 1972, relations between Soviet leaders and their brilliant
physicist were understandably getting a bit prickly. To make the
point that they considered his remarks unwise at best and treason-
ous at worst, they sent a few signals. His stepdaughter was expelled
from the University of Moscow in her senior year. Sakharov himself
was harassed by anonymous telephone calls and threats and, in
March 1973, was summoned to the office of the secret police for a
chat. Sakharov's response to this was to allow himself to be interviewed by a Swedish radio correspondent in July 1973. In this interview, he expressed doubts about the wisdom of socialism itself but
denied that he wanted to "reorganize the state" or see a revolution,
favoring a gradual change to avoid "the terrible destruction through
which we have passed several times."[20] This interview was followed
by a further official warning to Sakharov and a press campaign
against him in August and September 1973. Finally, forty members
of the Soviet Academy of Sciences, a group considered somewhat
immune to political pressure, signed a statement calling their colleague a "tool of enemy propaganda against the Soviet Union."[21]

While this particular attack on Sakharov ended soon after the
president of the American Academy of Sciences intervened on his
behalf, neither Sakharov nor the Soviet government immediately
changed its mind about each other. During the next six years until
1980, Sakharov continued to speak out on behalf of "prisoners of
conscience" in the USSR, often writing letters to Westerners, including one to U.S. President Jimmy Carter in 1977, which included
long lists of those imprisoned. More important, Sakharov continued to regard nuclear war as "the greatest danger threatening our
age" and in his 1975 Nobel Peace Prize lecture he proposed—much
as Teller had done thirty years earlier—an international agency to
effect disarmament and control the spread of nuclear weapons.[22]
Sakharov also continued to link disarmament with human rights.
Only a freer, more informed public in the USSR could put pressure
on the government to act more responsibly in military and foreign
policy, he wrote in 1978. The lack of freedom for citizens of the
USSR was not just an "internal matter" for him but, rather, "a men-
ace to international security."[23]

Unwilling to accept this view or to be further embarrassed by this man, who was too well known to be shot, the Soviet government, on January 22, 1980, formally stripped Andrei Sakharov of his medals and awards and exiled him to the city of Gorky, where he was closely watched and was kept from attending scientific meetings or associating with foreigners for six years. He was released from internal exile on December 16, 1986, informed of this by a personal phone call from President Gorbachev. During the remaining three years of his life, Sakharov was elected to the governing body of the Soviet Academy of Sciences and to the USSR's newly created Congress of Peoples' Deputies, where he served as a leader of the more democratic, or radical, wing.[24] He also visited the United States in November 1988, where he finally met Edward Teller at a dinner honoring the American physicist. At this meeting, the two men agreed on the wisdom of placing nuclear reactors underground for safety and on the need for openness in political and scientific matters. They disagreed on the value of the American plans to build a space-based missile defense system (SDI, or Strategic Defense Initiative), something Teller defended but Sakharov opposed as a "grave error."[25]

Now that the Soviet Union has collapsed, Sakharov's earlier positions on Soviet domestic reform, urging such things as the right to strike, free emigration, and "the right of Soviet republics to secede," seem prophetic rather than naive—as they would have appeared even in 1985.[26] This is perhaps due less to Sakharov's foresight than to the persistence with which Gorbachev pursued his reform of Soviet society and government in the late 1980s.

On the issue of nuclear power and disarmament, Sakharov was often as conservative as his American colleague Teller. In a 1978 essay, Sakharov expressed his support for nuclear power plants, pointing out that the Soviet Union would love to exploit energy shortages in the West. He even repeated Teller's earlier warning against "unfounded emotions and prejudices" in the discussion of nuclear energy. On the issue of disarmament, Sakharov repeatedly asked Western liberals during the 1970s not to be satisfied with a "false detente, a collusion-detente, or a capitulation-detente." They should be wary of unilateral disarmament or of anything less than strict parity in arms reduction. In 1983, Sakharov smuggled a statement out of the Soviet Union stating his opposition to a nuclear freeze and endorsing President Reagan's decision to build 100 MX missiles to counter the Soviet superiority in silo-based intercontinental ballistic missiles (ICBMs).[27]

Neither of these scientists-turned-political-activists fully fits the stereotype that many wished to impose upon him. Teller's support for a "world-wide government to which all owe allegiance and which guarantees freedom," expressed as late as 1962, did not please his conservative supporters any more than Sakharov's support for American arms build-up to achieve "strategic parity" with the USSR pleased the anti-nuclear movement in Europe or the United States.[28] That is one of the problems we encounter with intellectuals in politics; they are not always predictable.

Edward Teller said that scientists had no special political wisdom, yet he was quite willing to engage in political debates, winning some major political battles in his career. Andrei Sakharov, by contrast, believed scientists do have a "social responsibility." They could not fail, in his view, "to think about the dangers stemming from uncontrolled progress, from unregulated industrial development, and especially from military application of scientific achievements." Until the end of his life, Sakharov won only a few battles in his struggle with the government of the USSR, yet he exhibited great integrity in fighting, as he put it, "to preserve peace and those ethical values which have been developed as our civilization evolved."[29]

Despite the end of the cold war between the United States and the USSR, the question of nuclear dangers—whether in the form of power plant reactors or warheads on missiles—remains to bedevil us as we enter a new century. The struggle for a peaceful, uncontaminated world is not over; it is only entering another stage. Thanks to Edward Teller, Andrei Sakharov, and the human desire to explore the limits of the unknown, we continue to live and work in the shadow of the thermonuclear question mark.

Notes

1. Edward Teller with Allen Brown, *The Legacy of Hiroshima* (London: Macmillan and Co., 1962), 18.
2. Stanley A. Blumberg and Gwinn Owens, *Energy and Conflict: The Life and Times of Edward Teller* (New York: G. P. Putnam's Sons, 1976), 295.
3. Ibid., 4–10, 15–27; "Knowledge Is Power," *Time*, Nov. 18, 1957, 22.
4. Blumberg and Owens, *Energy and Conflict*, 28–63.

5. Ibid., 95–122; see also Robert Jungk, *Brighter Than a Thousand Suns: A Personal History of the Atomic Scientists*, trans. James Cleugh (New York: Harcourt, Brace and Company, 1958), 78–86.

6. Blumberg and Owens, *Energy and Conflict*, 153–163; Teller, *The Legacy of Hiroshima*, 13–15; many years later, in 1995, Teller said he was glad that the bombs had been dropped on the Japanese cities when he discovered that the Japanese had firm plans to kill all one hundred thousand prisoners of war in Japan if the islands were invaded. Dropping the bombs made invasion unnecessary. See "Dr. Teller Changes," *World Press Review* (August 1995): 16–18.

7. Blumberg and Owens, *Energy and Conflict*, 185–187, 199–214, 221, 230–231.

8. Harold Lavine, "H-Mystery Man: He Hurried the H-Bomb," *Newsweek*, Aug. 2, 1954, 23–26; Robert Coughlan, "Dr. Edward Teller's Magnificent Obsession," *Life*, September 6, 1954, 60–74. Teller's embarrassment is noted by Blumberg and Owens, *Energy and Conflict*, 369.

9. Blumberg and Owens, *Energy and Conflict*, 362–363; *New York Times*, March 25, 1983, 8; "The Old Lion Still Roars," *Time*, April 4, 1983, 12. See also "Edward Teller a controversial architect of the Nuclear Age, is dead at 95," in *The New York Times*. September 11, 2003, A22.

10. Edward Teller, "Back to the Laboratories," *Bulletin of the Atomic Scientists* (March 1950): 71.

11. Ibid., 72; Coughlan, "Teller's Magnificent Obsession," *Life*, September 6, 1954, 67; Lavine, "H-Mystery Man," *Newsweek*, August 2, 1954, 25; Edward Teller, "The Work of Many People," *Science*, February 25, 1955, 275.

12. Edward Teller and Albert L. Latter, *Our Nuclear Future . . . Facts, Dangers and Opportunities* (New York: Criterion Books, 1958), 116–126, 152–159, 167; A. D. Sakharov, *Memoirs*, trans. Richard Lourie (New York: Alfred A. Knopf, 1990), 203–204; Edward Teller et al., *The Constructive Uses of Nuclear Explosives* (New York: McGraw-Hill, 1968).

13. "Chief Opponent of Test-Ban Treaty: A Man Who Challenges the President" and "Another Round in the Test-Ban Debate," *U.S. News & World Report*, September 2, 1963, 12, 52–57.

14. Blumberg and Owens, *Energy and Conflict*, 1, 450.

15. Irwin Goodwin, "Changing Times: Sakharov in the US on Human Rights and Arms Control," *Physics Today* (February 1989), 91.

16. A. D. Sakharov, *Sakharov Speaks*, ed. Harrison E. Salisbury (New York: Alfred A. Knopf, 1974), 5, 167; Sakharov, *Memoirs*, 97. The firsthand autobiographical information on Sakharov in this work can be supplemented by "An Autobiographical Note" by Sakharov and "Some Events in the Scientific and Public Careers of Andrei D. Sakharov," in *On Sakharov*, ed. Alexander Babyonyshev (New York: Knopf Vintage,

1982), xi–xxix. For the sequence of the Soviet and American explosions and the secrecy surrounding them, see Blumberg and Owen, *Energy and Conflict*, 267–270.

17. A. D. Sakharov, *My Country and the World*, trans. Guy V. Daniels (New York: Alfred A. Knopf, 1975), 33–34, 73–74; *On Sakharov*, 175–177.

18. Sakharov, *My Country and the World*, viii–ix; *Progress, Coexistence and Intellectual Freedom*, with an "Introduction" and "Afterword" by Harrison E. Salisbury (New York: W. W. Norton, 1968).

19. *Sakharov Speaks*, 116–150.

20. Ibid., 50, 166–178.

21. Ibid., 180–192; George E. Munro, "The Case of A. D. Sakharov," *Midwest Quarterly*, vol. 20 (Winter 1979): 147–159.

22. A. D. Sakharov, *Alarm and Hope*, ed. Efrem Yankelevich and Alfred Friendly, Jr. (New York: Alfred A. Knopf, 1978), 5–12, 43–56.

23. Ibid., 99–105, 173.

24. See "On Accepting a Prize" by Sakharov in *New York Review of Books*, August 13, 1987, 49; "On Gorbachev: A Talk with Andrei Sakharov," *New York Review of Books*, December 22, 1988, 28–29; "Sakharov in US Puts in Plug for Perestroika" and "Sakharov Ought to Know," *Christian Science Monitor*, November 8, 1988, 3, 13.

25. Goodwin, "Changing Times: Sakharov in the US," 91–96; *Ethics and Public Policy Center Newsletter*, December 1988: 1, 3.

26. Sakharov, *My Country and the World*, 101–103.

27. Sakharov, *Alarm and Hope*, 124–128; *Sakharov Speaks*, 54; *My Country and the World*, 85–98; "A Plea for Nuclear Balance," *Time*, July 4, 1983, 15–16.

28. Teller, *The Legacy of Hiroshima*, 313.

29. A. D. Sakharov, "The Social Responsibility of Scientists," *Physics Today* (June 1981): 25–30.

Further Reading

BLUMBERG, STANLEY, and GWINN OWENS. *Energy and Conflict: The Life and Times of Edward Teller*. New York: G. P. Putnam's Sons, 1976. Honest yet critical biography. Best available.

LOURIE, RICHARD. *Sakharov. A Biography*. Hanover, N. H.: University Press of New England/Brandeis University Press, 2002. Full-scale biography of Sakharov by a man very familiar with his career.

SAKHAROV, A. D. *Sakharov Speaks*. Edited with an introduction by HARRISON E. SALISBURY. New York: Alfred A. Knopf, 1974. This provides a convenient look at Sakharov's political views.

TELLER, EDWARD L., and ALBERT LATTER. *Our Nuclear Future . . . Facts, Dangers and Opportunities*. New York: Criterion Press, 1958. Shows early scientific optimism about the potential peaceful uses of nuclear power.

CHAPTER 14

King and Mandela: The Prophet and the Politician

What are the best ways to correct fundamental social and political injustices in a complex industrial society? Which of these two men was the more successful, and by what standards should they be measured?

Both men told followers that they were willing to die to realize their dream. One did, violently, assassinated at thirty-nine, his dream unfulfilled. The other saw his dream largely fulfilled when he was seventy-six and has lived well into his eighties.

Martin Luther King, Jr. (1929–1968), and Nelson Rolihlahla Mandela (born 1918) are remembered, respectively, as the most famous African-American and most famous African leader of the second half of the twentieth century. Both were able to profoundly change the social and political systems in their countries; both struggled with the issue of whether violence or non-violence was the best way to bring about change. Both have been mythologized as larger-than-life heroes, King because of his assassination and Mandela because of his reputation for discipline and determination acquired during twenty-seven years in South African prisons.

King and Mandela were also profoundly different. King, a Baptist minister, spent his entire life trying to make real by Christian action the American promise of freedom and equality. Mandela, the son of a Xhosa chief in the Transkei region of South Africa, used the traditions of freedom and equality of the African National Congress, a leadership group for South African blacks founded in 1912, as his "bible." Both men, however, were protected in childhood against some, but not all, of the racism found in their respective societies.

Martin Luther King, Jr., was born Michael King, Jr. When Michael was five, his father, a Baptist preacher, changed both names to Martin Luther, in honor of the great Protestant reformer. As solid members of the black middle class in Atlanta, Georgia, the King family enjoyed privileges. Martin was spared the more brutalizing forms of racial discrimination as well as the poverty others experienced during the Depression of the 1930s. In King's later words, "the first twenty-five years of my life were very comfortable years."[1] And when the young man did encounter racism, he saw the resistance to it of the elder King. King, Sr., would not ride city buses because they were segregated, and abruptly left a shoe store when salesmen refused to serve him in the front part of the store. When father and son were stopped by a policeman who referred to Martin Luther King, Sr., as "boy," the elder King responded, pointing to his son: "That's a boy, I'm a man." When returning from an oratorical contest in south Georgia when in high school, Martin Luther King, Jr., stood on a bus for ninety miles, forced to give his seat to a white passenger. He had just delivered a prize-winning speech on "The Negro and the Constitution" and initially resisted giving up his seat until the driver threateningly called him a "black son-of-a-bitch."[2]

Like many male children with strong fathers, the young Martin both admired and resisted his father's strength and, like his father, was drawn to a profession in which he could help his people. When he entered Morehouse College in Atlanta in 1944 at age fifteen, Martin Luther King, Jr., wanted to become a physician or a lawyer, but not a preacher, as his father wished. He changed his mind during his junior year because he rejected the idea that one could discover truth through scientific, statistical analysis alone. He resisted "when an argument of his . . . was overwhelmed by force of sheer data" and wished to persuade "as much by sincerity as by fact."[3] Inspired by teachers who believed that a good preacher should also be a thinker, a philosopher, he found an alternative path to truth through the time-tested way of the ministry.

After graduating with a bachelor's degree in sociology from Morehouse in 1948, King entered Crozier Theological Seminary in Pennsylvania, where he earned a bachelor of divinity degree in May 1951. This was followed by four more years at another "white" school, Boston University, where King earned his Ph.D. in systematic theology in 1955. In both schools, King deliberately avoided "black" subjects and focused on the study of major Western social, political, and religious thinkers, past and present. He recounted engaging in "a serious study of the social and ethical theories of the great philosophers, from Plato and Aristotle down to Rousseau, Hobbes, Benthan, Mill, and Locke."[4] During these years, King rejected the ideas of Karl Marx, especially the "crippling totalitarianism" of communist government. He was, however, impressed by the "social gospel" of the nineteenth-century theologian and critic of capitalism Walter Rauschenbusch, who believed Christians should take the lead in demanding social justice for the poor. During these years King also encountered non-Western political theory emanating from India's independence movement and Mohandas Gandhi's practice of non-violent passive resistance. This would become the key to King's later successes as a civil rights leader. By the end of his educational journey, King believed that he had found a philosophical "grounding for the idea of a personal God," as well as a philosophical "basis for the dignity and worth of all human personality."[5]

Just prior to his the final year at Boston University, on June 18, 1953, Martin Luther King, Jr., married Coretta Scott, a talented singer and daughter of a prosperous storekeeper in Marion, Alabama, and on April 14, 1954, he accepted the pastorate at the Dexter Avenue Baptist Church in Montgomery, Alabama. In Coretta, he found someone who shared his passion for social justice, and in accepting the job in Montgomery, the young minister anticipated a relatively quiet pastorate. Such was not to be, for less than two years after he arrived in Montgomery, on December 1, 1955, Rosa Parks, secretary of the Montgomery NAACP [National Association for the Advancement of Colored People] refused to give up her bus seat to a white person and was arrested. The modern Civil Rights Movement began that month with a black boycott of Montgomery city buses.

A reluctant Martin Luther King, Jr., was drawn into the Montgomery bus boycott on December 5, 1955, when he was elected president of the Montgomery Improvement Association, formed to organize the action. He was only twenty-six and was selected, some say, because, as a newcomer to the Montgomery black community, he had made no enemies.[6] In his first speech (really a sermon) in this new role, King clearly demanded political justice on religious grounds:

. . . we are not here advocating violence. . . . we are a *Christian* people . . . but the great glory of American democracy is the right to protest for right. . . . And if we are wrong, the Supreme Court . . . is wrong. If we are wrong God Almighty is wrong. . . . If we are wrong Jesus of Nazareth was merely a utopian dreamer. . . . If we are wrong, justice is a lie. . . . And we are determined here in Montgomery to work and fight, until justice runs down like water and righteousness as a mighty stream!

Yet, despite these high-sounding words, the demands of the Montgomery Improvement Association were very moderate; they did not even ask for an end to segregated buses but only courteous treatment by drivers, a policy that whites would fill seats from the front to the middle of the bus, and blacks from the back to the middle (with no one forced to give up his or her seat), and that the city consider hiring black drivers on primarily black routes.[7]

Their demands for a modified system of segregation were rejected by the city, and so for the next year Montgomery blacks boycotted city buses, using black-owned taxis, carpools, or their feet to get to work. The buses were finally integrated in December 1956, after the U.S. Supreme Count declared unconstitutional Alabama's law segregating the races on buses.

Although the issue was finally settled in the courts instead of the street, this non-violent boycott did undermine the white power structure by exposing its abuses in the national media. This helped King mature as a man and emerge as a leader in the black community. By February 1956 white merchants had lost more than a million dollars due to the boycott. As this damage to white businesses became evident, white intimidation escalated. Martin Luther King, Jr., was arrested for speeding and threatened by phone, and a bomb was thrown on his porch.[8] Although King and his family survived the bombing, it was at this time that he began to brood about the inevitability of his death. During the Montgomery boycott, King, Sr. ("Daddy King," as he was known), made several unsuccessful efforts to get his son to move back to Atlanta; Martin Jr.'s resistance to this was psychologically important in helping him establish some independence from his father.[9] In the final analysis, the Montgomery boycott also gave King an opportunity to test his philosophy of non-violent passive resistance and made him aware that political rights, especially voting, was a condition of further progress for southern blacks.[10]

The six years after the Montgomery campaign, 1957 through 1962, were in the words of biographer Marshall Frady, a "wilderness time" for Martin Luther King, a prolonged season . . . of fitful and indefinite drift" as he tried to find the best role for a new organization he founded in 1957.[11] The southern Christian Leadership Conference, as the organization came to be called, was initially organized to put pressure on Southern leaders and on the Eisenhower administration to implement the Supreme Courts's decision declaring segregated busing illegal. The SCLC, which King headed until his death, helped organize protests against segregation and injustice throughout the South, and later the nation. The SCLC was not welcomed by leaders of other black organizations, such as Roy Wilkins of the NAACP, who favored seeking further black rights through court decisions rather than non-violent street protests. Black politicians such as Congressman Adam Clayton Powell of New York, also were suspicious of King's efforts to put pressure on the state and federal government from "outside" the system.

During the late 1950s, King made several foreign trips that broadened his horizons. He attended the ceremonies marking the independence of the west African state of Ghana in 1957, and visited India in 1959, a pilgrimage of sorts that strengthened his commitment to the principle of non-violent resistance. In a speech several years after returning from India, he noted that the vast majority of people there were desperately poor while the USA spent "more than a million dollars a day to store surplus food in this country." He suggested that we "store the food free of charge in the wrinkled stomachs of the millions of people who go to bed hungry every night" and added: "Maybe we spend too much of our national budget building military bases around the world rather than bases of genuine concern and understanding."[12] Both of these foreign trips made King more aware of how the problems of American blacks dovetailed with the poor, especially the non-white poor, in other nations.

In 1954 the U.S. Supreme Court declared "separate but equal" schools inherently unequal and ordered desegregation "with all deliberate speed." By 1960, with virtually no progress on this issue, the mood among young people in the civil rights movement was changing. In February 1960 several black youths requested service at a segregated department store lunch counter in Greensboro, North Carolina, and refused to leave until served, beginning the sit-in movement. This practice spread rapidly throughout the South, and was soon supplemented by Freedom Riders, black and white youth who rode buses together through the South, where angry whites often brutally attacked them and, on at least one occasion, burned their bus. In April 1960 the SCLC organized the Student Non-violent Coordinating Committee (SNCC) to help train the young pro-testors in non-violent techniques. However, tension soon developed between SNCC members, impatient for change, even if it required violence, and King's followers, who favored non-violent protests.

By 1960 both King and the SCLC were headquartered in At-lanta where Martin had moved to become a co-pastor at his father's Ebenezer Baptist Church. To position his non-violent direct action approach as an alternative to the gradual approach of the NAACP, King used the SCLC to aid local leaders in registering black voters in Albany, Georgia, in the summer of 1962. His goals were to call attention to the fact that most blacks could not vote and to help solve this problem by peacefully trying to register them. He also wanted to show the new Kennedy administration in Washington that federal intervention would be necessary for American blacks to receive full political and civil rights, something the President said he supported but had yet to act upon. Although hundreds of peo-ple were arrested as they tried to register to vote, white leaders met black protests with courtesy, and made sure that, whenever King and his close colleague Ralph Abernathy were arrested, they were soon bailed out, thus avoiding the attention of large northern news-papers. Even though King called the Albany Campaign a "partial victory" and "not an end but a beginning," this effort had failed to achieve his goals.[13] The SCLC campaign in Birmingham, Alabama, the following year would be much more successful.

In September 1962, the SCLC held its annual convention in Birmingham, where King's friend Fred Shuttlesworth, head of the SCLC affiliate, the Alabama Christian Movement for Human Rights, had been struggling for years to desegregate schools and public facilities in the face of repeated white bombings of their homes. Despite the bombing of Shuttlesworth's home and church in the fall of 1962, the ACMHR began a new boycott of downtown stores in March. Impressed with Shuttlesworth's courage and in need of a victory for non-violence that would bring federal help to his cause, King agreed to fight with the ACMHR in Birmingham, a place he called "the most segregated city in America."[14]

During April and May 1963, the SCLC led a series of non-violent protest marches in Birmingham. Unlike in Albany, where leaders of the white community carefully avoided confrontations that would attract outside media, Birmingham Police Commissioner Eugene "Bull" Connor attacked marching children with police dogs and with fire hoses "pressured to denude tree bark." Thousands of Americans watching the nightly news on television saw images of peaceful, well-dressed black youth blown across streets by blasts of water. It was a turning point in the civil rights movement of the 1960s. On May 20, the United States Supreme Court nullified the Alabama laws under which the Birmingham demonstrators were arrested. On June 11, President Kennedy addressed the nation on television to ask Congress to pass a major Civil Rights bill outlawing segregation. A settlement between protest organizers and Birmingham leaders was reached on May 10, but it was followed by a number of bombings, most famously the bombing of the Sixteenth Street Baptist Church (headquarters of the marchers) on a Sunday in September. Three young girls in Sunday school dresses were killed and many throughout the United States were shocked.[15]

The success in Birmingham was both political and moral. The Kennedy and Johnson administrations became fully engaged in the civil rights struggle on behalf of black Americans. The Civil Rights Act of 1964 would be followed, after a famous march from Selma, Alabama, to the state capital in Montgomery in the spring of 1965, by the Voting Rights Act of 1965. King's famous "Letter from a Birmingham Jail," in which he responded to a group of white clergymen who accused him of moving too fast in demanding an end to segregation, has acquired in thirty years the status of an important document in American history, included in college texts alongside the Gettysburg address of Abraham Lincoln and Franklin Roosevelt's first inaugural address in 1933. These major personal and political victories by Martin Luther King, Jr., earned him the Nobel Peace Prize in 1964, and made him *Time* magazine's "Man of the Year" for 1963. King was convinced, however, that the movement was successful, not only because it attracted national attention to injustice, but also because it did so using redemptive, non-violent resistance. In a speech in Detroit in June 1963, following the settlement in Birmingham, he explained that non-violence "has a way of disarming the opponent. It exposes his moral defenses . . . and he just doesn't know what to do:

If he doesn't beat you, wonderful! But if he beats you, you develop the quiet courage of accepting blows without retaliating. If he doesn't put you in jail, wonderful! But if he puts you in jail, you go in . . . and transform it from a dungeon of shame to a haven of freedom and unity. And . . . if a man hasn't discovered something that he will die for, he isn't fit to live.[16]

After the passage of the Civil Rights Act, King took his campaign for racial justice to the North, most notably Chicago in 1965 and 1966. In this setting, the tactics of non-violence were far less successful. Northern racism did not offer the simple and visible target offered by segregated public facilities. It was more "diffuse and anonymous," in the words of a contemporary black scholar. In Chicago, "King didn't have a loppy sheriff to outfox after he beat up defenseless blacks." Indeed, King said that he found the most "hostile and hateful" examples of racism he had ever seen in Chicago, especially when he marched for integrated housing. King also had attracted to his cause in the South many Northern liberals (who enjoyed using unenlightened white southern "rednecks" as scapegoats), as well as many whites. His philosophy of non-violence saw whites as redeemable, and this ultimately won over many Southern whites of goodwill, even if it came at great cost to blacks, who had to love their white neighbors even while they were being beaten. Neither blacks nor whites in the North were as susceptible to his religiously motivated message as were their southern counterparts.[17]

Martin Luther King's star dimmed in the popular press and imagination during the final three years of his life, not only because his non-violent tactics won no further significant victories for civil rights, but also because, by 1967, he began to publicly oppose American military involvement in Vietnam. King believed that the United States supported a new form of colonialism by propping up a corrupt regime in South Vietnam. He also noticed that American blacks suffered a disproportionate share of battlefield casualties in Vietnam—in 1964, 18.8 percent of eligible whites were drafted compared to 30.2 percent of eligible blacks. Polls showed that blacks as well as whites disagreed with King on the war, and he was attacked by the major American news magazines, *Time*, *Newsweek*, and *U.S. News and World Report*.[18]

All this changed dramatically and significantly on April 4, 1968, when King, in Memphis to try to help settle a strike of garbage collectors, was assassinated as he stood on the balcony of the Lorraine Motel. Riots broke out throughout the nation in the days following. With King's death, two things happened. Many middle-class whites that supported civil rights for blacks were left without their strongest contact in the black community. In addition, many white, and even some politically conservative, Americans who were beginning to have some doubts about the war in Vietnam lost the strongest black voice preaching non-violent protest. In the decades since his death, Martin Luther King, Jr., became an American hero, honored with his own national holiday. Had he not been martyred, this might never have occurred. Nelson Mandela also became a national hero to black and white South Africans alike, not by dying but by surviving decades in prison. He emerged from prison in 1990 with the status of a living icon.

Nelson Mandala, like King, enjoyed a childhood of relative privilege. He was born in a small village in the cattle-raising Transkei region of South Africa, 600 miles south of Johannesberg His great grandfather had been king of the Tembu people before British rule. His father Hendry Mandela, a hereditary chief, named his son Rolihlahla, a name that translates roughly as "troublemaker." Hendry was relatively prosperous until a local British official deposed him from his leadership position, and Rolihlahla (given the Christian name Nelson by his mother, one of Hendry's four wives) moved to a smaller village where he lived with his mother and enjoyed a happy childhood.[19] When Nelson was nine his father died and left him in the care of Jongintaba, leader of the Tembu people and head of the Madiba clan to which the Mandelas belonged. From the Regent, as Jongintaba was called, the young Mandela learned an African method of arriving at agreement on issues through consensus, with the leader guiding the group "like a shepherd, directing his flock from behind by skillful persuasion." He also absorbed as a child the African idea of *Umuntu ngumuntu ngabantu* ("a person is a person because of other people"), the notion that a person cannot accomplish anything of value without the support of others. This conviction he acted upon with great success later in life.[20]

Unlike most young Africans, Nelson was able to get an education at a series of missionary schools. He and Regent Jongintaba's son, Justice, attended a Methodist boarding school, and later Fort Hare University, the only college for blacks in South Africa. Although Mandela resented the British subjugation of his fellow

Xhosa tribesmen, he retained for the rest of his life a respect for the liberal education he received from the British missionaries. His career at Fort Hare was cut short, however, at the end of his junior year, when he joined in a student protest over food and was expelled by the headmaster. Returning home, he found that Jongintaba had decided that if he was going to leave school, it was time to arrange marriage for him with a local girl. To escape this, Nelson fled to the big city of Johannesberg in 1940. Had he not done so, Mandela would have probably lived the life of a respected rural leader of his people in Tembuland. Like King's in 1955, Nelson Mandela's life was changed by a single decision

Desperate for a job after several weeks in the big city, Mandela was referred to Walter Sisulu, a black real estate agent, who would become his lifelong friend and mentor. Sisulu introduced him to a while lawyer, Lazar Sidelsky, who hired him as a clerk and helped him begin his training to become a lawyer. Sisulu, "impressed with Mandela's air of command," also encouraged Mandela to join the African National Congress (ANC), which he did in 1944.[21] Mandela would devote the rest of his life to this organization. He also married Sisulu's cousin, Evelyn Mase, that same year. They were to have three children before their divorce twelve years later, which occurred because of religious difference (Evelyn became very religious, Nelson did not) and because Nelson, consumed by his work with the ANC, spent little time at home.

To understand the seriousness of Nelson Mandela's commitment to the cause of black equality and democratic government in South Africa, we must appreciate the reasons for and the nature of the system of racial separation (apartheid, or "apartness") constructed in that country in the generation after World War II. South Africa had been for centuries a multi-racial, multi-ethnic land. When Dutch settlers began moving into the cape in the seventeenth century, cattle-raising Bantu-speaking peoples had already completed their migration into the northern and eastern portions of what was to become South Africa, both groups putting pressure on the Khoisan people (Bushmen) in the western areas. Over the centuries, natives of India also settled in the southern part of the country, as did many British colonists Eventually, the British took political control of South Africa from the original Dutch and Bantu settlers, completing that process in the Boer War at the end of the nineteenth century.

The boom years of World War II temporarily improved black economic conditions while making many South African whites nervous with the increased black migration to the cities and black competition for urban jobs, not to mention overall population growth. From 1910 to 1946, the white population of South Africa had grown from 1.1 million to 2.4 million while the number of non-whites had increased from 4.5 to 9 million. This growth, as much as anything else, was the reason for apartheid. After the National Party, controlled by the descendants of the Dutch Afrikaners, won the election of 1948, it passed a series of laws over the next twenty years that controlled the lives of non-white South Africans and limited their movement. All South Africans had to register by race, and marriages were forbidden between blacks and whites and between whites and "coloureds" (mixed). The Group Areas Act of 1950 and later measures restricted black businesses and homes to specific areas. The Bantu Authorities Act of 1951 and later "Self-Government" measures created black homelands where chiefs enjoyed limited authority; in 1970 all South African blacks were made "citizens" of one of these homelands or "Bantustans." It was now legally impossible for them to live in the 80 percent of the nation reserved for whites. Since an educated black African leadership was a threat to apartheid, the government took control of all missionary schools, segregated all universities, and tried to limit blacks to jobs requiring menial labor. Passes were issued to all blacks to control their movement in white areas.[22] And this system was supported by a longstanding policy that only whites could vote and stand for election to the South African parliament.

As the apartheid structure began to develop, Mandela, Sisulu, and other young members of the ANC Youth League urged mass protests to reverse this development, but ANC elders turned this down as too dangerous. The Youth League first tried mass action on a large scale in the Defiance Campaign of 1952, systematically defying apartheid laws by ignoring pass laws and entering "white only" waiting rooms and restrooms. The South African government made thousands of arrests during the summer and fall, twenty-five hundred in September alone, banned fifty ANC and Indian Congress leaders, and created severe penalties for any civil disobedience.[23]

The government crackdown restricted Mandela to Johannesberg for six months and raised anew for Mandela and the Youth League the whole issue of multi-racial cooperation in the struggle for freedom. The multi-racial membership of the South African Communist Party impressed Mandela, but he opposed cooperation with the Communists or even with other white or Indian groups, arguing that black Africans should work alone for freedom and democracy. He even asked the ANC (without success) to expel members with allegiances to other organizations.[24] By the early 1950s, however, as the goals and methods of the National Party became clearer, Mandela changed his mind and came to the conclusion that cooperation with other groups was necessary to end apartheid and create a democratic government. Once he made this decision, his commitment to it never wavered. Although he was accused by the government and by foreign leaders (including those in the United States) of being a Communist, and did for a time accept the socialist belief that mines and mineral wealth should be owned by the government, Mandela also believed in the importance of a strong black capitalist middle class and in a "one-person, one-vote" democracy.[25] Although never a Communist, Mandela refused in the late 1980s to denounce the South African Communist Party as a condition of release from prison because decades earlier members of that party fought with him to end apartheid. He also refused to unilaterally reject the use of violence in order to be freed from jail, arguing that the South African government had not rejected apartheid, which he saw as inherently violent.

The question of violence versus non-violence continued to be divisive within the ANC. Headed by "middle-class and middle-aged men," the ANC remained opposed to violence, but Mandela, unlike Martin Luther King, Jr., was not philosophically committed to non-violence. "I saw non-violence on the Gandhian model not as an inviolable principle but as a tactic to be used as the situation demanded," he said in his autobiography.[26] Mandela believed that non-violent protests were preferable, but also that violence, or the threat of violence, could be an effective weapon to force the white minority government to accept change.

However, it was not until the 1960s, as conditions worsened for the ANC, that some members of the ANC, including Mandela, came to believe that it was time to engage in violent protest against apartheid. In March 1960, nervous South African police fired on a crowd of ten thousand blacks protesting the pass laws in the village of Sharpville, killing sixty-seven of them. This "Sharpville Massacre" caused the ANC to call a general strike that paralyzed the city of Johannesberg. The government responded by declaring the ANC illegal, and Oliver Tambo, Mandela's school friend at Fort Hare and his law partner since 1952, left the country to set up the ANC in exile.

By the middle of 1961, the leadership of the ANC somewhat reluctantly agreed to allow Mandela to form a military wing of ANC. It was called *Umkhonto we Sizwe* (Spear of the Nation, or MK). Mandela went underground to serve as its commander-in-chief, and during the first six months of 1962 traveled to Ghana, Ethiopia, and Algeria, where he engaged in some military training but discovered little support abroad for the ANC idea of a multi-racial democracy. Most African leaders wanted a black-dominated state in South Africa. Only the Communists joined MK in a sabotage campaign aimed, not at assassinating people, but at destroying government buildings, power plants, and railways. This campaign failed for several reasons. There was little support for the ANC in rural areas, where people preferred the Africanist solution of black rule for South Africa instead of multi-racial democracy and had formed themselves into the Pan-African Congress, or PAC. In addition, there were few safe places in the country for guerrillas to hide, and the South African government had a formidable security apparatus that finally captured Nelson Mandela in August 1962 after he returned from his trip abroad.[27]

Mandela was given a five-year prison sentence for incitement to riot and travel without a permit; then he and many of his colleagues were tried again in 1963 on the more serious charge of sabotage after South African security forces captured many ANC leaders and incriminating documents in a raid on a rural hideaway near Rivonia. Convinced that he would receive the death penalty, Mandela used the trial to demonstrate to the world the evils of apartheid. In a lengthy statement on April 20, 1964, opening the defense case at the Rivonia trial, Mandela acknowledged his role as leader of *Umkhonto we Sizwe,* and explained that he and others had only turned to violence as a last resort after fifty years of non-violent protest "had brought the African people nothing but more and more repressive legislation." He ended his speech, which has become as famous in South Africa as King's "Letter from a Birmingham Jail" is in the United States, with an often-quoted statement:

During my lifetime I have dedicated myself to this struggle of the African people. I have fought against white domination, and I have fought against black domination. I have cherished the ideal of a democratic and free society in which all persons live together in harmony and with equal opportunities. It is an ideal which I hope to live for and to achieve. But, if needs be, it is an ideal for which I am prepared to die.[28]

The Rivonia defendants were convicted of sabotage and sentenced to life imprisonment on Robben Island, a sort of South African Alcatraz off the southern coast of Africa.

It was his prison years, from 1964 to 1990, that helped Nelson Mandela refine the leadership skills that would eventually make him the first black leader of South Africa in 1994. Although prison conditions were very harsh in the early years (breaking rocks in a limestone quarry, for example), Mandela insisted that he be treated with respect, and in so doing became a model and leader for other prisoners while also earning the respect of his jailers. Mandela had always had the ability to project an air of confidence and dignity. During these years he also learned to control his temper, undertook a demanding daily fitness program, which included one hundred fingertip pushups and two hundred situps, and became more democratic in his demeanor. Mandela spent much time reading and arguing politics with the other political prisoners, many of them members of groups opposed to the ANC. He even learned to speak Afrikaans [a mixture of Dutch and African languages developed by the Dutch settlers] so that he could speak with his jailers in their own language. This would later help him when he met to negotiate his freedom and a new South African political order with National Party leaders in the late 1980s. As the number of prisoners grew during the 1960s, Mandela and other ANC leaders set up an internal organization to create a sense of community within the prison and maintain discipline.[29]

During the 1970s, the South African economic boom began to falter and a more radical black nationalism began to emerge in South Africa. The brutality of the apartheid state was revealed in 1977 when South African police beat black activist Steven Biko to death. By the end of the decade, the international community had embraced Nelson Mandela as the chief symbol of opposition to South Africa's increasingly embarrassing apartheid policy. In 1980 a South African newspaper ran the banner headline FREE MAN-

DELA. This slogan captured public attention and was repeated throughout the world, even in the United Nations Security Council.[30]

Responding to growing international pressure, the Nationalist Government under Prime Minister P. W. Botha moved Mandela off Robben Island to a mainland prison with better food, newspapers, and even better contact with the outside world through television. The government also began to improve housing conditions for blacks, eased apartheid restrictions that kept them from living in urban areas, and changed the South African constitution in 1983 to allow Indians and Coloured groups to elect their own representatives to Parliament. Mandela was offered freedom but he refused, choosing prison as long as apartheid policies were in place.

Meanwhile, violence increased in South African townships as the Inkatha Freedom Party Headed by Zulu chief Mangosuthu Buthelezi (aided with funds from the South African Security forces) engaged in frequent attacks on ANC members. Buthelezi, a tribal leader, cooperated with the "homelands" policy of the apartheid government, and opposed international economic sanctions against South African and the one-person, one-vote policy of ANC.[31] By 1985 the South African currency, the rand, was falling in value on the world market, and United States banks tightened their lending policy toward South Africa, "starting a chain reaction which pitched South African into a major financial crisis." South African government portrayals of the ANC and Mandela as Communist were no longer credible; even the Conservative Party Prime Minister of Britain, Margaret Thatcher, said in 1986 that the South African government should discuss a solution to their problems with Mandela.[32]

Between 1987 and 1990, the South African government conducted serious discussions about the future of South Africa with Mandela, who tried to remain in touch with Oliver Tambo, the leader of the ANC abroad. The government, led by P. W. Botha and (after August 1989) by F. W. de Klerk, favored a form of government that would allow voting by groups instead of individuals, and would thus give greater power to the white South African minority. Mandela, however, continued to insist on "a unitary state without homelands, non-racial elections to parliament, and one-person one vote." He said whites had nothing to fear from a black majority government because blacks did not want whites to leave but only to share a common homeland with the other inhabitants of South Africa.[33]

Finally, in a move that was not totally unexpected but still dramatic, on February 2, 1990, F. W. deKlerk announced to Parliament that the apartheid policy of three decades was being reversed. All political organizations, including the ANC, were now legal, and all political prisoners would be released. Nelson Mandela was released on February 11, 1990. Over the next four years, Mandela and deKlerk worked together (not always harmoniously, since deKlerk was still supporting Buthelezi's Inkatha Party as a counterweight to the ANC—trying to divide the black African forces) to create a new form of government. By the end of 1993, they had agreed on a multi-racial legislature whose members would be elected by simple majority vote and who would conduct parliamentary business in the same fashion. As a concession, the ANC agreed that Nationalist Party bureaucrats could maintain their jobs in the new government structure until they were eligible for retirement. This "sunset clause" eased white fears considerably and sealed the deal for a new government; it was ironically suggested by Mandela's old friend and ally, the white Communist Joe Slovo. Mandela and deKlerk were jointly awarded the Nobel Peace Prize at the end of 1993, and the following year Mandela was elected to a four-year term as President in the first free, multi-racial election in South African history. He governed with Nationalist Party and Inkatha Party colleagues in his cabinet and set an example by publicly forgiving his enemies, including the judge who had sent him to prison in 1964. Members of all parties, races, and ethnic groups welcomed him. Even hard-line Afrikaners understood that he cared about preserving their culture as well as his own.[34]

When Mandela left office in 1998, he was a man of larger-than-life proportions. During his campaign, one American news magazine said that the new president would have "to be both the father of his reborn country and the healer of its wounds: South Africa's George Washington and also its Abraham Lincoln." His principal biographer says Mandela was "a man of destiny" to both white and black South Africans.[35]

Each of these men has been and will continue to be remembered as much for what he represented as for what he accomplished. King and Mandela both clearly accomplished much in ending formal segregation of the races in their respective countries. Yet they are both thought of as symbols of racial harmony even though both the United States and South Africa have entered the twenty-first century with many unresolved racial antagonisms. Mandela has become a man of destiny who helped all South Africans avoid the race war that many had predicted would engulf that nation if whites were ever forced to give up power. Martin Luther King, Jr., is remembered mainly for his "I Have a Dream" speech given at the Lincoln Memorial in Washington in August 1963, in which he spoke of his dream of equality.

In a practical sense, Mandela, blessed with a life more than twice as long as King's, has been the more successful of these two leaders. He has seen his dream of a multi-racial democracy become a reality in South Africa. While South Africa still faces many economic problems, relatively few members of the white business community have fled since the country has turned to black rule and there is no danger of black-on-black or black-on-white civil war. Mandela's "essential integrity" has allowed his countrymen to believe, at least for a time, that members of all racial and ethnic groups do have a chance to create a nation that will, in time, reflect all of their values and bring a measure of prosperity to all.[36] By any of the standards we used to judge successful politicians, Nelson Mandela has been successful.

Yet as a prophet (like those in the Old Testament who called for justice) and as a radical (one who goes to the root of a problem), Martin Luther King, Jr., may be remembered longer than Nelson Mandela, even though his successes were not as complete as those of his African counterpart. King's belief in a "beloved community," one in which men really want to change morally in order to bring about a balance between freedom and equality, was a common feature of his early speeches on non-violence. King's quotation from the Old Testament referring to a world in which "justice runs down like water and righteousness as a mighty stream" makes him a modern prophet. The King we often remember today is the early King, the advocate of political changes in the late 1950s and early 1960s. The King holiday is not used today to remember the more challenging King of 1965–1968, the King who opposed the Vietnam war and the civil rights leader who linked equality to economic opportunity as firmly as to the political promises of the American constitution. Even in *Why We Can't Wait*, published in 1964, King proposed "some compensatory consideration of the handicaps [blacks] have inherited from the past," something we today call affirmative action. By 1967, when King's *Where Do We Go From Here; Chaos or Community* was published, he was proposing a guaranteed income at the median level, tied to inflation, for all poor people in the United States, two-thirds of whom were white.[37] By the time of his death, according to Michael Dyson, King had moved from believing that non-violence could be used to *persuade* men to change to the conviction that non-violent mass demonstrations should be used to *force* people to change. He believed further that the changes had to be fundamental ones that guaranteed a measure of economic equality.[38]

In the final analysis, Martin Luther King, Jr., was not able to compel or inspire American society to change as much or as deeply as he believed it should. Nelson Mandela did bring about dramatic changes in South Africa. But then, King, one could argue, was asking for something much more fundamental than was Mandela. How then should we judge leaders of social and political movements: by their practical political accomplishments or by the depth and quality of their dreams?

Notes

1. *The Autobiography of Martin Luther King, Jr.,* edited by Clayborne Carson (New York Warner Books, 1998), 5. Other accounts of King's early years are in Stephen B. Oates, *Let the Trumpet Sound. The Life of Martin Luther King, Jr.* (New York: Harper and Row, 1982), 3–17, David L. Lewis, *King A Critical Biography* (New York Praeger, 1970), 6–17; Marshall Frady, *Martin Luther King, Jr.* (New York: Viking Penguin, 2002), 12–17.
2. Oates, *Let the Trumpet Sound,* 12, 16; Lewis, *King,* 6–7.
3. Lewis, 19.
4. Clayborne, *Autobiography,* 17. For a fuller account of the subject of King's studies at Crozier and Boston University, see Lewis, *King,* 27–45, and Oates, *Let the Trumpet Sound,* 24–41.
5. Lewis, *King,* 39; see also Oates, *Let the Trumpet Sound,* 24–28, 31–33, 37–41.
6. Frady, *Martin Luther King, Jr.,* 30.
7. Frady, *Martin Luther King, Jr.,* 35–36.
8. Lewis, *King,* 55, 66–67.
9. Oates, *Let the Trumpet Sound,* 92–95.

10. King described the Montgomery boycott in *Stride Toward Freedom: The Montgomery Story* (New York Harper and Row, 1958). A useful, condensed summary of this book is contained in an article King wrote in 1956 and published in April 1957 as "Our Struggle." This has been reprinted in Martin Luther King, Jr., *I Have a Dream Writings and Speeches That Changed the World* (New York: HarperCollins Publishers, 1992), 3–13.

11. See Frady, *Martin Luther King, Jr.*, 57–97, for a concise description of King's activities and issues during these years.

12. Clayborne, *Autobiography*, 124.

13. Clayborne, *Autobiography*, 169; King, *Why We Can't Wait* (New York: New American Library 1964) 43–44; see accounts of the Albany Campaign in Frady, *Martin Luther King, Jr.*, 88–96, Lewis, King, 140–170.

14. Oates, *Let the Trumpet Sound*, 209–210; see the following 33 pages for a fuller account of the Birmingham campaign. Most of the chapters in King's *Why We Can't Wait* also deal with the Burmingham campaign; see chapters 3–5—the last of these is the now-famous "Letter for a Birmingham Jail."

15. Lewis, *King*, 192–195, 198–205; see also Frady, *Martin Luther King*, 100–120.

16. Lewis, *King*, 211; see his comment on King's Birmingham "Letter" on 187–191.

17. Michael Eric Dyson, *I May Not Get There with You: The True Martin Luther King, Jr.* (New York Simon and Schuster, 2000), 37, 34–35.

18. Dyson, *I May Not Get There*, 55–64.

19. Anthony Sampson, *Mandela: The Authorized Biography* (New York: Random House, 2000), 5–15.

20. Sampson, *Mandela*, 9, 12.

21. Sampson, *Mandela*, 32–33; Meredith, *Mandela*, 39.

22. Meredith, *Mandala*, 76; Sampson, *Mandala*, 96–100; for a quick summary of the Apartheid laws, see *http://www.africanaencyclopedia com/apartheid/apartheid.html.* [accessed 7-18-2003]

23. Meredith, *Mandela*, 93–94, 97; Sampson, *Mandela*, 69–75.

24. Meredith, *Mandela*, 47–49, 66–67; the "Manifesto" of the ANC Youth League was clearly an Africanist document, one that argued that native Africans should rule African in general and South Africa in particular. See "ANC Youth League and Programme of Action 1944–49," in Nelson Mandela, *The Struggle Is My Life* (New York: Pathfinder Press, 1986), 11–30. This is a useful collection of ANC documents and of Mandela's writings and speeches before he was imprisoned in 1964.

25. The ANC was criticized by non-communist white liberals and by Africanists [those who wanted an African state ruled solely by blacks]

when it, under Mandela's leadership from 1954–1956, worked with the Indian Congress, the South African Coloured People's organization, and Communists to create a "Freedom Charter" that would serve as a manifesto for a democratic, multiracial South Africa. See Sampson, *Mandela*, 88–95; Meredith, *Mandela*, 131–137; a copy of the "Freedom Charter" and an article by Mandela in support of it can be found in *The Struggle Is My Life*, 50–58.

26. Sampson, *Mandela*, 40; Mandela, *Long Walk to Freedom*, 147.
27. Meredith, *Mandela*, 200–216, 219; Sampson, *Mandela*, 147–157, 170–171.
28. Mandela, *The Struggle Is My Life*, 161–181.
29. Meredith, *Mandela*, 287–289, 297–301, 314; Sampson, *Mandela*, 208–215, 241–242, 289–293; Mandela, *Long Walk to Freedom*, 379–449.
30. Sampson, *Mandela*, 311–314; Meredith, *Mandela*, 341–343.
31. Sampson, Mandela, 319–322, 324–325, 330. For a brief biographical sketch of Buthelezi, see the Columbia Encyclopedia, 6th edition (2001) online at *http://www.bartleby.com/65/bu/Buthelez.html*. [accessed 7-20-03]
32. Meredith, *Mandela*, 360–361; Sampson, *Mandela*, 346.
33. Meredith, *Mandela*, 358–359.
34. Sampson, *Mandela*, 449–468; Meredith, *Mandela*, 448–452, 466–484, 490–494.
35. Eric Ransdell and Jerelyn Eddings, "The Man of the Moment," *U.S. News and World Report* (May 9, 1994), 34–35; Sampson, *Mandela*, 497.
36. Sampson, *Mandela*, 577.
37. Martin Luther King, Jr., *Why We Can't Wait*, 134, 136–138; Martin Luther King, Jr., *Where Do We Go from Here: Chaos or Community?* (New York: Bantam Books, 1968), 190–193.
38. Dyson, *The True Martin Luther King, Jr.*, 43.

Further Reading

DYSON, MICHAEL ERIC. *I May Not Get There with You. The True Martin Luther King, Jr.* New York: The Free Press, 2000. An excellent interpretation of the changes in Martin Luther King's image in the years since his death.

FRADY, MARSHALL. *Martin Luther King Jr.* New York: Penguin, 2002. A short, readable account of King's life and career by a journalist who knew him.

MANDELA, NELSON. *Long Walk of Freedom: The Autobiography of Nelson Mandela*. Boston: Little, Brown and Company, 1994. Includes much detail from his life and gives the reader a good feeling for his personality.

SAMPSON, ANTHONY. *Mandela: The Authorized Biography*. New York: Vintage Random House, 2000. Despite the word "authorized" in the title, this lengthy work gives a clear and fair picture of Mandela's strengths and weaknesses.